3·20

CLIMATE, SOILS
AND
VEGETATION

A landscape, like this flood-plain of the Rio Grande in New Mexico, usually reflects the interactions of *Climate* (notice the arid environment), *Soils* (here azonal, alluvial, with humus from native and introduced plants, and moist—but, thanks to man's conservation, not too moist), *Vegetation* (trees line the channels, old and new, and lower forms thrive on sands and gravels, while man's introduced plants cover the flats), and *Man* (whose pattern of settlement is clearly imprinted). (*U.S. Soil Conservation Service.*)

CLIMATE, SOILS
AND
VEGETATION

BY

D. C. MONEY, M.A., F.R.G.S.

UNIVERSITY TUTORIAL PRESS LTD

842 YEOVIL ROAD, SLOUGH SL1 4JQ

Published 1965

Reprinted 1966, 1968

Reprinted (*with minor alterations*) 1970

Second Edition 1972

Reprinted (*with minor alterations*) 1974, 1976

Third Edition 1978

ISBN: 0 7231 0769 6

Printed in Great Britain by Fletcher & Son Ltd, Norwich

PREFACE

THIS book introduces climate, soils, and vegetation as major components of man's environment. These, with their many accessory features, are considered in turn; although their inter-relations, their influences on man, and ways in which men modify them, consciously or otherwise, are particularly stressed in subsequent chapters. Emphasis is also laid upon their *dynamic* nature: such as the change and variability of climatic features and their causes, the processes involved in soil formation, and the struggle for dominance in plant communities.

The chapters which deal with climate present many facts of meteorology. The properties of air, its heat and moisture contents, the nature of its movements, its stability, and other features are described first, so that the characteristics of the air masses and the cyclonic systems which affect the weather, and hence the climate, may be better understood. The later chapters show that purely local meteorological conditions, prevailing for short periods over small areas—a hollow, a hillside, a field with crops—are often very different from those of the surrounding atmosphere; and that such conditions may vitally affect crops or natural vegetation. For this reason, too, explanations of the significance of relative humidity, lapse rates, soil capillarity, and other physical facts are given in the introductory chapters.

Climatology is, of course, really a branch of geophysics, and a study of any depth calls for a knowledge of many physical principles and the use of advanced mathematics. Any broader treatment, to suit the purposes of geographers, entails much simplification—with the inevitable dangers of over-simplification. All too often, descriptions of rigid patterns of "wind belts", and the over-emphasis of purely convectional processes when dealing with atmospheric circulation, confuse perceptive students, because there are so many apparent anomalies. Here, the treatment of such facts as the translation of heat energy into energy of motion, and surface movements in terms of air masses, aims to provide a more realistic

v

picture of atmospheric circulation, without requiring the student to possess any detailed technical knowledge. However, the simple physical principles are outlined at appropriate places in the text.

The treatment of atmospheric circulation is presented in two parts. The first part leads from the more familiar idealised patterns of air circulation to the concept of air masses. The second, following considerations of the physical properties of the atmosphere, outlines the relationships between heat exchanges and upper air movements and pressure distributions; it then deals mainly with the characteristics and movements of specific air masses in the lower troposphere.

The characteristics of various types of climate are described in Chapters VI and VII, after first considering some of the ways in which climates may be classified and examining the defects and limitations of the more usual methods of regional sub-division.

As with climates, so with soils: the descriptions of soil types and their distribution are preceded by explanations of the *causes* of soil formation, and of physical and chemical processes which are vital to soil structure, and which may be unfamiliar to geography students.

Climatic factors are extremely important in the development of soils and vegetation, but climatic-vegetational correlations are often over-simplified. The relationships of plants with climate, soils, and biotic factors, including other plant members of their own community, are extremely complex, and are usually changing. Therefore, the numerous elements which make up the environment of individual plants are considered first, and then the ways in which plant communities may change in composition until they form a relatively stable unit of vegetation.

By describing plants in relation to their environment, and introducing the idea of plant successions, and the possible effects of man's interference, a platform is provided from which to view broad patterns of vegetation over the earth's surface. The following Chapters XII and XIII, therefore, describe types of vegetation on a world-wide regional basis, but also consider the form and variety of many of their component plants, communities, and associations.

While a student may thus acquire a reasonably realistic picture of the climates, soils, and vegetation of regions with which he is not familiar, it is hoped that he will be encouraged to undertake more detailed local studies. The final chapter adds emphasis to this by directing attention to the immense importance to plants of their "microhabitat" and its various elements, and to inter-relationships between natural and human features in relatively small rural and urban areas.

The book, necessarily, touches on a wide range of topics, so that the reader may find the list of papers and books for further reading, which follows Chapter XIV, particularly useful. References to the papers are arranged in the order of the chapters, but grouped together according to the subject-matter.

Conversion Tables, showing equivalents for ° C/° F., km/ft, and ins/mb., follow the Book References.

I am most grateful to the many individuals and members of Government and University Departments, and business firms, who helped me with diagrams and photographs, and provided information and assistance with material. My thanks are particularly due to the Librarian of the Royal Meteorological Society, and to Mr Lennart Larsson, Mr W. F. Parrish, and Mr V. C. Robertson, for their efforts to obtain particular information or illustrations for me; and also to Mr J. A. Taylor for his permission to use material, duly acknowledged in the text.

D. C. M.

CONTENTS

LIST OF ILLUSTRATIONS

CLIMATE, SOILS, AND VEGETATION

CHAPTER I

THE ATMOSPHERE AND AIR CIRCULATION (I)

The Composition of the Atmosphere

A mixture of gases surrounds the earth; gases which are in ceaseless motion, but which are retained by the force of the earth's gravity. This is the atmosphere, densest at sea-level, with all but 3 per cent. of its mass within 30 kilometres of the surface, and about half of it below 6 000 m.

Dry surface air consists mainly of nitrogen, about 78 per cent., and oxygen, 21 per cent., by volume. Among the smaller quantities of other gases, carbon dioxide, some 0·03 per cent., and the varying amounts of water vapour in moist air, are very important indeed as far as climates, and animal and vegetable life are concerned. Variable amounts of tiny particles, such as dust, smoke, and salt crystals may have high local concentrations and affect weather in a number of ways. At high levels ozone, another form of oxygen, is present in small but important quantities.

We are principally concerned with, and directly affected by, the lower, denser part of the atmosphere, known as the *troposphere*. In this air there is usually a fairly rapid fall in temperature with altitude, until an overlying layer of relatively warm air causes an abrupt change, at a height of about 8 000 m near the poles and 17 000 m in the tropics; this is known as the *tropopause*. The actual height of the tropopause varies also with the season and weather conditions. Immediately above this, temperatures cease to decrease with altitude, and there may be a slight increase in temperature. In general, the temperature between 12–22 km remains at about −50° C.

This upper part of the atmosphere, known as the *stratosphere*, is dust-free and cloudless, and above the height reached by con- vectional movements of the troposphere. However, there are marked temperature differences between parts of the stratosphere in higher latitudes and those in lower latitudes. The consequent variations in the density of the upper air results in strong meridional air movements at great heights. The ozone concentration at this height absorbs radiation from the sun. This concentration is

1

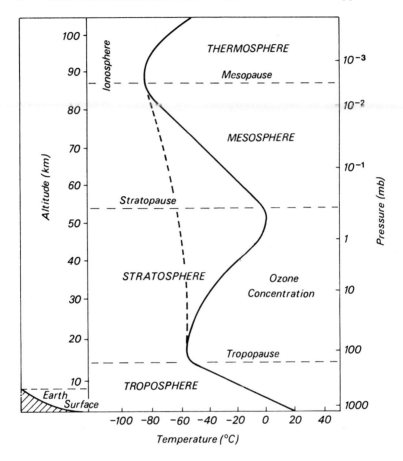

Fig. 1.

Human activities are most directly affected by turbulent activities within the troposphere.   Nevertheless there are strong air movements in the stratosphere, where there are seasonal changes in temperatures and density and consequent meridional differences.   Under polar winter conditions temperatures above the tropopause continue to decline with height (dotted line), to a minimum approaching −90° C, while elsewhere in the stratosphere the temperature may rise as shown.

Above this absolute atmospheric minimum the temperature rises again in the Thermosphere, where photo-chemical effects in the thin air create a high proportion of ions.   This ionised zone (Ionosphere) reflects radio waves.

greatest over polar regions where, as a result, the ozone layers of the stratosphere tend to be particularly warm in summer. In winter, the lack of insolation results in particularly cold upper air over the polar regions. These seasonal contrasts between upper air in the higher and lower latitudes means that in parts of the stratosphere there are strong horizontal winds (p. 76).

But our familiar weather phenomena, including the massive towering thunderclouds, are confined to the troposphere, even though their causes may not be. So to provide a background to a study of climatic conditions we turn first to the troposphere, where vertical convection currents do disturb the atmosphere, and masses of air flow horizontally from one latitude to another, as "advection" currents, taking with them their contents of moisture and heat energy.

AIR CIRCULATION IN THE TROPOSPHERE
Air Movements and the Transfer of Heat Energy
Energy Received and Energy Lost

The earth and its atmosphere receive heat energy from the sun (*solar insolation*). Some is returned by scattering and reflection, and much is lost by their own radiation to outer space. An energy balance has been established, which, as far as present climatic conditions are concerned, is being maintained; so that the earth and the atmosphere taken as a whole are becoming neither hotter nor colder.

Fig. 2 considers factors which contribute to this heat balance and illustrates average conditions for both earth and atmosphere. The figures are, necessarily, only approximate estimates, based on data which in part can be accurately assessed, but involve factors variable with time and place. Short-wave radiation from the sun passes through the atmospheric gases fairly effectively. It is not absorbed by most of them; though at high altitudes ozone is a good absorber, and at low levels carbon dioxide and water vapour absorb a certain amount. Yet, in fact, only about half this short-wave radiation is absorbed by the earth's surface; for much is reflected, by cloud surfaces and by the earth itself, and tiny particles, such as dust, scatter it, so that some is lost into space. The loss by scattering and reflection, which averages something like two-fifths of all the incoming short-wave radiation, is sometimes called the *albedo* of the earth. On a local basis the term "albedo" is used to express the ability of a surface to reflect insolation. Fresh fallen snow has an albedo of some 85 per cent., while for various forms of vegetation it ranges from 10–25 per cent. (p. 260).

Though the atmosphere absorbs little energy direct from incoming radiation, it receives much from the earth; and is thus mainly heated from below. As the surface of the earth absorbs energy its temperature increases. It, too, radiates energy, though in this case with a long wavelength, which can be strongly absorbed by the atmosphere. The water vapour in the air and water droplets, and hence clouds, take up a great deal of this energy emitted by the

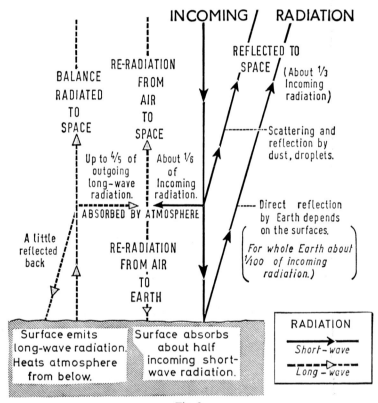

Fig. 2.

On the right of the diagram is shown the reflection, scattering, and absorption of short-wave radiation received from the sun. On the left is represented the loss of energy by long-wave radiation from the surface; and in the centre the absorption and re-radiation by the atmosphere of both long- and short-wave forms of energy (see also Figs. 15 and 16).

earth. As the atmosphere absorbs energy, its own temperature is raised, and it too radiates heat, some downwards to the earth and some outwards to be lost in space.

The overall picture, therefore, is of an atmosphere relatively transparent to short-wave radiation but gaining energy rather from long-wave radiation; resulting in the maintenance of fairly high temperatures at and near the surface—often known, for obvious reasons, as a "greenhouse effect".

Energy Transferred Horizontally

So far we have generalised about the earth as a whole: but though there is an overall balance between heat energy received and lost into space this does not mean that there are uniform conditions in the troposphere. The insolation received varies, of course, with latitude. In low latitudes, where the midday sun is high in the sky and insolation is strong, the daily amount of incoming radiant energy exceeds the outgoing; but in the middle and high latitudes, where the sun's rays are oblique to the surface and the insolation is less intense, more energy is lost from the earth than is received. If, therefore, there is an overall heat balance, and if the low latitudes are not to become hotter and hotter, and the high latitudes colder and colder, some of the heat energy must be

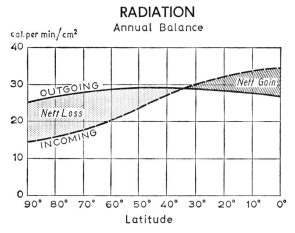

Fig. 3.

When comparing heat energy lost and gained by different parts of the earth, remember that the surface area between latitudes 35° N. and 35° S. is much greater than that of the rest of the surface of the globe.

transferred horizontally, by advection, from lower to higher latitudes.

The unequal heating of the earth's surface is not, however, simply a matter of gradual change from low to high latitudes. The location of the hottest parts of the earth's surface vary according to the seasons; land and water masses absorb and radiate heat at different rates; and variations in the topography and texture of the surface affect its own temperature and that of the air above. Nor does air circulation only depend on such temperature differences. The physical make-up of the atmosphere varies from place to place: masses of air acquire different properties *as* they circulate, moving both vertically and horizontally, and changing their density and water content. The direction of rotation of the earth also affects the pattern of air circulation.

We cannot hope to appreciate all the causes nor investigate all the influences which are responsible for the complex and changing atmospheric movements; meteorologists are only at the beginning of their investigations into the mechanisms of such circulations. However, it is possible to observe that there are types of atmospheric movement which occur, and recur, in place and time with some regularity; and it is possible to map average conditions, and to investigate the properties of the air which gives rise to these conditions. We may thus build up a picture of the distribution of various types of climate, and can then investigate the more changeable features of those climates. Let us start, therefore, with some elementary considerations of *patterns* of air circulation: in the first instance those which stem from unequal heating at lower and higher latitudes.

Idealised Circulation Patterns

Most students will already be familiar with a generalised picture of air movements over an imaginary, uniform globe, in which air is depicted as rising from the strongly heated lower latitudes—the equatorial low pressure region known as the Doldrums. The ascending air moves outwards at high levels and descends in the flanking sub-tropical high pressure zones about latitude 30°, the "Horse Latitudes". From these sub-tropical highs surface air returns towards the equator as the Trade Winds, completing the Hadley Cell (p. 78). These are urged to the right of their course in the northern hemisphere by the deflection force due to the earth's rotation (p. 8), and to the left in the southern hemisphere.

In this idealised plan of circulation each of the sub-tropical highs is also the source of air moving polewards along the surface into a broad trough of low pressure situated between themselves and a polar high pressure zone. These air flows, also deflected as a result of the earth's rotation, are the Westerlies of the higher middle latitudes. At the same time, air sinking from thermal causes in the polar regions flows to lower latitudes as cold Polar Easterlies, which meet the Westerlies and ascend with them in the low pressure trough. This air then moves outwards at high levels and once more feeds the adjacent highs.

This simple pattern of air circulation is a far from accurate description of actual conditions. Many causes act to modify it, and the thermal and mechanical processes involved are grossly over-simplified. Nevertheless it is a starting point already familiar to beginners, with sufficient germs of truth to enable us to examine the modifying factors, step by step, and come nearer to the realities of atmospheric circulation.

Seasonal Changes and the Idealised Surface Circulation

This simplified circulation pattern has not even allowed for seasonal changes. At midday on June 21st the sun is at the zenith over the Tropic of Cancer, at the angle of $23\frac{1}{2}°$ from the zenith when viewed from the equator, and at 47° from the zenith at the Tropic of Capricorn. This by itself means that the hottest parts of the imaginary, uniform surface will be north of the equator at

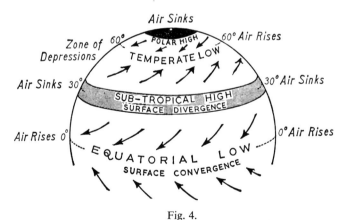

Fig. 4.

A simplified picture of global atmospheric circulation over a uniform surface.

this time of the year; also during the northern summer the period of daylight is longer in the northern hemisphere. Thus on a seasonal basis the idealised wind pattern should show the air moving towards a zone of maximum heating which is north of the equator in June, about the equator at the equinoxes, and the south of the equator in December.

Fig. 5 shows the consequent seasonal swing of the zones of high and low pressure over the uniform surface, and the resulting winds. The tendency of the air to change direction on crossing the equator is shown as a result of the earth's rotation. This needs some clarification, and an explanation of the nature of what is sometimes called the "Coriolis Force".

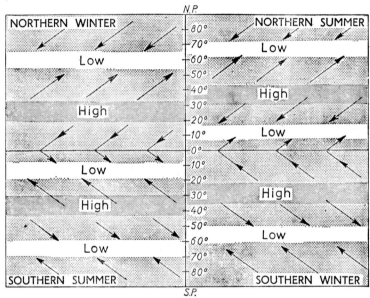

Fig. 5.

A diagrammatic representation of the seasonal shift of the pressure zones and prevailing winds over a uniform surface.

Wind Deflection due to the Earth's Rotation (Coriolis Force)

When air flows over the surface of the earth from an area of high pressure to one of low pressure—down a "pressure gradient" —it is deflected to the right-hand in the northern hemisphere and to the left-hand in the southern hemisphere. The deflection is greatest at the poles and diminishes to zero at the equator.

The force due to the pressure differences causes air to travel in a straight line with respect to a point in space. However, directions on earth are not fixed with respect to such a point, but are related to meridians, which constantly change their position as the globe rotates. As a wind moves across the surface of the earth the meridians, in a sense, rotate from under it, so that to an earth-bound observer the wind apparently changes direction.

Consider a point P at latitude θ on a given meridian (Fig. 6). When this is in the position P_1, the direction in space of true North is the tangent P_1N. After the earth has made half a revolution, this point is at P_2 and the direction of true North in space has changed to P_2N; the angle between these directions is seen to be 2θ.

The reason for an apparent deflection of a wind is difficult to visualise; but mathematicians have shown that we can allow for this effect due to the earth's rotation by *assuming* a force F acts on the wind according to the following equation, where V is the wind velocity, θ the latitude, and ω the angular velocity of spin of the earth (i.e. 15°/hour; usually expressed as $7 \cdot 29 \times 10^{-5}$ radians/sec.)

$$F = 2 \omega V \sin \theta.$$

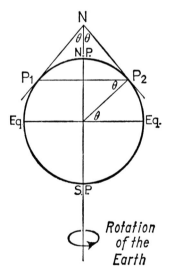

Fig. 6.

This apparent deflecting force acts at right angles to the wind direction and is called the "Coriolis Force". But remember that this force is used only as a mathematical convenience, to allow for the apparent deflection of the wind due to the earth's rotation.

On a map showing pressure distributions and winds, air moving simply as a response to the pressure gradient would be shown as a wind crossing the isobars at right angles. The effect of the Coriolis Force is to deflect the air so that it tends to flow *along* the isobars. High in the atmosphere, where there is no friction, this *geostrophic wind* (p. 69) does blow parallel with the isobars. But near the surface frictional drag tends to act against the deflecting force, so that the air flows at an angle to the isobars. The result is that a wind spiral is produced with height—the "Ekman Spiral" (Fig. 7). The surface wind is seen blowing at an angle to the isobars, with a velocity reduced to well below that of the geostrophic wind at 500 metres. The deflective force is dependent on the velocity.

For the moment, all we need to consider is the result of these forces, which has been summed up as *Ferrel's Law*: "A body moving horizontally in the northern hemisphere tends to be

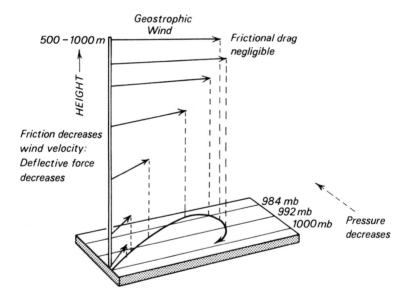

Fig. 7.

deflected to the right of its path of motion, and to the left in the southern hemisphere". Our revised scheme of air circulations appears, therefore, as in Fig. 5.

Atmospheric Pressures—Average Sea-Level Values

A glance at the maps (Figs. 8, 9, 10, and 11) which show the *average* atmospheric pressures and the generalised paths of the surface winds in January and July, is sufficient to stress that over much of the earth the "belts" of high and low pressures do not exist in the way we have depicted: yet there are many features of similarity.

A broad zone of low pressure is seen extending across the low latitudes; while lying over the sub-tropics, especially in the southern hemisphere, are well defined regions with high pressure. Poleward of these are low pressure zones, certainly forming a recognisable "belt" in the southern hemisphere. Associated with these pressure distributions, the low latitude Easterlies, and the Westerlies of the higher middle latitudes, can be easily identified.

The much more regular "zoning" in the southern hemisphere is clearly due to the fact that the expanses of ocean are interrupted by relatively narrow land masses, so that the surface is more nearly uniform. Conversely, the properties of the large continental masses of the northern hemisphere—their low specific heat, large ranges of temperature, mountain barriers, and frictional effects—contrast with the ocean's high specific heat, small temperature ranges, and surface uniformity. And so an average pressure map of this kind tends to show pressure "cells" rather than belts of pressure: thus the area of low average pressure in January, which is centred about latitude 60° N. in the north Atlantic, is flanked by considerably higher pressures over the continents.

Such figures and maps of *average* pressure conditions, and winds drawn to show movement resulting from the *average* gradients, still give us only a generalised picture of the air circulation and tell little of the properties of the moving air. Nevertheless, like the idealised circulation maps of Figs. 4 and 5, they are useful stepping stones towards an understanding of the world's climates, and it is worthwhile summarising the characteristic features of these average conditions.

Pressure Conditions Characteristic of Various Latitudes

(a) The most striking features are those belts or cells in the vicinity of 30° N. and 30° S. where throughout the year the average pressures are high. These *sub-tropical highs* receive air subsiding

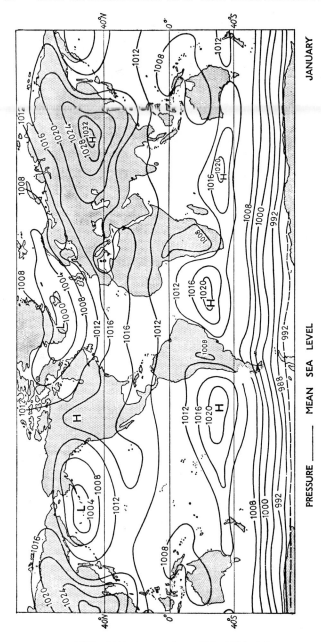

Fig. 8.

The January map emphasises the intensity of the Euro-Asian high pressures built up over the cold land mass.   Notice also the strong sub-tropical cells of high pressure over the southern oceans.

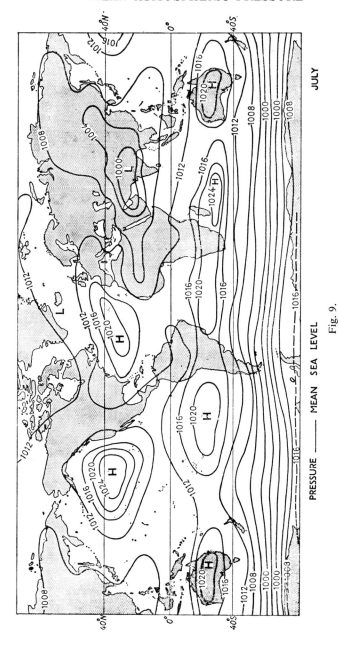

PRESSURE ——— MEAN SEA LEVEL

JULY

Fig. 9.

The mean pressures for July show an almost continuous sub-tropical belt of high pressure in the southern hemisphere, and strong high pressure cells in the eastern sub-tropical parts of the northern oceans. The thermal "low" centred to the north-west of the Indian sub-continent can be readily identified.

from high altitudes, due to dynamic causes rather than thermal ones; although part of the excess of heat energy in the lower latitudes is carried upwards and outwards to the extra-tropical regions.

In January, cells of high pressure are well established in the southern hemisphere, while in the northern hemisphere an almost continuous belt extends eastwards across these latitudes from the thermal high over central Asia [para (c) below]. In July, in the southern hemisphere a more continuous belt of high pressures extends its influence further north than in January; while in the northern sub-tropics very strong high pressure cells over the North Atlantic and North Pacific contrast with thermal lows over the land areas.

(b) *The near-equatorial trough of low pressure* is more in evidence to the south of the equator in January, when the southern land areas, with higher temperatures, show particularly low average pressures. In July the lowest pressures are generally north of the equator, with especially low pressures, of thermal origin, over the land masses in the sub-tropics, particularly in south-east Asia.

(c) *In the higher middle latitudes,* maps of average pressures for January show cells of low pressure over the oceans of the northern hemisphere, but well developed areas of high pressure over the very cold eastern interiors of the Euro-Asian land mass; in North America average pressures are high, but much less intense and less clearly defined than the Asiatic highs. In the northern hemisphere in summer, lows of thermal origin are created over the land masses; but low pressure cells, as such, are less in evidence in oceanic areas. In the southern hemisphere a continuous deep trough lies across the sub-polar regions, and these low pressure conditions persist throughout the year over the vast stretches of the southern oceans.

(d) *In polar latitudes,* thermally-induced high pressures over Antarctica are clearly shown on zenithal maps of average pressures, and highs do persist for most of the year. The Arctic highs appear less intense; they are, in fact, less persistent, and pressure conditions are irregular in the north polar latitudes.

Air Movements Associated with Average Pressure Conditions

Examining these pressure conditions we can see that air movements associated with them appear on our generalised maps (Figs. 10 and 11) as the prevailing winds in various latitudes.

(*a*) *The tropical easterlies,* or Trade Winds, have their origin in the sub-tropical highs from which the warm, dry, sinking air moves across the pressure gradients towards the equatorial trough. The persistence of these pressure conditions on the seasonal maps underlines the fact that these winds are noted for their remarkably constant force and direction, especially over the oceans.

(*b*) *The equatorial trough* is the area with weak and variable winds and long periods of calm which was known in the old days as "The Doldrums". When the pressure gradients to the north or south are steep the tropical easterlies stream into it more rapidly, and sometimes small disturbances form in this zone of convergence, deepen, and give rise to squally storms with strong winds.

(*c*) Poleward of the sub-tropical highs air flows across the barometric gradients as the *mid-latitude Westerlies.* In the southern hemisphere these form a belt of almost uniform width between latitudes 35°-60°, the so-called "Roaring Forties" and "Furious Fifties". In the northern hemisphere their constancy is affected by the land masses and the varying pressure conditions associated with them. Moreover, in these latitudes the convergence of these westerlies of sub-tropical origin and air from the polar regions cause atmospheric disturbances; the resulting depressions pass eastwards with rotational air movements, so that a place may experience wind from any direction, though the prevailing movement of air, and of the disturbances, is from west to east.

(*d*) *Monsoonal air movements* associated with the changing thermal conditions of the great land masses can be seen on the maps, with very different wind directions to those described in (*a*), (*b*), and (*c*). The persistence of the air flows moving into the Asiatic lows of the northern summer, and away from the high pressures of central Asia in winter, indicate the powerful controls exerted by the great land masses. Changes of wind direction with the seasons are seen also over northern Australia and in south-central parts of North America.

(*e*) There is some evidence on the maps of easterly winds moving from the polar regions to lower latitudes; but in Arctic regions these are hardly regular winds. Nevertheless, the irregular outward movements of polar air have a great influence on weather conditions and climates experienced in the higher middle latitudes.

Pressure Variations and Associated Air Movements
So far we have considered only the *average* pressure distributions for certain periods during the year. For a better appreciation

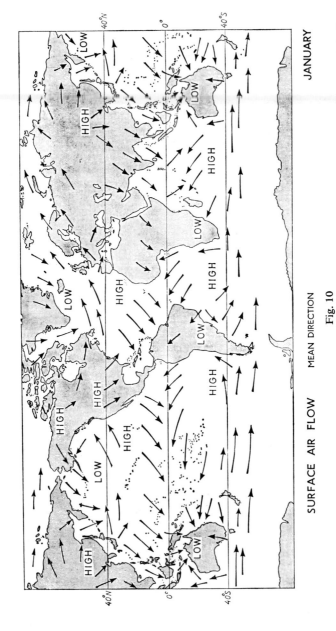

SURFACE AIR FLOW   MEAN DIRECTION

Fig. 10

The prevailing winds in January.   (Air movements in near-polar latitudes are not shown, but are discussed on pp. 143–6.)

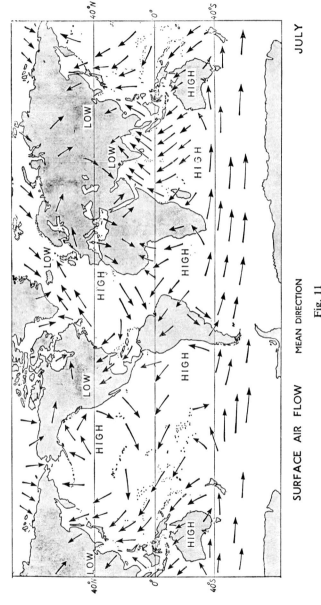

SURFACE AIR FLOW   MEAN DIRECTION   JULY

Fig. 11

The prevailing winds in July.   (Air movements in near-polar latitudes are not shown, but are discussed on pp. 143–6.)

of the climate of a place we need to know not only the average pressures, rainfall, temperatures, etc., over a given period, but also the nature of the day-to-day variations which are likely during the period considered. One may then study climate in terms of the average weather conditions at various times of the year, and yet be aware of *likely* variations in climatic elements at those times. Some parts of the world, Western Europe is one, have very variable weather; for these, particularly, our maps of, say, average pressure are not likely to represent the actual pressure distribution at any given time. We need to examine the causes of these deviations.

Even the apparently persistent belts and cells of high pressure in the sub-tropics seen on maps showing average conditions are not stationary systems, but a procession of "highs" separated by troughs; and, in the southern hemisphere especially, these systems move fairly regularly from west to east. Such sub-tropical fluctuations not only affect local weather but also cause variations in the strength, temperature, and humidity of the trade winds, which have their source in the "air masses" of these latitudes.

Similarly the cells of low pressure which appear on maps of average pressures over the northern oceans in the higher middle latitudes, are really the mean conditions resulting from the passage of successions of eastward-moving troughs, with a relative "high" between each low pressure system (depression). Apart from intervening ridges of high pressure, extensive high pressure systems may also persist there for days or weeks at a time, yet Figs. 8 and 9 give no indication of these. Westerly surface winds may prevail in these regions, but day-to-day winds associated with the frequent pressure changes vary a great deal in strength and direction. These are regions of very varied weather conditions; but in all parts of the world we find greater or lesser variations from average pressures and average wind directions. It is air in motion we are considering, and the time has come to look at the properties of moving masses of air.

The Origins and Nature of Air Masses

We have seen that one way that heat energy may be transferred from one part of the troposphere to another is by moving masses of air. At first we considered the wind systems as air movements over fairly predictable courses, under the influence of pressure differences. Now we see that masses of air are apt to move irregularly. So, to understand the nature of the climate of any place, we must try to find out the likely movements of air masses, their characteristics of temperature and humidity, their stability, and the probable frequency of their movements over the area concerned.

The mass of air brings with it characteristics it has acquired at its place of origin and on its way. On arrival it may replace completely, or mask, more local climatic elements, and so come to determine the weather of the whole region. The place of origin of each air mass, and the nature of the surface over which the air moves, are therefore significant. In many cases, the place of origin and direction of movement is what we might expect from our previous concepts of pressure conditions and belts of winds; and certain types of air masses tend to be associated with the particular zones considered above.

Characteristics Acquired in Source Regions

An air mass is a portion of the atmosphere of considerable depth, whose characteristics of temperature and humidity are remarkably uniform in a horizontal direction at any level, at or above the earth's surface. In certain parts of the world air accumulates, for reasons which will be considered later, and remains stationary at its place of origin long enough to acquire specific characteristics. The air is conditioned from the earth's surface, so the properties of warmth or coldness, humidity or dryness, become strikingly homogeneous when it rests over an extensive uniform surface. Its stability depends mostly on the temperatures at various levels within the mass—its vertical temperature distribution. If such air remains over a particular surface for a long time, any vertical movements will help to distribute the surface characteristics throughout it. Those parts of the earth where air masses develop and acquire such characteristics are called "source regions".

Source regions are likely to be found in parts of the world where, as we have seen, high pressure (anti-cyclonic) conditions tend to persist for long periods: such as the great expanses of ocean in the sub-tropics, the cold interiors of Euro-Asia and northern North America in winter, and in Antarctica. Here air subsides and diverges at the surface. With only light movements over the surface within these regions, uniform horizontal temperatures can be established throughout the source of air. This immediate influence of the surface is seen in the sub-tropics, where air subsiding and moving outward over the ocean rapidly acquires a high water vapour content; while air sinking on to an adjacent land mass, such as the Sahara, remains dry whilst *in situ*. In air masses developing over the cold land areas the humidity is usually very low.

Air Movements and Modifications in the Air Masses

As air moves away from the source area, in response to pressure differences, it affects the weather of the regions it invades. The modifications it introduces are relative to the prevailing local conditions. The encroaching air might appear warm and humid in a locality hitherto affected by cold, dry air; but might have a cooling effect if it replaced tropical humid air. The air mass may retain its general characteristics for a long time; but gradual changes will occur as the lower levels are affected by the surfaces over which it passes. It may also be modified to some extent by radiation received. Temperature and humidity changes usually take place slowly, unless vertical movements are set up, and hasten the changes within.

The actual path of movement of an air mass is firstly in response to the prevailing barometric gradients, though really outstanding relief features exert their influence. Air from a given source does not always move in the same direction; but it is obviously a great help in understanding weather and climatic conditions to know the *most likely* paths followed by certain air masses, and their usual frequency of passage at a given time of the year. The chief sources of air masses are the high pressure regions of the sub-tropics and the polar regions; "tropical" and "polar" are descriptions used to indicate air from these sources. The importance of modifications from the surface has been stressed, and the additional terms "continental" and "maritime" are used to describe the nature of the air affected by land or oceanic surfaces. The highs of thermal origin over the great land areas are important sources of "continental" air during winter. Fig. 12 shows, diagrammatically, some of the air masses which affect North America and the British Isles, and Fig. 47 gives a generalised picture of these sources of air movements on a world basis. They show also the system of letters used to describe them.

The idea of the global wind system is still a valid and valuable one, but a knowledge of the origin and characteristics of air masses helps us understand other atmospheric motions superimposed upon the general circulation. Apart from the movements of the air masses themselves, air also circulates as a result of the *interaction* of air masses, whose sloping boundary surfaces form "fronts" along

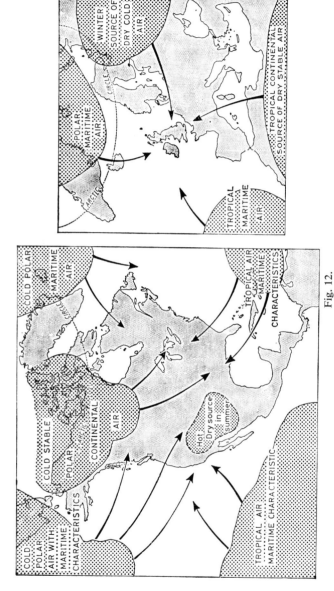

Fig. 12.

The diagrams show the source regions whose air may affect North America and the British Isles at various times during the year; and indicate why these parts of the middle latitudes may be regarded as a "battle ground" between air masses of very different characteristics. We must remember that air from these sources is modified *en route*; and, in the case of the British Isles it may not reach the country by a direct path.

which many of the weather conditions have their origin. In Chapter IV we turn again to air masses, their fronts and resultant disturbances, and their effects on weather and climate. In the meantime we need to know more about those very important elements of climate—air temperature and moisture in the atmosphere.

CHAPTER II

INSOLATION AND AIR TEMPERATURE

THE INFLUENCES OF LOCAL FACTORS

The air temperature at a given place is affected by a number of local factors, and those of particular importance are described below. But, of course, the temperature at any moment may be very largely due to the invasion of an air mass which has transferred air conditions from its source.

The Sun's Altitude

Rays falling obliquely to the surface of the earth give less energy per unit area than those striking vertically, on account of

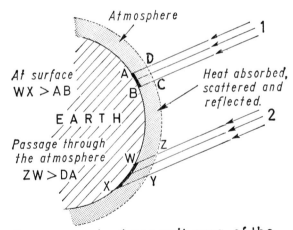

Energy received per unit area of the earth's surface is greater at A B

Fig. 13.

the spread of energy over the larger area, and because of the increased absorption, scattering, and reflection which occurs during a more lengthy passage through the lower layers of the atmosphere.

Day and Night—Energy Gains and Losses

During darkness, with no incoming energy, the loss by radiation causes a fall in temperature. The amount lost depends on the length of the night, the temperature of the radiating surface, the nature of the surface, the amount of moisture in the atmosphere, and, above all, cloud (remembering its ability to absorb and re-radiate heat). Generally, temperatures are lowest just before sunrise and highest, over land, about two hours after noon. However, all these considerations may be upset by the arrival of imported air.

As the length of the day varies with the latitude and season, so, therefore, does the amount of energy received. At the equator the longest period of continuous daylight is 12 hours, but the altitude of the noon-day sun is always high. Within the Arctic and Antarctic circles the longest daylight periods are from 24 hours at latitude $66\frac{1}{2}°$ increasing to six months at the poles; but the noon-day sun is never within 40° of the zenith, and at low altitude for much of the year; during the long period of darkness the loss by radiation mounts steadily and, all else being equal, temperatures fall progressively

HEAT ENERGY PER UNIT AREA FROM INSOLATION

SEASONAL VARIATIONS

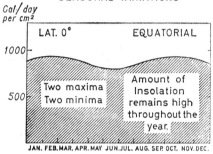

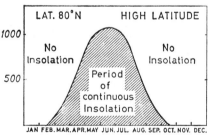

Fig. 14.

as winter continues. Elsewhere over the globe there are various combinations of shorter winter days with the sun relatively low in the sky and longer summer ones with a higher noon-day sun. Fig. 14 shows the combined effects of the length of day and altitude of the noon-day sun on the energy received at the outer limits of the atmosphere, at certain latitudes.

The Nature of the Surface

The specific heats of the various land surfaces are all much less than that of water; so that, for a given amount of heat energy received, their temperature rises much more rapidly than that of equivalent amounts of water; and as they lose heat by radiation their temperature falls more rapidly. Since the heating of the lower parts of the atmosphere depends on convection, turbulence, and the acquisition of long wave energy from the earth, the nature of the surface is important to air temperatures. The atmosphere in turn, by its "greenhouse" effect, helps to keep surface temperatures higher than they would otherwise be, allowing much short-wave radiation to reach the earth, while absorbing and re-radiating much out-going long-wave radiation.

Land and Water Differences

The amount of heat transferred by conduction from a solid surface through the ground is small compared with that carried away from an oceanic surface by the water; for convection currents in the latter can transport heat freely through the body of the liquid (though conditions frequently do not favour vertical mixing to any great depth). Soil particles enclose a great deal of air, which is an effective heat insulator. For these reasons, therefore, a relatively thin surface layer of land heats and cools quickly. In hot deserts the surface temperatures may become very high indeed, of the order of 90° C (a potent factor in weathering).

Water, distributing energy through its mass, not only has a slower rise of surface temperature, but cools slowly, and as a whole; for as cooling surface-water increases in density (down to 4° C) it sinks and is replaced by warmer water from beneath, until the whole mass is gradually cooled. Its supply of heat is therefore available to the atmosphere for a longer period, and oceans are sometimes referred to as "heat reservoirs". As the land does not store heat in this way, and cannot have a similar long-term effect on the atmosphere, there are often striking differences between continental and oceanic temperatures.

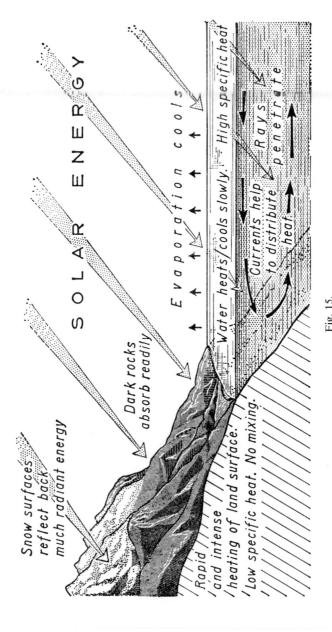

Fig. 15.

The ways in which radiation falling on a land surface and on water is redistributed.

Minor factors also operate differently in respect of land and water. Evaporation from open water and from moist land cools the evaporating surfaces, the extent depending on existing temperatures and air humidity: dry land, obviously, cannot share this effect. The effects of transparency and surface reflection also vary with the type of surface. Water, in the liquid state, allows some energy to penetrate to great depths. Water, as ice and snow, with its high albedo, may reflect back some four-fifths of the solar energy received, and warm but slowly; whereas a grassy land surface may reflect only a fifth, and a dry, black soil as little as one-tenth.

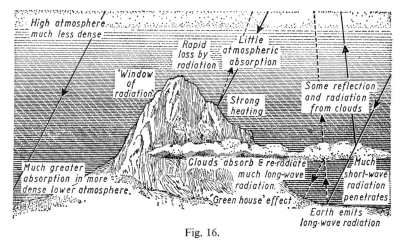

Fig. 16.

High mountains act as "windows of radiation" in the rarer conditions above the lower, denser levels of the atmosphere.

Water Vapour and Water Droplets

We have already seen that water vapour is the chief absorber of incoming radiation in the atmosphere, and also of radiation emitted by the earth. Therefore, in dry air, with clear skies, the ground receives much energy; but the long-wave radiation losses into space are also considerable. By contrast, the droplets of a low cloud cover reflect back some of the incoming solar radiation and thus reduce surface heating, but can be very effective in absorbing and returning energy to the earth. In the British Isles with 8/8 low cloud the diurnal variation may be only 1-2 C °; but with clear skies ten or fifteen times as much.

Topographical Effects

The smaller heating effect of the sun's rays striking obliquely, rather than vertically, affects the surface temperatures of sloping ground. Also, sunlit and shaded slopes in close proximity may show striking differences in surface temperature. The surface of an enclosed, flat or gently concave, valley in the low latitudes can become excessively hot and, by transferring its heat to the air above, may cause considerable turbulence (p. 32). On the other hand valleys and hollows can become collecting places for cold dense air if, under still conditions, radiation losses are great, and local winds may again develop (pp. 64–65). In connection with this, high mountain surfaces extending into a thin, dry atmosphere act as "windows of radiation"—for the radiation received and lost in a given time is much greater above the lower absorbing layers of the atmosphere (Fig. 16).

VERTICAL DISTRIBUTION OF TEMPERATURE

The Lapse Rate

The rate at which temperature decreases with altitude is known as the lapse rate. An average figure for this, the "normal lapse rate", is about 0·6 C° per 100 metres; but, of course, the rate varies from place to place, and with season, time of day, water vapour content, and other factors. There is almost always a variation of lapse rate with height. The actual temperature decrease in height in the air about you, at any moment, is the *environmental lapse rate* (ELR).

The cooling rate with "dry" (unsaturated) air—the *dry adiabatic lapse rate* (DALR)—is about 1·0 C° per 100 metres; dry sinking air gains in temperature at the same rate. But the atmosphere is never completely dry. Its moisture content has no direct effect on the rate so long as no condensation occurs, but causes important modifications on condensation: for as the rising air is chilled to saturation (at its dew-point) much of the water vapour condenses to form droplets, and so liberates heat into the air (the latent heat of vaporisation). This has a considerable effect if a large amount is condensed, for the heating acts against the adiabatic cooling, so that the overall cooling is slower—at a rate called the *saturated adiabatic lapse rate* (SALR). This is a variable rate, and at first this is only about half the rate in dry air, about 0·5 C° per 100 metres. Higher up, with lower temperatures and a low moisture content, the rate again increases. It is about 0·75 C° per 100 metres for temperatures between 0° C and —40° C. At about 12 000 metres the value may approach that of the dry adiabatic rate.

The actual observed decrease of temperature with height at any moment, the ELR, is usually between the DALR and the SALR. As the chief source of heat is the earth's surface, the lapse rate in air near the ground often far exceeds the normal rate. Because of this

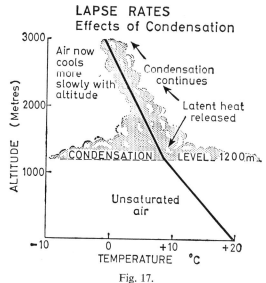

Fig. 17.

The break in the curve indicates the height at which latent heat of condensation is given out; above this the rising air cools at a slower rate.

the first hundred millimetres or so may be said to have a "climate" of their own (p. 260). In sunny weather in the low latitudes, by early afternoon a steep gradient may exist up to several hundred metres. On the other hand rapid cooling on clear, still nights may cause a lapse rate much below the normal. The invasion by new air masses with their own temperature characteristics may cause air flows at different levels, of different temperatures and speeds, so that the lapse rate may change frequently. An advance knowledge of the lapse rates in the invading air gives an indication of the likelihood of strong vertical movements, with turbulence and mixing of air in the lower troposphere. Where air near the ground is cooler than the air above, normal conditions are inverted and a negative lapse rate is recorded.

Temperature Inversions

Near the Surface

When radiation losses are great, and the cold surface chills the air immediately over it, air at the lower levels may be colder than that aloft, an "inversion" of the normal conditions. This is usual during long nights when the air is relatively dry, skies clear, and movements slight; so that the near-surface air remains in contact

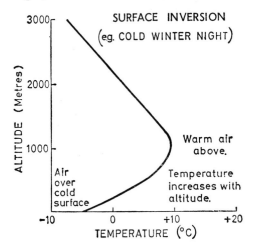

Fig. 18.

The coldest air is in the lowest levels, where it is being chilled from the cold surface. This is a very deep inversion; most purely surface inversions extend upwards only for 50-100 metres.

long enough to become really cold. Snow-covered surfaces enhance this effect, so that in polar regions inversion at low levels is common; whereas "surface inversion" is not likely over the oceans. The depth of such inversions is usually only up to a few hundred metres.

Under inversion conditions the cooler, denser air near the surface is apt to flow to neighbouring lowlands, valleys, or hollows. Fruit farmers in temperate regions are well aware of the need to plant orchards on slopes above potential "frost-pockets" of this kind; settlements in the Swiss mountains are generally clear of cold, foggy, valley bottoms; and in the Brazilian state of Parana the coffee is almost entirely high on the sunny, northern slopes of the rolling uplands.

In the Upper Air

Subsiding air masses gain heat by compression and in this way may become warmer than the air beneath; so that even when the lower air is turbulent they may come to overlie it and prevent convectional updraughts reaching any great height. With such a blanketing effect the air as a whole may become stable, and dry conditions prevail.

Inversions of this kind are common in relatively stationary high pressure systems, such as the sub-tropical highs and those over the continents in the cold winter months. The eastern parts of the sub-tropical high pressure cells over the oceans usually have strong inversion conditions, and subsidence and upper-air inversion remain strong over the poleward parts of the Trade Wind zones, giving stable conditions.

Less permanent inversion conditions occur in other circumstances, such as the formation of a spreading layer of warm air aloft as part of an occlusion, during the later stages in the life history of a depression (pp. 55–9).

Stable and Unstable Air

Vertical air movements are of prime importance in producing weather conditions; strong vertical movements are apt to result in water vapour condensation followed by precipitation; whereas lack of vertical movements may lead eventually to droughts or to prolonged foggy periods. We need to know as much as possible about conditions which are likely to affect the lapse rate at any place. When any "parcel" of air is caused to move vertically, the difference between its properties and those of the surrounding air may result in further upward movement: this part of the atmosphere is then in an *unstable* condition. On the other hand, where air is forced to rise vertically but tends to return to its former level the conditions are obviously *stable* and vertical motion is resisted.

Air in contact with a hot surface may be heated to a temperature well above that of the surrounding air. It will have a high lapse rate, and will continue to rise as long as it remains warmer and less dense than the environmental air. Air of only moderate instability may not begin to rise unless some local cause sets it in upward motion, as when it is flowing horizontally but is forced to rise on encountering a mountain-side or mass of cold, dense air. Extremely stable conditions may persist in cold, dense air with little moisture content, such as accumulates over the northern heart of the Euro-

Asian and North American land masses in winter.   The cold stable
air may have warmer air overlying it: there is thus a strong *inversion*,
indicated by the negative lapse rate.   Under general conditions of
stability any mechanically caused uplift is resisted and the air tends
to subside again.   Subsidence in an air mass, with a gain of heat
aloft, makes for increased stability.

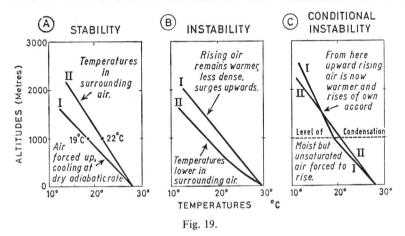

Fig. 19.

In each case curve I represents the rising air (forced upwards—perhaps by a
physical obstacle—in diagrams A and C).   In A this air has no further incentive
to rise and would sink when allowed to.   In C heat gained by condensation
during the enforced uplift, is sufficient to make it unstable above about 1 500
metres.   The development of instability is conditional on the relative humidity
of the air.

Fig. 19 shows a comparison of lapse rates for stable and unstable
air, and also for the state of *conditional instability* which is likely
in moist air.   In A the volume displaced and forced to rise remains
cooler than its surroundings, and thus denser.   After displacement
it returns to the lower levels.   In B the rising air has a lower lapse
rate than the surrounding air, and as long as it remains warmer
and less dense it continues to surge buoyantly upward.   This is
absolute instability, which is a rare state.   In C moist air is forced
upwards and is at first cooler than the surroundings; but soon
condensation occurs and heat is released into this ascending air, so
that it cools rapidly; eventually it becomes warmer than its surroundings and hence unstable, and continues to rise by virtue of its
own buoyancy.

Above: An aircraft above a stratocumulus layer covering central Sweden records the results of vigorous updraughts during a summer afternoon. Billowing clouds form and spread as rising air penetrates the stable layer. (*L. Larsson*).

Below: Summer clouds over a Swedish lake. The base of stable air, under inversion conditions aloft, is marked by the layer of stratocumulus cloud. Beneath, cumulus forms over warm ground. Towering cumulus rises above islands in the cooler lake, but flattens out on reaching the stable layer. (*L. Larsson.*)

Above: Air subsiding over the western central Andes creates inversion conditions. Cloud forms in the cold air in the deep valleys. Eastwards, however, moist unstable air rises up the steep eastern slopes creating towering cumulus. (*D. C. Money*)

Below: Banner cloud forms above Brent Knoll, Somerset, as westerly air (relative humidity 94 per cent.) disturbed by the knoll reaches condensation level. Air descends in the lee, so that a 'banner', rather than a line of cloud, is formed. (*Meteorological Office—H.M.S.O. Copyright.*)

In general, saturated air, with a slower rate of cooling, is more likely to be unstable than unsaturated air; also, by nature, air containing water vapour is lighter than the same volume of dry air. Warm, damp air may rise to great heights, and produce the towering clouds and heavy rain storms seen on a hot humid summer's day and in moist conditions in the tropics. Clouds can be a useful indication of relative stability: layer clouds generally suggest stable air, and cumulus clouds some degree of instability.

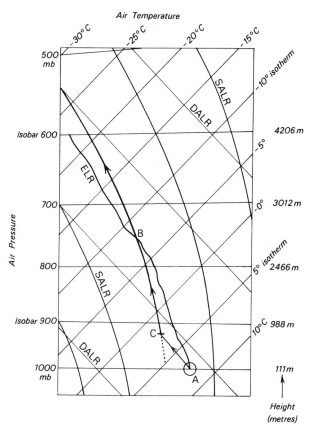

Fig. 20.

A more detailed view of conditional instability.

Fig. 20 shows lines related to various properties of the atmosphere: *isotherms* (air temperature); *dry adiabats* (parallel lines of constant potential temperature aligned according to the DALR; *saturated adiabats* (curved lines reflecting the variation of SALR with height).

This is part of a *tephigram*, which normally also shows lines related to the saturated mixing ratio used to determine the condensation level. Here we see, more realistically, the state of conditional instability, which is a common one in the atmosphere. The heavy line indicates the environmental lapse rate (ELR) *as observed* at a particular time.

The line AC indicates air ascending from A, and cooling at the DALR. At C, the condensation level, its temperature is seen to be below that of the environmental air. The line CB shows the rate of cooling of the saturated mass of displaced air—at the SALR. At B its temperature equals that of the environmental air. Up to this point there has been a stable situation. But above B the state of the local atmosphere is such that a rising mass of saturated air (continuing to cool at the SALR) remains warmer and more buoyant, and so surges upward.

HORIZONTAL DISTRIBUTION OF TEMPERATURE

Isotherms—Their Uses and Limitations

An isotherm is a line drawn joining places having the same temperature at the time of observation or the same mean temperature over a period of observation. Isothermal maps are often made showing the air "shade" temperature distribution at various levels on or above the earth's surface; others can show mean vertical temperature distributions (Fig. 43).

The reader will, of course, be familiar with isothermal maps. Yet it is easy to be casual when interpreting such maps; perhaps by failing to understand exactly what the figures so plotted refer to—whether to actual temperatures as read, or temperatures reduced by calculation to represent those at, say, sea-level; or by failing to realise that mean temperatures for a period are being used. There are other types of temperature maps, dealing with ranges and variations of temperature; and so it is as well to bear in mind a number of points when referring to "the temperature" of a place, and when using isothermal maps.

(1) Where temperatures have been recorded near ground-level in, say, a Stevenson Screen, at a number of scattered stations,

isotherms may be drawn using the actual readings taken, or using temperatures amended to show what they would have been at sea-level. The map of actual temperatures will in many cases resemble a relief map. The "sea-level" isotherms have the virtue of eliminating some of the effects of relief and so demonstrating other influences, such as those of a prevailing wind, ocean current, or "continentality".

Upper air temperatures are now recorded regularly at many stations, and isothermal maps can be drawn for horizontal surfaces at various altitudes.

(2) It is essential to realise, and to make clear, the instant or period to which temperature figures and isotherms refer. A mean daily figure is calculated from the day's maximum and minimum readings by adding them and dividing by two. But a daily mean of 27° C may conceal a maximum of 40° C and a minimum of 14° C, or a maximum of 32° C and a minimum of 22° C, and will mask small local peculiarities of temperature during a day—a sudden drop, which might conceivably be vital to a given crop.

To obtain a mean monthly reading, say, for a particular July, the mean readings for all the days of that July are added, then divided by 31. But here again the monthly mean of, say, 20° C may well hide a hot spell when the daily averages soared to 30° C, or a cool spell when the days' temperatures failed to average 15° C. The limitations of the figures quoted for the mean July temperature of a place, calculated by averaging the July figures for the past thirty-five years, if available, are now obvious; though the usefulness of a mean climatic figure varies with the region considered. If the weather is variable, as in cool temperate oceanic regions, a large number of observations are needed; whereas fewer readings are usually required to give reasonably reliable mean temperature figures for places in the lower latitudes.

(3) The same caution is needed when dealing with ranges of temperature. The annual range, taken as the difference between the mean temperatures of the hottest and coldest months, may be far from the figure of the absolute range in that year. A mean of 5° C for the coldest month may hide a temperature of – 15° C, and 15° C for the hottest may hide a temperature of 35° C; here the annual range would be 10 C°, yet the absolute range 50 C°.

(4) Besides these yearly ranges, the *mean* annual ranges and the *mean* absolute maximum and minimum figures may be obtained; the latter is usually a more significant figure for engineers and agriculturists than the mean annual range. Such men may also be

interested in figures showing the mean duration, or frequency of occurrence of certain temperatures.

(5) Many other types of temperature map may be drawn on an isothermal basis to give necessary climatic information; showing, for example, variations from the mean temperatures for a given latitude, or emphasising similar variations from the mean in other parts of the world by isoanomalous lines (Figs. 24 and 25).

When referring to temperature readings, or isotherms, it is therefore absolutely essential to make quite clear what the figures quoted represent—whether actual figures or mean ones, surface temperatures or upper air ones, absolute ranges or mean ranges, and whether or not figures have been reduced to sea-level. So often geographers are guilty of referring to "*the* temperature" without qualification.

Seasonal Variations—Mean Monthly Temperatures on World Map

Figs. 21 and 22 show the mean monthly sea-level temperatures for January and July, and bring out many of the facts of thermal distribution discussed on previous pages. Apart from the effects of latitudinal differences in insolation and the physical differences of oceans and land masses, the influences of oceanic circulation, which also transports heat energy, are very noticeable. These and other climatic influences of ocean currents are considered in more detail on page 89.

In general the east-west trend of the isotherms reflects the overall decrease of insolation from equatorial to polar latitudes. The isotherms are more nearly parallel to one another in the southern hemisphere, where the expanses of ocean make a more uniform surface. The wider spacing in the tropics emphasises that large areas of the world have relatively similar mean temperatures; the spacing is wider again in the polar regions than it is in lower-middle latitudes.

The east-west run of the isotherms changes where oceans meet continents, stressing once more the contrasting heating and cooling properties of land and water surfaces. *The January map* reflects the great loss of heat from the northern land masses, especially from north-eastern Asia, and the poleward trends of the isotherms over the northern oceans are striking. The effect of ocean currents on air temperatures are seen where the influence of the relatively warm North Atlantic Drift exaggerates this poleward trend off north-west Europe. Oceanic influences are also seen in the differences in the mean air temperatures at the same latitudes to the east and west of South America; in the east, heat carried southwards by the Brazilian current is transferred to the air above it; in the west, the air is in contact with the cold upwelling waters off the coast and with the relatively cold streams which make up the Peruvian current. Similar effects may be seen off the coasts of southern Africa. The tropical parts of the southern African and Australian land areas have particularly high mean temperatures at this time of year.

The summer and winter mean temperatures in North Polar regions can be seen in Figs. 21 and 22, and the large mean annual ranges are also illustrated in Fig. 23. There has been a great increase in the number of polar meteorological stations in recent years and some of the results of their observations are discussed more fully on page 89.

The July map shows that the contrasts in mean temperatures of continents and oceans are less marked. There are certainly not the same temperature contrasts between summer and winter in the southern hemisphere that there are north of the equator; yet comparison does show a marked general latitudinal shift in the isotherms from one season to the other. The northern tropical and sub-tropical continental areas have very high mean average temperatures in July, when the sub-tropical anticyclones are well developed over these lands.

A comparison of the two maps gives an idea of the *mean annual temperature ranges;* though, of course, the months chosen are not necessarily the hottest and coldest at any particular place. Fig. 23 shows the mean annual ranges, which are obviously smallest over the oceans and in the low latitudes, and largest over the continents in the middle and higher latitudes. Terrestrial controls are also shown in Figs. 24 and 25, which depict the temperature anomalies.

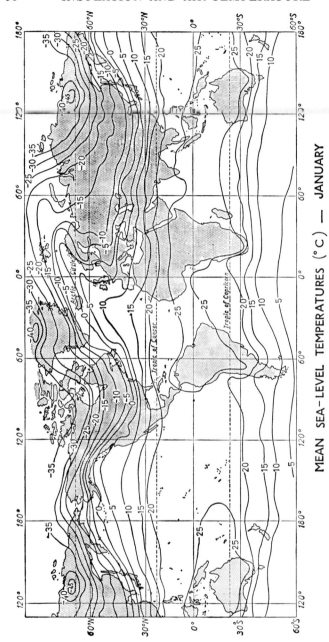

MEAN SEA-LEVEL TEMPERATURES (°C) — JANUARY

Fig. 21.

Mean annual temperatures in the Antarctic are shown in Fig. 60.

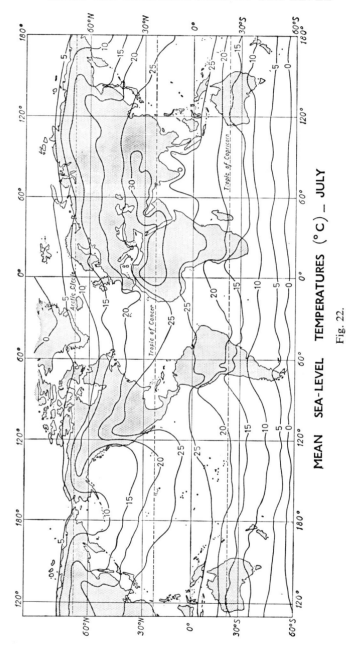

MEAN SEA-LEVEL TEMPERATURES (°C) – JULY

Fig. 22.

Mean annual temperatures in the Antarctic are shown in Fig. 60.

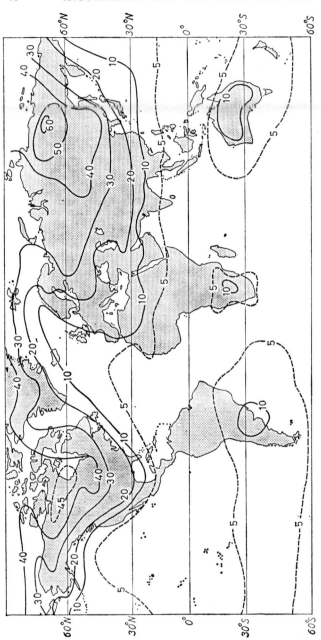

MEAN ANNUAL TEMPERATURE RANGES   (C°)

Fig. 23.

Notice the obvious contrasts between air temperature ranges over the continental areas of the higher and middle latitudes and those over the oceans; also notice the low ranges in maritime land areas affected throughout the year by winds from the ocean, and the generally low ranges in the southern "oceanic" hemisphere.

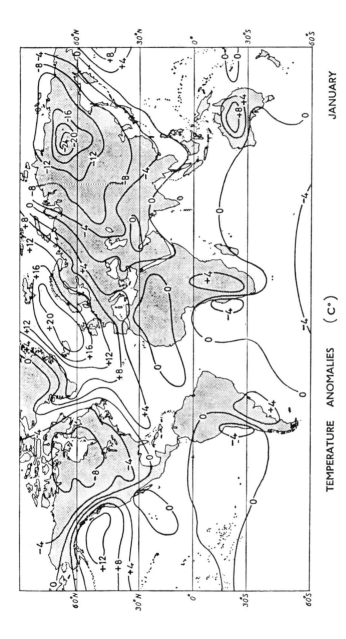

TEMPERATURE ANOMALIES (C°)

JANUARY

Fig. 24.

The temperature anomalies shown here represent the difference of the mean monthly temperature from the *average* of the mean monthly temperatures for that latitude. Above all, these maps stress the great differences in temperatures of the air over the land and sea areas of the northern hemisphere during the northern winter.

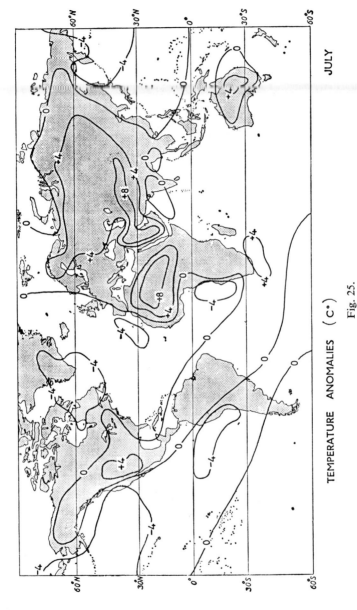

TEMPERATURE ANOMALIES (C°)

JULY

Fig. 25.

The land/ocean contrasts are no longer so marked in the northern hemisphere. In both January and July large areas of the southern "oceanic" hemisphere have very similar temperatures.

CHAPTER III

ATMOSPHERIC MOISTURE AND PRECIPITATION

The Humidity of the Atmosphere

The atmosphere gains water vapour as a result of evaporation from exposed water surfaces and moist ground, and from plant transpiration. The amount present at any time varies greatly, and decreases rapidly upward; so that the mean vapour content at 1 200 m is only about a tenth of that near sea-level, though the actual amount at any height is always varying. The water vapour content of the lower air tends to be some 2 per cent. of its volume, but varies from very little to about 5 per cent.

The *absolute humidity* of the air may be expressed as the mass of water vapour in a unit volume of air (*e.g.* g/m^3). But rather than use volumetric measurements, meteorologists usually refer to the *mass mixing ratio* (x): this is the mass of water vapour in grammes per kilogramme of dry air (g/kg). The water vapour content may also be stated in terms of that part of the total atmospheric pressure which is solely due to the water vapour. Thus, if the atmospheric pressure were 1 000 millibars (mb) the water vapour may well contribute 20 millibars of pressure to the total (something like 15 mm of a total pressure of 760 mm of mercury). Cold dry air may have a vapour pressure of less than 2 mb; whereas in warm, moist tropical air water vapour may exert a pressure of 15–20 mb.

For any given temperature there is a limit to the amount of water that can be held as vapour, and once this limit of saturation is exceeded condensation usually occurs. The absolute humidity of the air does not alter unless water vapour is added to or taken from the body of air concerned, but the *relative humidity* varies with the temperature: it is expressed as a proportion of the actual weight of water vapour contained in a given volume of air to the maximum amount that could be contained at that particular temperature. It may also, of course, be expressed as a percentage. The water vapour present may be measured in terms of the pressure it exerts; so that a comparison of the actual vapour pressure with that in *saturated* air, at the temperature concerned, will also give us the relative humidity. Consider air which is saturated at 4° C, and its relative humidity therefore 100 per cent.; as it warms up the value falls to 70 per cent. at 10° C, 50 per cent. at 18° C, and is as low as 20 per cent. at 31° C. We can now see why very dry air over a hot desert may contain as much, or more, water vapour as saturated air over Arctic waters.

Condensation

When unsaturated air is cooled, its relative humidity rises until it is completely saturated. This is its *dew-point*, and any further cooling leads to condensation. If the dew-point lies below 0° C, some of the condensation may appear as ice crystals—as snow, white frost, or high (cirrus) clouds. In practice, liquid condensation often occurs at temperatures well below freezing point.

In order for water droplets to form in the atmosphere it is necessary for tiny particles to act as nuclei of condensation. These may be microscopically small, such as dust particles or salt crystals, which are common in the lower troposphere. Particles with an affinity for water (hygroscopic substances) are the most effective nuclei of condensation. Salt particles over the ocean are particularly suitable, and, of course, plentiful. Where nuclei are absent, cooling may continue far below the dew-point without condensation, and the air becomes "super-saturated" with water vapour. These conditions are obviously less likely to occur below say, 6 000 m than in the higher atmosphere.

CLOUDS

When countless millions of very tiny droplets, or minute ice crystals, are maintained in the atmosphere by slight upward movements, they are seen as clouds. When the sun shines on their outer surfaces, or through thin layers, they appear white by reflected or refracted light; the shaded sides appear grey, or black when the cloud mass is dense.

Clouds are of wide variety and have many different forms. A study of cloud forms can tell us a great deal about probable weather changes in the near future.

Apart from observing cloud form, we may be able to estimate whether clouds are building up or dispersing by observing the outer edges of clouds in the lower levels of the atmosphere. Turbulent conditions may be irregular, perhaps as the result of friction effects, and such eddying in humid air may cause it to rise and fall above and below condensation level. Clouds may thus form in an up-current and disperse in a down-current. In other words, behaviour as well as shape may tell us something of atmospheric conditions. Certain cloud types are typical of various parts of the world, and also of particular seasons. Therefore we will briefly consider a number of representative types of cloud, their appearance, chief characteristics, and the conditions under which they are likely to be formed.

High Clouds [forming generally above 6 000 metres (ca. 20 000 ft)]

Cirrus. These are composed of ice-crystals and are usually wispy or feather-like in appearance. They may be seen in isolated groups in fair weather conditions, but when regularly banded or associated with cirrostratus may be due to air rising at a sloping front, and presage bad weather (p. 58).

Cirrostratus. This is a thin sheet of ice crystals covering the sky; so that, instead of the deep blue, there is a hazy or milky appearance, and a halo may be seen around the sun or moon, as its light is refracted through the crystals. Such clouds tend to form from the moisture of air ascending at a front, so that precipitation is likely to follow a thickening of this layer.

Cirrocumulus. Where the air ascending at a front is unstable, these cirrus clouds may develop as small masses with some vertical development and have a globular appearance. They are often in lines, giving the appearance of a "mackerel" sky, and hinting at unsettled weather conditions.

Middle Clouds [usually between 2 000-6 000 metres (ca. 6 500-20.000 ft)]

Altostratus is a thick cloud layer of water droplets, which may merge with the cirrostratus. Formed at lower levels than cirrostratus, the more abundant water vapour generally gives a denser, darker cloud, though the sun may gleam faintly through the grey layer which often blankets the sky. It forms most frequently where uplift and condensation are associated with the warm front of a depression, and fairly steady precipitation frequently follows its development.

Altocumulus forms generally under fair weather conditions and the cloud masses have some vertical development. There are often layers or lines of individual altocumulus clouds, with blue sky visible between. These may be caused by layers of air of different density and humidity flowing one over another, with a billowing effect. The clouds themselves may appear white, or grey on the shaded sides.

Low Clouds [from the surface to about 2 000 metres (ca. 6 500 ft)]

Stratus is a low, dense, uniform, dark-grey layer of water droplets, similar to blanketing, ground-level fog, but does not rest on the ground, and often forms well above the surface. Ragged in appearance, and usually shallow, it may drift swiftly along; or it may form rapidly in moisture-laden air when weather conditions otherwise appear fair, and blot out a hillside, or hang close to the

CLOUD TYPES

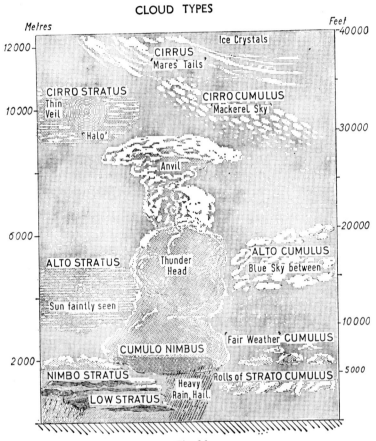

Fig. 26.

summit. Thicker stratus associated with rainfall or snow is known as *Nimbostratus.*

Stratocumulus clouds are usually low, soft-looking masses with a somewhat globular or roll-shaped appearance. Open sky shows between them, and there is often a regular pattern, particularly when rolls of cloud form at right angles to the general direction of cloud movement. This type of cloud is mostly associated with clearing weather.

Clouds with Marked Vertical Development

Cumulus of the fair-weather type is formed when convection is strong and rising air condenses out at a particular height, which is indicated by the flat base of the cloud. Above this it develops vertically until it meets stable air at higher levels: the force of updraughts result in the "bumps" and domed masses of its upper surface, which resembles a cauliflower. In less stable air moist, warm, rising currents can be strong enough to cause continuous condensation for tens of thousands of feet in cloud masses of this kind. Where illuminated by the sun they appear white, but grey on the shaded sides. As convection currents lose strength, usually towards evening, these clouds tend to die away.

Cumulonimbus. In these, where the air remains unstable to considerable heights, the vertical development is very great, and clouds may extend from about 500 m to towering summits at over 10 000 m, their tops dazzlingly white, but with thick, shaded masses giving the typical threatening appearance of a thunder-cloud seen from the ground.

As ice forms in the higher parts of these clouds, more latent heat is released, which helps to increase the rate of upward movement (p. 32). Eventually a cirrus mass forms at the top, spreading out in the typical anvil shape as it encounters the strong inversion of the tropopause; at last there is stability with the environment, and winds carry the particles forward. Torrential rain and hail (p. 50) are often the result of these vertical movements, and lightning and thunder the result of discharges of accumulated static electricity between cloud and cloud, or cloud and earth. The discharge heats the air and causes great expansion, so that the resulting contraction produces the initial sound of thunder. The charges themselves result from the updraught, causing the separation of positive and negative charges, possibly by splitting water droplets or by friction between ice-crystals: the mechanism is still not satisfactorily

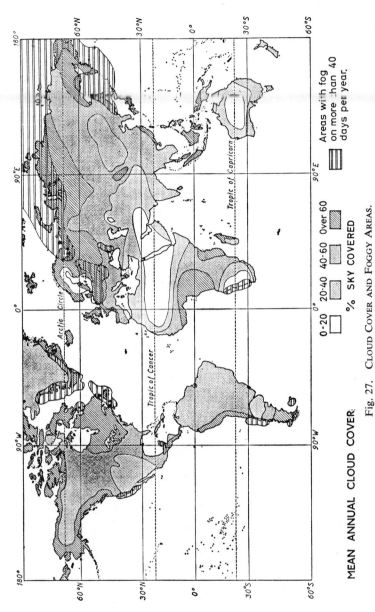

MEAN ANNUAL CLOUD COVER:

0-20   20-40   40-60   Over 60   % SKY COVERED

Areas with fog on more than 40 days per year.

Fig. 27.   CLOUD COVER AND FOGGY AREAS.

Notice the distribution of sea fog over the cool currents in sub-tropical and tropical latitudes off the west sides of the continents, and where warm and cool waters converge in the north-eastern parts of the northern oceans.

Above: Cumulus clouds develop as moist air rises in convectional updraughts (thermals) over the northern coastland of Tasmania. Over the cooler waters of Bass Strait the sky remains clear. (*D. C. Money*)

Below: Towering cumulonimbus with heavy rain at the rear of a depression which has moved eastward over the Fraser delta; downtown Vancouver stands out in the clear, cooler air. (*D. C. Money*)

Above: A persistent saucer-like layer cloud forms a thick cover over Mt. Egmont, North Island, New Zealand, as moist westerly air rises up uniform slopes. Under stable conditions the descending air warms and clear skies surround the conical mountain. (*D. C. Money*)

Below: A Föhn arch, followed by other thick cloud belts, seen over the foothills west of the Canterbury Plains, New Zealand. Moist westerlies passing over the Southern Alps acquire a 'bouncing' wave motion. Thick cloud forms at the crests, followed by lighter cloud, or clear skies, as the air descends in the troughs. (*D. C. Money*)

explained. The charges then become concentrated in certain parts of the cloud.

Fog

Fog is a dense layer of droplets lying close to the ground. It forms when very moist air is cooled below its dew-point, or sometimes as a result of an addition of water vapour to the mass of air. The cooling in this case does not involve the rising and expansion of the air concerned, but condensation occurs *in situ*. When clear skies freely permit radiation loss, and the air, maintained in contact with the ground by inversion conditions, becomes chilled below the dew-point, condensation occurs and *radiation fog* is formed. Such fog remains close to the surface when inversion conditions persist, and there is little horizontal or vertical movement.

Gravity plays a part in building up such fog belts, which are especially likely to form in valleys receiving cold dense air from adjacent highland. This fog develops and thickens from the bottom upward, but usually disperses rapidly when the sun's heat breaks up the local inversion conditions. When an inversion of temperature occurs up to a higher altitude, the fog may be more persistent, or else become low stratus cloud by day, thickening and lowering again at night. Much of what is known as "hill fog" is, however, cloud at hill level.

Where fog results from the movement of warm moist air over a cold surface it is termed an *advection fog;* such are the many dense fogs which form off the Newfoundland coast, where warm moist air from above the Gulf Stream passes over the cool waters of the Labrador current. Such fogs are also common along, or near, sea coasts. They are also likely in winter when warm air is caused to move over cold surfaces, especially snow-covered ones; then they may turn to drizzle, or in very cold weather to hoar-frost or freezing fog. Advection fog is a common occurence when a warm front displaces a winter anticyclone which has given a very cold spell.

PRECIPITATION

The Nature and Types of Precipitation

The term "precipitation" includes such condensation forms as rain, snow, sleet, hail, dew, hoar-frost, and rime. The most common cause of air being chilled until saturated with water vapour is its ascent, resulting in expansion and adiabatic cooling. As we have seen, unsaturated air may rise and cool at the dry adiabatic rate until condensation begins within its mass. Clouds now form, but the mass may continue to rise, its heat energy gained from condensation helping to counteract cooling due to expansion. The temperature of enormous masses of air may be lowered below the dew-point, and condensation may occur throughout the body of air concerned on such a scale as to cause precipitation.

Droplet sizes between 0·001 mm and 0·05 mm are common. Very small droplets tend to avoid each other if set in motion. But less small droplets may collide and coalesce into larger and larger drops, until they are able to fall by gravity to earth as *rain*, often against considerable updraughts. The maximum size of a raindrop is of the order of 5 mm.

The rate of fall of droplets varies. A drop of 0·5 mm radius may take four minutes to fall one kilometre, that of 2·0 mm radius may take less than two minutes. Evaporation will occur below the cloud base, so that much fine rain may evaporate before reaching the surface. The terms *warm rain* and *cold rain* are often used. These may be taken as meaning that when rain falls from clouds with no ice crystals it is "warm rain". "Cold rain" comes from ice crystals which have melted.

As temperatures fall below freezing point, ice crystals may be formed, either by the freezing of droplets or directly from vapour to the solid state. As the crystals coalesce they fall as *snow*. Very cold air has little moisture, and heavy falls are then unlikely; but when warm moist air meets really cold air, as a warm front encroaches on cold anticyclonic air in mid-winter, the fall may be really heavy, with large flakes in the warmer air, and fine, hard snow under colder conditions. About 300 mm of light, packed snow is the approximate equivalent of 25 mm of rain.

Hoar-frost is formed in calm conditions, when temperatures fall well below freezing point and the water vapour is super-cooled. As a result, minute ice crystals are deposited on grass, leaves, and cold surfaces, though there may also be frozen droplets of super-cooled water. *Rime* is usually a heavier deposit formed when the air is in motion, and often when foggy conditions occur under clear skies. Crystals build up on the windward side of objects. *Glazed frost* is rather different, in that it is a smooth icy deposit formed from air droplets or very light rain brought by a breeze into contact with very cold surfaces.

Hail is formed under different circumstances, usually in clouds of the towering cumulonimbus type described on page 47. With the updraughts, raindrops are carried to high altitudes, where they freeze. Further condensation occurs on the ice particles as they fall, before being carried up again in vertical currents. This process may be repeated many times until the resulting hail-stones escape the updraught, or are large enough to fall to the earth, cushioned to some extent by the uprush of air. The hail-stone's interior shows concentric shells of ice formed by these processes.

CAUSES OF AIR ASCENT AND PRECIPITATION

There are a number of reasons why air should rise and, if moist enough, cause precipitation.

Convectional Causes

Air is heated from the surface, and so on warm days instability is to be expected. We have already seen that moist, unstable, rising air may reach a level when condensation begins and then rise at a retarded rate of cooling. Under hot humid conditions such vertical development. is great, and towering cumulus or cumulonimbus clouds develop, separated by blue sky as cooler air descends between the cloud masses. Short but heavy downpours are a usual result of these conditions, though convection storms do not only occur on hot sunny days. Sometimes a stream of cold air, or the base of a polar air mass (p. 80), receives warmth and moisture from a warm sea, so that with a high lapse rate, convection may be vigorous. If a warm land surface, or outstanding relief, provides an additional uplift, very heavy rain may occur.

Orographic Causes (Forced Ascent Due to Relief Barriers)

When landforms, such as mountains, scarps, or plateau edges, force air upward, condensation and precipitation may follow, and may be heavy in unstable air. In the tropics the heaviest falls are usually close to the cloud base level on the windward side of high mountains, where the number and size of drops falling from warm rain clouds are greatest. In temperate regions the maximum fall is usually slightly leeward of the summit, as air rises for a while after it has crossed the line of the crests.

But, beyond this, the leeward, "rain-shadow", side of the barrier is much drier. Air descending leeward slopes will be warmed at the dry adiabatic rate, and resulting Föhn winds (p. 66) may produce very dry conditions.

The amount of precipitation depends on the direction of movement, the moisture content and stability of the air, and on local relief, such as steep slopes, re-entrants, funnels, and other topographical features. This is illustrated on a large scale by the effects of the hot, humid monsoon air sweeping up the Western Ghats of India. In a few months over 5 000 mm of rain falls on some of the seaward-facing heights, while adjacent slopes receive less than half this total, and places on the lee-slopes a few miles inland have less than 750 mm. In Assam the local topography in parts of the Khasi Hills funnels the moist air upward to give Cherrapunji an average of over 7 500 mm in the three wettest months: more than 1 000 mm of rain has fallen there in a single day.

Rainfall Intensity

The intensity of rainfall, that is the amount divided by the duration, during a storm, is of great importance because of its effect on physical landforms and on settlement. Rapid run-off as sheet-wash, or in gullies, can remove and transport top-soil and regolith, causing soil erosion, floods, and subsequent deposition (which can be harmful or beneficial).

The average intensities for short periods are much greater than those for longer ones. In downpours high-intensity rain is associated with increased drop size rather than an increased number of drops. In a fifteen-minute storm affecting north-western Jamaica 200 mm of rain was recorded.

CYCLONIC STORMS

There are three main types of cyclonic storms: (i) *Depressions* of the middle and higher latitudes; (ii) *Tropical cyclones* with origins in the low latitude oceanic areas, where disturbances can become intense, and move rapidly as violent hurricanes or typhoons; (iii) *Tornadoes*, which are smaller systems, but extremely violent and destructive.

Each of these is a low pressure system with a fairly strong gradient towards the centre; hence, with converging winds modified by friction, and in higher latitudes by the Coriolis Force, air moving towards the centre of the "low" does so obliquely—as an anticlockwise swirl in the northern hemisphere, and with clockwise rotation in the southern hemisphere.

The eastward-moving depressions of the higher and middle latitudes, and the resulting unsettled weather, are so much a part of the climate of these zones that it is as well to treat them in some detail.

CAUSES OF UPLIFT

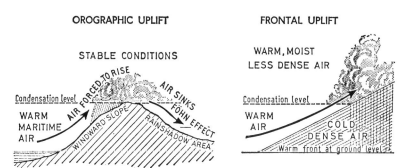

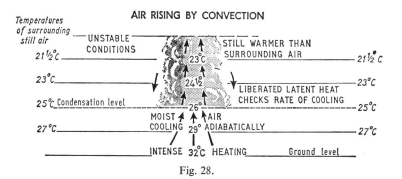

Fig. 28.

Depressions in the Middle Latitudes

Such depressions do not necessarily comprise a complete revolving wind system, so that it is better to use the term "depression" or "low" rather than "cyclone".

The Mechanism of Depressions

It now appears that the formation of these depressions is closely connected with the mechanisms operating as part of the general atmospheric circulation. Their mode of formation is studied by meteorologists in relation to upper-air movements and the transfer of energy from one zone to another. Here we are concerned chiefly with the nature of a depression system at ground-level and with its effects. However, we can see that the presence of low pressure at the surface means that there is a reduction of the total weight of atmosphere above it, and that air will move in from all sides as a result of the pressure gradient created. The converging air then moves vertically upward and, to maintain the "low", must be removed from the system by upper air divergence at higher levels; removal at a rate greater than the surface convergence will lead to a "deepening" of the depression. (In a high pressure system, of course, air subsides and diverges at ground-level.)

The surface circulations are closely linked with fluctuations in the upper-air flow. If we consider only surface phenomena, it is difficult to decide whether a fall in pressure is the result of air flow being distorted into circulation, or whether such circulation occurs as a result of a drop in pressure. In fact depression systems develop where a region of upper air divergence overlies a frontal zone.

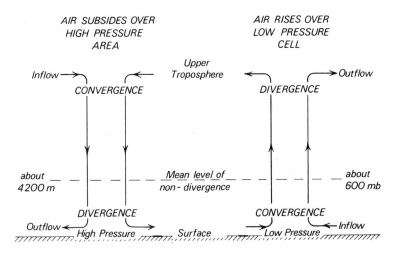

Fig. 29.

Horizontal inflows or outflows of air are accompanied by compensating vertical movements. A shows how air converges towards the near surface low pressure centre, ascends, and diverges aloft. B shows upper air convergence, air subsidence, and near-surface outward flows from the high pressure area. Notice that, in the middle troposphere, there is a level at which horizontal divergence or convergence is effectively zero. The mean level is about 4 200 metres.

Middle latitude depressions mostly develop along a fluctuating front of contact (the *polar front*) between cold air of polar origins and warm maritime tropical air; air masses unlike in temperature, density, and direction of movement. With such contrasting air side by side, and at angles of contact which depend on the temperature differences, speeds of movement, and latitude, any disturbance (however caused) may act to create a wave along this front. The wave sometimes develops to reach a stage where cold air moves into the warm air along the surface (as a *cold front*), and the displaced warm air readily rises above it. Further along the main front of contact warm air moves forward at the surface (as a *warm front*), and again rises over the adjoining cold air, as if ascending a gently inclined ramp. Fig. 30 shows how the warm, tropical maritime air comes to form a sector, or wedge, with a centre of low pressure at the apex. A cyclonic circulation develops, with the temperature contrasts of the air masses, and heat liberated by condensation, adding energy for movement. The cold front advances more quickly than the warm front, and cold air replaces warm air at the surface, until the latter is completely raised aloft—a state of *occlusion* which begins where the warm sector is narrowest, and develops outward from the low pressure centre.

Fig. 30 shows the typical closed system of isobars and the gradient towards the centre. Warm air moves polewards over what, relative to its own movement, is a retreating slope of polar air. At the surface circulating cold air moves parallel with the warm front, circles about the centre, and moves in behind the cold front. None of the air moves entirely around the system. Some is carried along by the depression in its general movement (usually eastward), and rises as it reaches the centre: much never reaches the centre, but moves off in other directions. In a sense it is, in its early stages, a wave which moves along the surface of discontinuity between the cold and warm air masses. In its later stages it remains a vortex until the air ceases to be removed quickly enough at the higher levels.

The Passage of a Depression—a ground-level view

We are considering the depression as a source of precipitation, and there is usually a period of prolonged precipitation as the warm air rises, cools, and its moisture condenses some way ahead of the warm front; a shorter, heavier downpour is a feature of the passage of the cold front at the rear of the system.

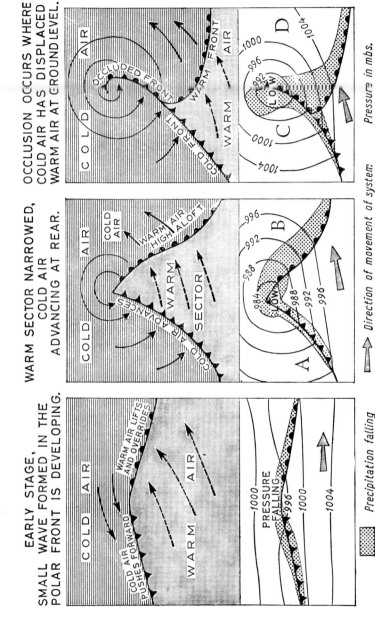

Fig. 30.

Stages in the development and occlusion of a depression of the middle latitudes.

As the first signs of an approaching depression, we are likely to see the wisps of cirrus, as feathery "mare's tail", where, perhaps, several hundred kilometres ahead of the front, the air still retains enough moisture after ascent to cause ice-crystals to form at 8 000 or 10 000 m. There may be a sun halo in the thin veil of high cirrostratus which follows. The watery blue then gives way to lower, thicker altostratus, and spots of rain may fall as the main rain belt ahead of the warm front approaches. Steady persistent rain sets in as the dark nimbostratus masses, with their base fairly near the ground, come in ahead of the warm front. The duration of the rain belt depends on the rates of movement of the system and the front. The heaviness of the rain and form of the clouds mainly depend on the nature of the warm air. Relatively dry air may give little precipitation; but moist unstable air may give rise to vertical development and cumulonimbus, with cirrocumulus ahead: in this case the "mackerel sky" will be a sign of a heavy downpour to come.

As the warm front passes, we soon feel a rise in temperature and notice a veering of the wind. The barometer stops falling, or falls more slowly. The continuous rain ceases, though the humidity remains high, and there is often much shallower layer cloud in the warm sector. There may, however, be scattered convection showers, and short periods of rain over hilly country.

At the cold front, the warm air is being forced upward by the advancing wedge of cold air, and the slope of the surface of discontinuity is greater than at the warm front, being of the order of $1:25$ to $1:80$ (rather than between $1:100$ and $1:400$). Here the vigorous uplift results in huge cumulonimbus clouds, and we experience a relatively brief, but violent, downpour. Sometimes the cold air advances so rapidly as to overrun the warmer air, so that very strong vertical movements occur and brief violent "line-squalls" may develop.

As the cold front passes, with its "clearing-up storm", the wind veers sharply, the barometer rises, the skies clear, visibility improves, and the temperature falls as cold air moves in from a poleward direction—air which is usually colder than that in front of the depression.

The central diagram in Fig. 30 shows how such fully-developed depressions appear on the weather map: notice the different spacings of the isobars according to whether warm or cold air is at the surface, and the sharp angles where the isobars cross the line of the fronts. Depressions tend to move forward along the line of the iso-

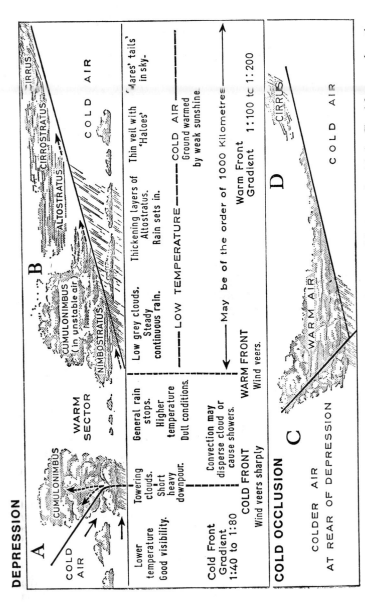

Fig. 31.   Profiles of a Mid-Latitude Depression and Occlusion.   (Moving to the right.)   Cloud forms and weather depend on the stability or instability of the warm air; here unstable and rising at the fronts (Ana-fronts)   Stable subsiding air forms a "lid" over rising currents.   At such Kata-fronts precipitation may only be light.

bars in the warm sector. The fronts are apt to move anti-clockwise about the centre, with the warm sector becoming smaller and smaller until occluded. Sometimes a second wave develops on the cold front in the rear of the depression and a "secondary depression" forms. More than one secondary may develop; and sometimes a whole "family" of them may circle slowly around the primary depression; moving anti-clockwise in the northern hemisphere. The long spells of changeable weather in the British Isles are often due to the passage of series of secondary depressions, with belts of rain, followed by a day or two of brighter weather in the high pressure ridges between the lows.

Tropical Cyclones (Hurricanes / Typhoons)

These cyclonic whirls of strong winds about a calm centre have no marked fronts of warm and cold air, and tend to be symmetrical swirls. They form over oceans in the low latitudes, and their centres move from east to west. They are usually between 50 to 1 000 km across, and are most frequent over the western parts of the oceans in summer and autumn. In the Indian Ocean they are most frequent before and after the wet Monsoon, in the periods

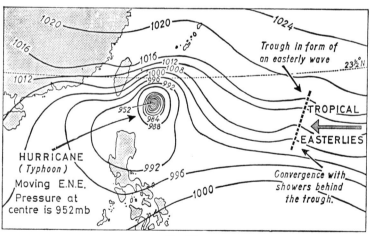

Fig. 32.

A typhoon formed in the western Pacific and is swinging away to the north-east of the Philippines. Shallow troughs, such as the one to the east of the hurricane area, are not uncommon in the low-latitude oceanic regions. Occasionally some deepen and form a closed circulation, and a few develop into a hurricane system.

April to June, and October and November. Severe tropical hurricanes can cause great damage, and so can the tidal waves which may be generated by the winds of an approaching hurricane. Sometimes the winds converging on the centre of the system uplift the water there into a "wave surge".

Tropical cyclones form close to the Inter-Tropical Front (p. 82) rather than near the equator, where the Coriolis Force is too small to cause sufficient deflection for such a system to begin circulating. They form only over very warm tropical waters, usually with temperatures above 25° C, and appear to start for a number of reasons. Essential conditions appear to include a supply of heat and moisture and low frictional drag at the sea surface. Sometimes air convergence with resulting upward movements seem to be the cause; but occasionally a trough may cause polar air to enter the tropics and initiate cyclonic movements. But in each case convection plays a part, and additional energy is released by condensation, creating spiral bands of towering cumulonimbus about the storm centre. Air ascends in a warm vortex about the centre and is removed by outwards movements at high altitude. Air descends, and warms adiabatically, in the "eye" of the storm.

Areas of cloud and rain form about the centre, especially in nearly stationary systems. The rainfall, which varies considerably in amount, is usually torrential in character; there may be up to 250 mm at a time, but sometimes five times that amount is recorded.

Tornadoes

These are much smaller systems, sometimes only a few hundred metres across, and may be very violent. On a local scale they are extremely destructive. Air spirals at tremendous velocity, with a vigorous updraught in this narrow vortex. They form over land in the outer tropics and in near-tropical regions, mostly when air is moist and unstable, especially in the hot afternoons. As they writhe their way across country at some 50 kph they suck up much loose, or detached, debris. Frequently a funnel-shaped cloud accompanies them, opening out to a heavy cumulonimbus mass above. Thunderstorms, heavy rain, and large hailstones are typical of such systems in hot moist conditions. They occur in many parts of the world, and occasionally develop over parts of Britain. An area with frequent tornadoes is the southern U.S.A., especially in the Mississippi valley. When such systems move out over the sea

ALMOST CIRCULAR SYSTEM

Lack of contrasting air masses. No fronts.

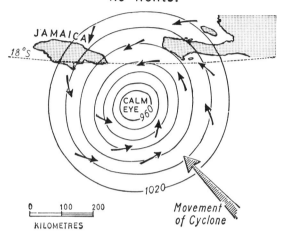

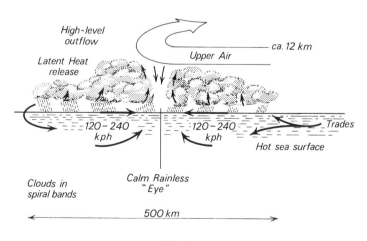

Fig. 33.

A deep tropical cyclone is moving towards Jamaica. Likely wind strengths are shown in the section below.

a water-spout may develop, carrying the water upwards towards the overhanging cloud, and flinging it out again by centrifugal force; and very often taking fish up with it.

TROPICAL CYCLONES — AREAS WITH FREQUENT HURRICANES

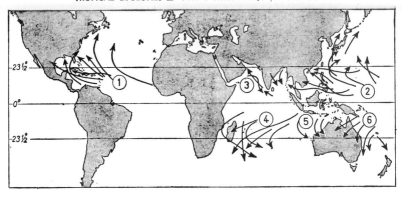

1	Caribbean, Gulf of Mexico.	2	W. Pacific — Off China, Philippines.
3	Arabian Sea, Bay of Bengal.	4	South Indian Ocean.
5	Off·N.W. Australia (Willi Willies)	6	South Pacific — Off N.E. Australia.

Fig. 34.

THE RETURN OF WATER TO THE ATMOSPHERE

We have just seen a number of processes which result in water, precipitated from the atmosphere, falling to the earth's surface. This, of course, is part of a general "hydrological cycle"; for the water is returned to the atmosphere by evaporation from moist surfaces, such as free water, damp ground, and vegetation. During such circulation, water may be held for various lengths of time away from the surface, beneath the ground, or within a water mass, or in plants and animals; but eventually by percolation, convection, transpiration, or some other appropriate mechanism, it again becomes available to pass as vapour into the atmosphere. Fig. 35 shows parts of this kind of circulation diagrammatically.

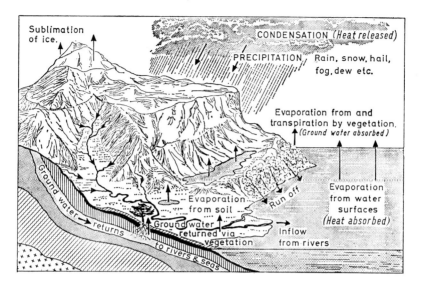

Fig. 35.

Some of the processes of water circulation in the "hydrological cycle". ("Sublimation" means the conversion of a solid direct into vapour without melting—in the case of ice, melting may also take place, of course.)

CHAPTER IV

ATMOSPHERIC CIRCULATION (II)

Now that we have seen something of the ways in which the heat content and humidity can affect air movements, and help to produce cyclonic disturbances and forms of precipitation, we can look at the movements themselves in a little more detail. The weather at any place can be affected both by air moving under the influence of huge air masses, and by winds of a more local origin. Before again considering air circulation on a global scale, we will look at some of the local air movements which may have considerable effect on regional climates, soils, and vegetation.

LOCAL AIR MOVEMENTS

While a certain part of the world may often be affected by a particular air mass, or the results of a "conflict" of air masses, it may also experience frequent air movements, typical of that location, caused by features of the local environment. These may be frequent enough to modify the local climate, soils, or vegetation. Some local winds we have seen already, such as the movements of cold air into low-lying frost pockets in parts of mid-latitude countries, and the funnelling of moist air up valleys on a windward slope to give abnormally high precipitation. These and a host of other regional influences act to modify the general climatic pattern.

Mountain and Valley Winds

If during the daytime fairly calm conditions prevail in a mountainous region, local thermal differences can cause air currents to move towards and up the mountain slopes. In the northern hemisphere this effect is well marked on south-facing slopes; for as the sunny parts of the valley and slopes become hot, they heat the air immediately above, which expands and moves up the mountainsides, sometimes concentrated by gulleys into a strong current. Such an updraught may cause cumulus clouds to form above mountain summits. In wide, deep valleys air tends to move up-valley on sunny days for the same reason.

On clear, calm nights, the air is chilled from the ground, which is continually losing heat by radiation; this cold dense air then tends to flow down the hillsides and valley slopes.

Land and Sea Breezes

Near seas or large lakes, when the weather is warm or hot, and conditions calm, an on-shore wind sets in during the day, but is replaced by an off-shore wind at night. Generally the on-shore

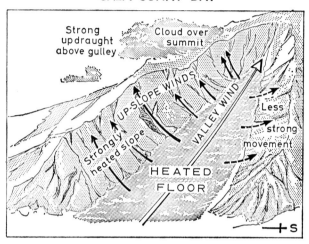

Fig. 36. MOUNTAIN AND VALLEY WINDS. (Here seen in the northern hemisphere, with south-facing slopes strongly heated.)

wind is stronger than the off-shore one. By day the near-coastal land becomes much hotter than the adjacent water surface. Air rises over the land, so that a pressure gradient is established between the cooler air over the water and that over the land, thus causing the on-shore "sea breeze" by day. The movement is reversed aloft, with a flow of air from land to water. In the tropics these effects can result in a strong sea breeze moving as far as 100 km inland, sometimes causing much cloud and perhaps precipitation. In temperate latitudes the effects are much slighter, and they are often overshadowed by even light general winds.

At night land temperatures fall rapidly to below those of the water surface, so that air cooled over the land drifts towards the water in a "land breeze".

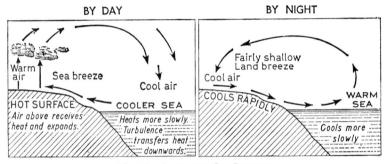

Fig. 37.   Land and Sea Breezes.
The on-shore wind is generally stronger than the off-shore one.

Gravity Winds

Where extensive surfaces are much colder than their surroundings, as on an elevated ice-cap, cold dense air accumulates at the surface, and may drain to the lower areas by gravitational pull. Sometimes in Antarctica and Greenland the downward flow becomes a really strong wind; but even in mountain country with small isolated ice surfaces, cold winds of this type are noticeable.

Föhn Winds

Air may be caused to move from one side of a high range to another in response to pressure differences over areas flanking the mountains. As unsaturated, moist air moves on to a mountain mass it is forced upwards, and cools adiabatically at about 1·0 C° per 100 metres. But eventually its water vapour is chilled to condensation point, when latent heat is released; so that further ascent is at the slower saturated adiabatic rate of about 0·5 C° per 100 metres.

On the lee slopes, the air descends and gains heat at the dry adiabatic rate; and so, being warmed more rapidly, has at equivalent altitudes, higher temperatures than it had on ascent. Thus a wind may blow down and away from the lee slope with a temperature 10-20 C°, and sometimes approaching 30 C°, higher than the air on the windward side. Its absolute water vapour content is small; and with higher temperatures, the relative humidity may be very low indeed. In fact, other processes may also be

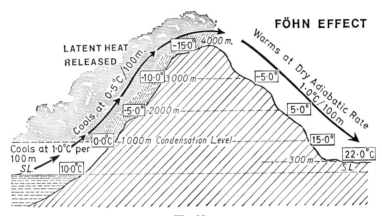

Fig. 38.

The air sinking in the lee of the mountains is gaining heat at the dry adiabatic rate, which is considerably higher than the rate of cooling of the saturated air during the greater part of its ascent.

involved, such as turbulence and eddying on the lee slopes, which may bring about a *forced* descent of the air. This may help to account for temperature increases on the lee flanks when no condensation occurs on the windward side. Considerably greater heating can occur when part of a warm tropical air stream is forced to descend, and is thus further warmed by compression.

Föhn winds are common in the European Alps in spring and autumn. Air crossing the Alps from the south usually produces the most marked temperature contrasts. Such winds tend to set in when a depression lies over north-central Europe, so that a gradient is established from the Mediterranean towards the low pressure to the north. Similar winds occur in other mountain systems under appropriate pressure conditions. The "Chinooks" of the Rockies, like the Alpine föhn winds, tend to cause rapid snow-melt in spring and help to open grazing land; föhn winds of the Southern Alps of New Zealand have a desiccating effect on farmland in the Canterbury Plains, which, in any case, lie in a rain-shadow region, so that wind-breaks are a familiar part of their landscape. In Alpine regions the sudden onset of a föhn wind, with rapid thawing, is apt to cause avalanches.

Pressure Changes Resulting in Local Winds

Fairly abrupt changes in the direction of air movements may bring remarkable changes in weather. These may be due to the rapid passage of ridges of high pressure or low pressure troughs, but may also be the result of moving depressions whose centres are located far from the place of observation.

When the centre of a depression travels eastward over the Mediterranean Sea, the air in front of the system moves northward from the deserts of North Africa and north-westward from Arabia. Places in the northern Mediterranean may then experience an unusually hot, dry, and sometimes dusty wind, which can set in for several days at a time. In spring the change from coolness to heat can be abrupt. In the southern lands themselves such winds are dry, and known as the Sirocco; in Egypt as the Khamsin. Their influence is felt in northern Mediterranean lands; where, as they tend to acquire moisture from the sea, they may bring heavy rain to the eastern Adriatic.

In the rear of such a depression the air moves from the north, so that, in spring especially, polar continental air, or cold air from the mountains of Alpine Europe, is sometimes funnelled through gaps in the high relief to reach the Mediterranean. The Mistral of the Rhône valley is such a strong cold wind, and may persist for days: despite clear bright skies its chill blast can have disastrous effects on early-flowering trees and shrubs, and wind-breaks are necessary precautions in the lower Rhône valley. Another gusty wind of this type is the Bora of the north-east Adriatic; this moves from high pressures over the Danube lands to join in the circulation at the rear of a Mediterranean depression.

In southern Australia the eastward passage of a well-defined trough can bring hot dry air from the interior to the south coast as the scorching "brickfielder": these northerly winds with their desiccating effect on vegetation, greatly add to the danger of bush fires. Behind the troughs, southerly air suddenly replaces the "brick-fielder"; temperatures drop rapidly and heavy rain may occur at the onset of these "southerly busters".

ATMOSPHERIC CIRCULATION

Upper Air Movements

We have seen that low pressure systems involving air converg-ence require the removal of the ascending air at high levels, and

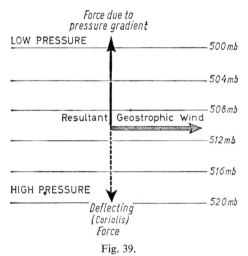

Fig. 39.

Air moving as a result of a pressure gradient at high altitudes is deflected (to the right in the northern hemisphere) to move, as a geostrophic wind, almost parallel to the isobars. The velocity of this wind is inversely proportional to the latitude.

that divergence at the surface is fed by air sinking from aloft. We need also to know something of the relations between such vertical movements and the general atmospheric circulation. Observations of upper air conditions have only recently been possible on a scale sufficient to be of real value, in this respect, to meteorologists; and obviously, even now, much more regular information is needed. Nevertheless, charts of high level conditions are now regularly prepared for certain parts of the atmosphere; some of the forms in which these are now plotted are briefly described below.

High-level winds move in relation to different, but related, pressure gradients to those at the surface. They do not experience friction drag as the surface winds do, and are generally of greater

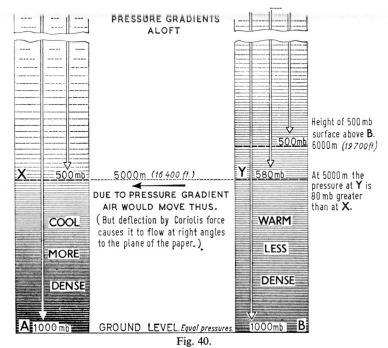

Fig. 40.

Air moving according to the pressure gradient at 5 000 metres altitude. Notice the different heights of the 500 mb. surface: by plotting a "contour" map of the varying heights of this surface we can obtain an indication of likely upper air movements.

velocity. Hence, under the deflective force of the earth's rotation, they tend to remain closely parallel to the isobars, as geostrophic winds (Fig. 39), except near the equator, where the Coriolis deflective force approaches zero.

Pressure Gradients Aloft and Thermal Winds

In Fig. 40 we see two places A and B on a horizontal surface; at each the atmospheric pressure is the same, say, 1000 mb. This means that the air "column" above A has the same weight as that above B. But the air immediately above A is cooler and denser than that above B. Now consider the level XY in column A. The pressure of the air above this level is 500 mb; for the lower, denser air, from A to X, itself exerts a pressure of 500 mb. In the air column B, the pressure of air above the level XY is 580 mb, for the air below this height (being warmer and less dense than that in column A) contributes only 420 mb of the total pressure. The arrow indicates the consequent direction of movement of the upper air.

Looking at Fig. 40 once more, we see that the height of the surface of 500 mb pressure is 5 000 m in A and 6 000 m in B. It is possible, therefore, to plot the varying heights of this surface for any given pressure, and obtain a kind of contour map which will give an idea of the upper air movements: the 500 mb map is one used much by meteorologists. Another method makes use of the vertical distance (thickness) between selected pressure levels, say the 1 000 mb and 500 mb surfaces. This is recorded at a large number of stations, plotted, and contours drawn. In Fig. 40 this thickness at A is 5 000 m, at B, 6 000 m: the thickness is a response to the mean temperatures. Direct readings of the wind speed at these heights can now be obtained regularly on a global scale, and these too can be shown on upper air charts.

Upper Air Winds and the Jet Streams

As temperatures decrease polewards, the accompanying thermal winds in the upper troposphere move as strong westerlies; their speed becomes great where the temperature gradient is steep. The velocity of the upper westerlies is therefore very high indeed above the fronts of air masses of contrasting temperature in the middle latitudes. Thus the general poleward gradient gives rise to a high-level west wind vortex around each of the poles, and embedded in these westerlies are narrow air streams of high velocity above the various fronts, following snaking courses as they move eastwards (Fig. 42).

The narrow belts of high velocity winds are known as *jet streams.* Wind speeds along their meandering courses vary greatly from place to place; but at their core may be from 100-200 knots, sometimes faster. Differences in the temperature gradients in the northern and southern hemispheres lead to variations in the pattern of upper air flow in each; and there are also, of course, seasonal variations in the average positions and strengths of the winds.

SPECIMEN VERTICAL CROSS SECTIONS

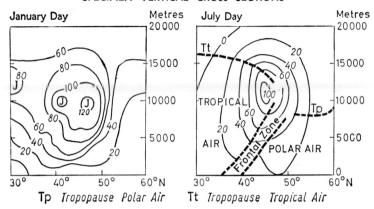

Tp *Tropopause Polar Air*   Tt *Tropopause Tropical Air*

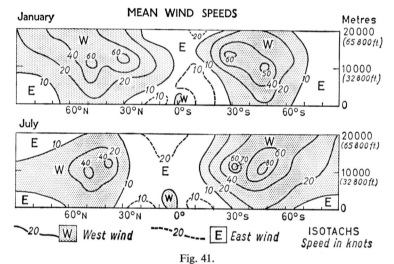

~20—— W *West wind*   ----20---- E *East wind*   ISOTACHS *Speed in knots*

Fig. 41.

The specimen vertical cross-sections of the atmosphere show typical upper air conditions over eastern North America in January and July. At about 10 000 metres above the fronts air is rushing *towards* the observer at over 100 knots. The right-hand diagram (July) shows the divisions between the troposphere and stratosphere, and the front between polar and tropical air. Fronts have been omitted from the January diagram to show the concentration of these high westerlies in the middle latitudes.

The sections below show in a more general way the average positions and mean speeds of the global winds up to 20 000 metres. (These sections are not *directly* related to the specimen sections above, and, to avoid confusion, the westerlies are shown moving *away* from the observer.) [*After Lamb.*]

72

FLUCTUATIONS IN SPEED OF JET STREAMS

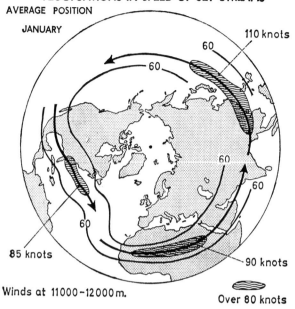

AVERAGE POSITION

JANUARY

110 knots

85 knots

Winds at 11000–12000 m.

90 knots

Over 80 knots

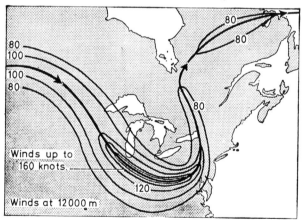

WINDING PATH OF JET STREAMS

80
100
100
80

80

80

Winds up to 160 knots

120

Winds at 12000 m

Fig. 42.

The map of the northern hemisphere shows average speeds and positions of the sub-tropical westerlies at about 11 000 metres. That below, a typical upper air chart for north-eastern U.S.A. in June, gives some idea of the concentration and high speeds of the moving air in certain parts of these latitudes.

73

Sub-tropical Upper Westerlies and Atmospheric Circulation

The jet streams of the sub-tropical westerlies undoubtedly play important roles in the maintenance of the general atmospheric circulation and distribution of heat energy. We have seen that they are particularly intense winds corresponding to steep temperature gradients— with cold air on the poleward side and much

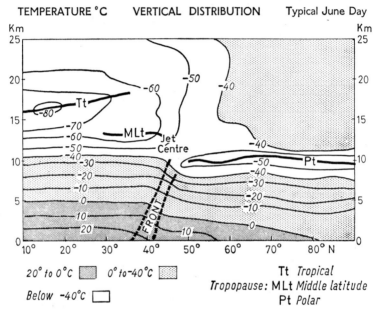

TEMPERATURE °C   VERTICAL DISTRIBUTION   Typical June Day

20° to 0°C ▨   0° to -40°C ▨   Tt *Tropical*

Below -40°C ☐   *Tropopause:* MLt *Middle latitude*
Pt *Polar*

Fig. 43.

The vertical distribution of temperature shows that at the front a strong temperature gradient extends to the upper troposphere and the centre of strong winds above the front (the jet centre on the map). The gradient is between the cold air on the northern side and the much warmer air to the south.

warmer air equatorwards. The thermal differences seem to be converted into the tremendous energy of movement concentrated in these upper westerlies. The mechanisms by which air is transferred meridionally (from one latitude to another) at high levels are being closely studied, but are far from being fully understood. As the speed of the jet stream varies, air enters or leaves it. Thus an accelerating stream will draw air into its high speed flow, and so affect pressure distributions in the lower troposphere, while its waving path enables its effects to be felt over a wide range of latitude.

Circumpolar Upper Winds

As already indicated (p. 3), the ozone concentration at between 15 and 35 km, in the stratosphere, absorbs radiation from the sun. This concentration is greatest over the polar regions. But in winter there is little incoming radiation, so that there is a gradual fall in temperature from about $-50°$ C at the tropopause to $-80°$ C at some 80 km above the surface. The resulting meridional temperature differences cause strong westerlies, of up to 70 knots, about the cold polar core. A "polar-night jet stream" of this type, at 15–20 km above the surface, is particularly well developed about Antarctica (p. 146), where it persists until spring. Like all strong meridional air flows, such movements tend to minimise the interchange of

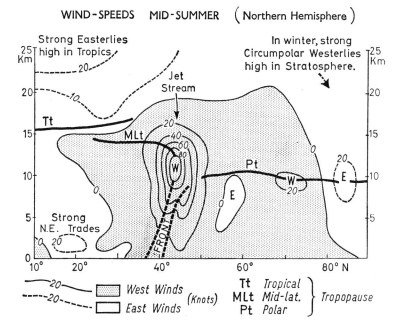

Fig. 44.

This emphasises the features shown in Figs. 40 and 42, and indicates the position of the strong circumpolar westerlies which in winter encircle the polar regions of sinking air. [*After Hare.*]

energy between the high and low latitudes; and so, indirectly, they help to increase the severity of the Antarctic winter.

In summer the concentrated ozone layers of the stratosphere tend to be particularly warm. The result is that strong easterly winds of up to about 40 knots encircle the warm polar core in the upper atmosphere.

High Relief and Upper Air Flow

The world's highest mountain systems extend into the middle and upper troposphere, and such outstanding relief features can even affect the flow of the strong upper westerlies of the middle latitudes. Air flowing over regions of high relief seems to impose ridges and troughs on the upper pressure surfaces. A tendency exists, for instance, for deep troughs to occur over eastern North America and to the east of Japan, while ridges are formed in the longitude of the American Cordilleras. In parts of the subtropical upper westerlies there are two or three characteristic streams of particularly stong flow, and the general jet movement seems to become deformed and to have a number of separate "cores" as the westerlies pass above the Tibetan plateaux and the ranges of southern central Asia. The position of this composite "sub-tropical jet stream" over southern Asia fluctuates with the seasons, and has a marked influence on the climate of northern India at the time of the summer monsoon. The jet stream moves from its winter position over the northern Indian plains and the Himalayas northwards, to a mean position over central Tibet, which has a dry summer.

Upper Air Movements and Weather in the Lower Troposphere

The jet streams are, therefore, not currents of uniform strength, nor are they continuous in their general eastward flow. Their average positions vary with the seasons. As surface high pressure systems on the warmer flanks of the jet streams are fed by air from above, and as the location of these highs, and of the low pressure systems of the higher middle latitudes seem to be associated with the various troughs and ridges in the upper westerlies, such seasonal movements must have considerable bearing on climatic variations in the lower troposphere.

Surface heating over the oceans and continents, and the release of large amounts of latent heat at times of widespread

PRESSURE DISTRIBUTION __ UPPER ATMOSPHERE

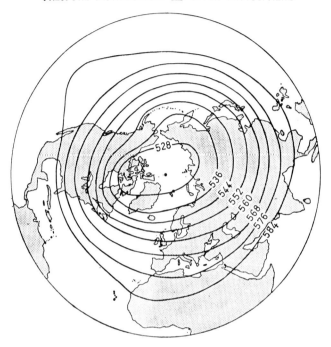

500 mb Level plotted to show pressure distribution
and indicate circumpolar air circulation.

(Mean height __ Dekameters)

Fig. 45.

A specimen map to show the advantage of plotting the height of the 500 mb
level. A clear picture is obtained of upper air circulation. Fig. 40 shows how
the height of this surface is related to the pressure gradient and upper air
movements.

condensation and precipitation, also seem to modify the general
pattern of movement of the upper air. The huge quantity of
energy released by a period of exceptionally heavy rainfall in
Hawaii, say, may well increase the amplitude of swing of the
meandering jet streams, causing unusual climatic conditions in
north-west Europe on the other side of the hemisphere. But cause
and effect are often inextricably mixed, and our knowledge of upper

air conditions in the past is slight. It would obviously be a great step forward if it were possible to calculate and forecast accurately the position, movement, and strength of these strong upper-air currents. Once enough data is available and plotted for study, the advantage of maps of the 500 mb surface, with their simpler and bolder patterns than the sea-level isobaric maps, ought to lead to more accurate forecasting. The places of maximum wind speeds are, in fact, at a rather greater altitude than this surface: at about 9 000 m in temperate latitudes (near the 300 mb surfaces) and 12 000 m in the sub-tropics (about 200 mb).

A Summary of Meridional Circulation

Fig. 46 shows a schematic representation of the upper air meridional circulation. In the low latitudes air rises, with much vertical heat transport effected in huge cumulonimbus clouds. In the sub-tropics subsidence, with the formation and regeneration of anticyclones, fed by fast moving upper air streams, occurs to the west of the continents, S(W). Air tends to rise at the eastern edge of these great anticyclones, U(E), so that the eastern oceans, and western parts of the continental masses, have ample precipitation.

Air returns equatorwards as the Trade Winds, and rises in the low-latitude zone of convergence, especially in convective storms, TrC. So that, in effect, the system of circulation suggested by G. Hadley, as long ago as 1735, does exist.

The graph of the mean latitudinal precipitation shows peaks in the middle and higher latitudes, where the wave cyclones are active along the polar front, MLC. There is no direct equivalent of the Hadley cell in the high latitudes, although a weak mid-latitude cell exists. At the polar front the cold, dense easterlies flowing from the polar areas of subsidence, PS, meet air from the sub-tropical anti-cyclones which has travelled polewards. The latter rises over the cold air. Part of it returns at high level towards the equator, although the Coriolis force tends to reinforce its westerly momentum. Much of the polar air, warmed by its journey equatorwards, and mixed with warmer air, rises in the cyclonic systems and returns polewards, as a westerly flow aloft.

Air Masses and Their Fronts in the Lower Troposphere

We now turn once more to air masses as experienced at lower levels. Fig. 12 shows that an area may be affected at different times by the advent of air masses from various directions. But the movements of these bodies of air are irregular; and though

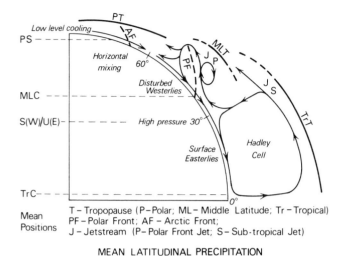

Mean Positions

T – Tropopause (P – Polar; ML – Middle Latitude; Tr – Tropical)
PF – Polar Front; AF – Arctic Front;
J – Jetstream (P – Polar Front Jet; S – Sub-tropical Jet)

MEAN LATITUDINAL PRECIPITATION

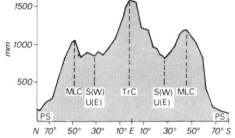

PS – Polar Subsidence; MLC – Mid-Latitude Cyclonic;
S(W)/U(E) – Subsidence to West of land masses / Uplift to East;
TrC – Tropical Trade-wind Convergence

Fig. 46.

certain air masses may be more dominant in one season than in others, there is often a conflict between air from the different source regions, especially in the parts of north-west Europe shown. Boundaries between neighbouring air masses can be identified, and, as we have already seen when considering temperate depressions, the gain of one type of air at the expense of another can be shown on a map as a moving front. The location both of air masses and their fronts are important weather features, and are plotted as such in daily weather maps.

From the climatic point of view we can show *average* positions of both air masses and fronts, and study seasonal, or other periodic variations in these average positions. The maps in Fig. 47 show such average positions for January and July, and give some idea of the characteristics of the air moving in the directions shown in Figs. 10 and 11 as "mean winds". We now have a much better picture of lower atmospheric conditions than we could obtain from the "pressure and winds" maps of Figs. 8–11 alone.

Characteristics of the Air Masses

Arctic and Antarctic Air (Ac or Am). This type of air has its origins over the frozen land or ice-caps of the very high latitudes. It is very cold at the place of origin and the moisture content is low; as a result it is very stable, with inversion conditions. But as it passes over warmer seas, heat and moisture are taken up, and contrasts are established which lead to instability and convectional stirring.

Polar Air (Pc or Pm). This has its origin over cold land or water in high latitudes. The polar continental air is naturally very dry, and cold in its lower layers, often with strong inversion. Polar maritime air is soon modified by the warmer seas and, again, tends to be less stable as a result.

Tropical Air (Tc or Tm). The source regions are chiefly in the lower middle latitudes, or sub-tropics. The air which sinks onto, and then diverges from, a large land mass like North Africa is very warm and very dry (tropical continental air). The tropical maritime air has stable characteristics at its place of origin, but picks up much moisture on its passage over the oceans; and the stability of the air depends a great deal on the surface over which it passes. Where it moves over a surface colder than the temperature of the lower air, the latter is chilled, giving a surface inversion which adds stability. Where the lower layers are warmed by a surface hotter than themselves, the air tends to become unstable. The letter "w" may be used to show that the air mass is warmer than the surface, "k" (kalt) to show that the air mass is colder. Thus as air flows outwards from sub-tropical sources over the oceans, some moving polewards and some equatorwards, the symbols Tmw or Tmk tell us something of the likely weather conditions associated with that air.

As we have seen already, the moisture content may lead to instability by releasing latent heat of condensation, and is likely

to affect subsequent weather in warm air of the Tm type. Nevertheless, violent contrasts in temperature between air and surface
are less likely in tropical than in temperate regions; so that the

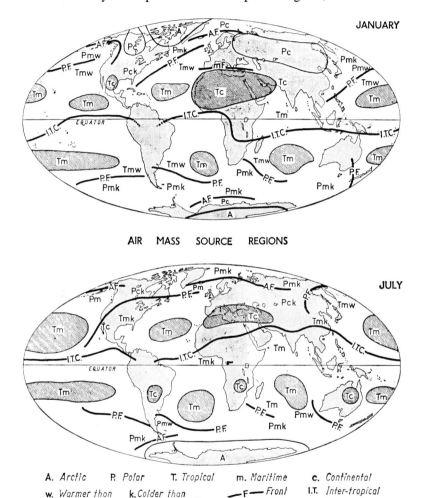

Fig. 47.

The average positions of air masses and fronts in January and July, with
symbols to indicate the dominant types of air at that time of year. In January
there may be a "Mediterranean Front", shown by the line MF.

tropical maritime air often remains in a fairly stable state for a long time (fine weather, with scattered cumulus is a particular feature in the "Trade Wind belts" over the oceans). However, forced uplift, due to convergence or higher relief, may bring heavy rain.

The Inter-Tropical Front (I.T.F.) or Zone of Convergence (I.T.C.)

The meeting place of the tropical air masses is often termed a *zone* of convergence (I.T.C. zone), rather than a *front* (I.T.F.), for the air masses are very similar in character, especially when they meet over the ocean. There are not the density differences that are apt to exist between converging types of air in the middle latitudes, nor the well defined fronts between contrasting types of air that there are in the higher latitudes.

But, partly as a result of such convergence, the equatorial weather is not as uniform as one might think, and various disturbances do occur. The tropical air flows converge, as the Trades, in conditions of warmth and humidity that spell potential turbulence, but may lack the "trigger effect" to set off strong uplift. Their mutual uplift adds to the instability, but the real disturbances often come from "waves" in the air flows themselves. Sometimes air from higher latitudes penetrates as far as equatorial regions to set tropical cyclones in motion. The tendency of air to be lifted by convergence is greater on the western side of the oceans, and adds to the frequency of storms in those waters within the tropics (though these seldom occur within five degrees of the equator). Sometimes, however, weak lows, associated with air convergence, do develop in the heart of the equatorial trough of low pressure, and swirls of air may then move against the normal surface flow, with accompanying storms.

The Polar Front

Polewards of the sub-tropical air sources, the tropical and polar air masses meet; as we have seen (p. 55) their strong temperature contrasts favour the birth and development of depressions. The position of the "polar fronts" varies from day to day, but the average positions are shown in Fig. 47. The presence of the fronts between these converging and contrasting types of air over the oceans is a regular feature of the weather maps in these latitudes. The winter build-up of pressure over the northern Euro-Asian land mass occasionally gives rise to a meeting of polar continental air in the vicinity of the Mediterranean, and this is sometimes referred to as a "Mediterranean Front".

The Arctic Front

A well established front of this type is more likely to occur as an "Antarctic Front", where the very cold air from the Antarctic, usually Am or Pm air itself, sometimes meets warmer air originally of a Pm source, but which has been greatly modified by waters further south: this may happen because this now warmer air has rotated to some extent as part of the system of a depression. The contrast between the air masses may be marked, but less so than between Pm and Tm air.

These then are some of the more regular features of the air mass pattern, and Fig. 47 shows that when average positions of sources, areas, and fronts are recorded, seasonal "swings" can be noticed which, naturally, resemble those seen on the maps of average pressure conditions, Figs. 8 and 9.

Monsoon Systems

We shall now consider in more detail those parts of the world where winter and summer air flows are reversed. These are the monsoon areas where thermal effects cause pressure changes; though the depth of the atmosphere involved in the resulting air flows is not great. The upper air flows appear to retain their general pattern, especially over eastern Asia; and the tendency of air to descend in the lower middle latitudes seems to exert a blanketing effect on unstable air of the summer monsoon in southern Asia, especially on the landward perimeter of the thermal low pressure centre.

A *monsoon* effect is so well developed in southern and eastern Asia that we will consider the seasonal changes in these great areas in some detail: but there are other parts of the world where air flows are sometimes described as "monsoonal". Among these are northern Australia, the southern part of West Africa, and the Gulf states and south-eastern U.S.A. The seasonal contrasts are well marked in northern Australia. In the others there are complicating factors: in the south-east of the U.S.A. there is not a well-developed outflow of air in winter.

The Monsoon in Southern Asia

This is in many ways a separate system from that of eastern Asia, and the Himalayas are a very real climatic barrier. During the winter, air subsides over the northern plains of the Indian sub-continent and drifts generally southwards as north or north-east winds. On an average pressure map air is often shown as flowing from the exceptionally high pressures of central Asia outward over India and China. But the strong outflow of cold air over eastern China is very different in character to that which descends, warmed by compression, over northern India, though both are "continental" in origin. In a sense, the normal trade-wind flow is established over India, and air moves towards the inter-tropical zone of convergence, now south of the equator.

From November to February the mean monthly temperatures of the northern plains average between 10° C -16° C. Apart from precipitation accompanying weak depressions which move into north-west India from the west, skies are clear, mid-day temperatures very warm, and nights crisply cool. It soon becomes hotter, however; and from March the mid-day heat becomes intense, and mean temperatures rise rapidly. Pressures fall over the northern plains, and maps of average pressure show this as a region of low pressure separated by a declining high from the very warm, humid, tropical maritime air over the Indian Ocean. By the end of May a zone of convergence becomes established in the region of the intense thermal low, and the maritime air is able to advance as far north as latitude 30°. The "burst" of the monsoon occurs at almost the same time each year; so regularly that agricultural practices become geared to its average time of arrival, and the occasional delay can cause widespread crop failures. The source of the tropical maritime air is in the southern hemisphere, so that this Tm air moves across the great expanses of ocean in equatorial latitudes. Sometimes this air, which has crossed the equator, is classified as an "Em type".

Moist air from the oceans moves in and over much of the Indian sub-continent; but the idea of a simple flow bringing heavy rain to the affected areas is not sufficiently accurate. In fact, daily conditions vary a great deal: pressures fluctuate, the winds change direction, and shallow cyclonic disturbances arise in the maritime air and move across the land, giving variations in the occurrence and intensity of rainfall from place to place.

Where the main body of the unstable tropical maritime air meets relief barriers, exceptionally heavy rain occurs; where, for instance, air from the south-west is forced up by the Western Ghats, and where southerly air, moist from the Indian Ocean and Bay of Bengal, meets the Khasi Hills. Convection above the heated

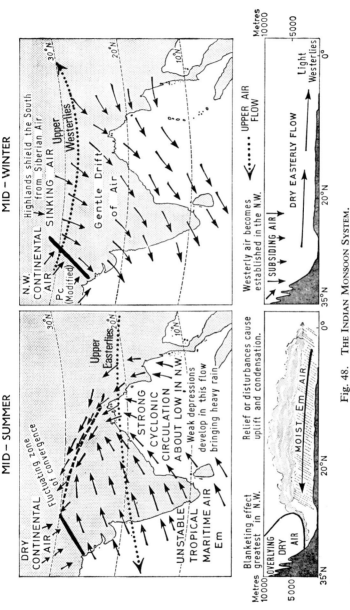

Fig. 48. The Indian Monsoon System.

From June to early September the relative shallow in-flow of very warm moist air brings heavy rain to many parts of the sub-continent—though in the north-west sinking continental air acts against thermal uplift, and dry, conditions result. Dry, sinking air moves equatorwards from the sub-tropics during the winter months.

plateaux and plains also adds to the intensity of precipitation. We have already seen the control that relief exerts over the amount of precipitation, especially where there is conditional instability. The total rainfall received decreases markedly from the Bay of Bengal to the north-western plains, and the hottest parts of the sub-continent have, in fact, a low rainfall. The westerly jet stream, which passes high above northern India during winter, has moved northwards; but subsiding upper air advances aloft from the north-west, and overruns the moist shallower monsoon air. It thus provides a blanketing effect which prevents excessive vertical movements of the moist air, Fig. 48.

The rainy period lasts in most places until mid-September, though during the "rains" there are breaks, which vary in length from place to place, and from year to year. Upper easterlies overlie the south-west monsoon. Subsidence on the south side of these can cause dry spells. The presence of this upper air also helps to enhance the aridity of the central Deccan plateau, where there is little rainfall in late summer.

Gradually the continental air re-establishes itself over northern India, and the low-pressure zone of convergence is now further south. During the "retreat" of the monsoon, tropical cyclones are apt to develop within the low pressure zone, and violent storms are likely to affect southern India during October and November. Storms are also likely during April and May, before the break of the monsoon.

The Monsoon of Eastern Asia

During summer, humid air tends to move in from the east and south-east; while in winter, strong, persistent flows of cold stable air reach eastern Asia from the west and north-west. The *summer* monsoon is weak compared with that of southern Asia, and in the northern parts of this huge area the inward air flow is fairly shallow. In places, in south-eastern China for example, prominent relief helps to cause heavy rainfall in summer; but over much of eastern Asia the rain appears to be of frontal origin; weak disturbances cause much of it, and typhoons bring almost a third of the summer rainfall to the coastal south-east. In the extreme south-east, Em air, hot and humid, arrives from the southern hemisphere. In the southern interior, near the Burmese and Indo-Chinese borders, some air arrives from the Indian monsoon system; and though

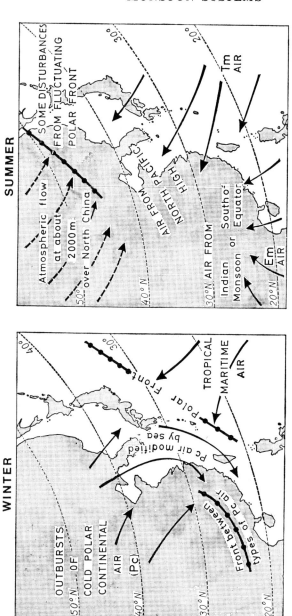

Fronts whose actual positions fluctuate greatly.

Fig. 49.

In summer, warm moist unstable air is brought in by the equatorial south-westerlies and the south-easterlies from the Pacific, as a shallow monsoonal flow: most of the rainfall comes from disturbances within these flows, producing heavy tropical storms. In winter, cold dry air surges over eastern Asia from the interior, but precipitation may occur at fronts formed as shown. In north-western China there is a westerly flow at no great height, even in summer, when, occasionally, rainfall there is associated with the polar front.

this has lost much of its moisture content already, it gives occasional thunderstorms.

In the north, plentiful rainfall occurs about the mean position of the polar front, where tropical maritime air of Pacific origin meets polar maritime air from the Sea of Okhotsk. The high mountains and plateaux are the limits of penetration of the Tm air into Asia; inland of this, dry continental air moves eastwards, though very occasional surges of moist air may produce some of the meagre rain which falls in the interior.

During the *winter* months, cold, dry, polar continental air arrives in outbursts from central Asia. This is stable air; the skies are clear and the weather bitterly cold. Some of this air swings clockwise around the anticyclonic system as a whole and, in fact, reaches much of eastern China with moisture gained from the western Pacific. Its origin is polar continental, but its modifications give it sufficient instability to give rise to cloud and precipitation over the coastal regions, notably where relief causes uplift, and especially in the south. In central and southern China, disturbed weather may result from fronts between this air and that coming directly from the interior. The true polar front, with Tm air involved, lies to the extreme south of China and Indo-China.

At higher levels, westerly winds persist over China as a whole, and air from the high Tibetan plateaux has a westerly flow throughout the year, warming on descent and giving bright, sunny weather in Yunnan.

Other Monsoon Areas

These Asian monsoon systems have been described in some detail as being huge modifications of the pattern of circulation at low levels, and involve air moving from the air mass sources already described. Even here the actual weather may be affected by air from a number of different sources. The other so-called "monsoon systems" mentioned above can be explained even more clearly in terms of the main air masses described on pp. 80–2. The West African seasonal changes, for instance, can best be seen in terms of a northward migration of the inter-tropical zone of convergence in summer, with Tm (or Em) air meeting Tc air far inland; and as a retreat of this front in the cooler months, when dry continental air extends southwards, as the Harmattan, over all but the coastal districts.

OCEANIC INFLUENCES ON CLIMATE

We have already recognised that there are close connections between oceanic "reservoirs of heat" and the general Atmospheric Circulation; and have observed some of the interactions of the oceans and atmosphere. So that this is a suitable place to review, briefly, the inter-relationship between the oceans and climates.

Interactions of Atmosphere and Oceans

The atmosphere and oceans have a relationship which is in a state of dynamic equilibrium. Air passing over the ocean moves surface waters, and helps to create and maintain an oceanic circulation. The heating and evaporation of the tropical surface waters, and the cooling of polar waters, also give rise to vertical and horizontal movements in the ocean. The moving waters themselves help to transfer heat from lower to higher latitudes, and thus play a part in maintaining the atmospheric heat balance. In the higher and middle latitudes, especially, the warm currents yield vast amounts of heat energy and moisture to the air above them. Oceans, with their convectional movements, can act as heat reservoirs, in a way that land areas cannot.

We have already seen many of the results of the transfer of heat energy and moisture from oceans to the atmosphere; and need only recall here the fundamental role of the ocean reservoir in the processes of the "hydro-cycle", in the condensation, cloud formation, and precipitation which result from the meeting of contrasting types of maritime air, or the passage of unstable maritime air over a region of high relief, and in the creation and maintenance of hurricane systems.

Air Over Cold Waters

The presence of relatively cold waters off-shore may result in fog and low cloud near the coasts, and generally does little to relieve the aridity of coastal regions. Offshore winds tend to initiate the upwelling of cooler water from several hundred metres beneath the surface. Prevailing winds may thus influence the surface water temperatures, which in turn may affect the local climate of the littoral region. This is especially so off the tropical west coasts, where air moving onshore, as a daily sea-breeze, is chilled by the cool waters, becomes saturated with water-vapour, and tends to form fogs. For instance, fog, or low cloud, which is more likely when light winds cause turbulence, are common features along these cold-water coasts of California, northern Chile and southern Peru, and south-west Africa. Inland, over the warmer surfaces, the relative humidity of the air falls and fog disperses: turbulence is unlikely to do more than cause a higher cloud-layer; often skies clear completely, so that bright sunshine contrasts with the dull conditions immediately off-shore. Little rain results from these conditions, and, though the Peruvian coastlands gain some moisture where the persistent cloud level meets the hillsides, almost complete aridity is maintained. The summer fogs of San Francisco are notorious. They pour in through the Golden Gate at such low levels in the cold dense air, that at this time of the year the hill summits to the north, remaining in bright sunshine, have an average temperature of 5 C ° above that of the city beneath. The strong advective movement through the break in the coastal hills is influenced by the thermal low pressures over the hot surfaces of the Great Valley to the east. Inland the fog clears rapidly.

Air Over Warm Waters

In the examples above, both the waters and the atmosphere make their own contributions to the general climatic or oceanic conditions. This is further emphasised by their relationships in the outer Tropics. By providing warm, dry, stable air with water vapour, the oceans also give it, potentially, a degree of instability. While at the same time such air affects the waters beneath. For instance, as warm, dry air moves outward from its source region, as a Trade Wind, the skies to begin with are clear, allowing strong sunlight and heat energy to reach the ocean beneath, and causing rapid evaporation. Thus the surface temperature of the ocean increases, and receiving little rainfall and losing water to the atmosphere, its salinity increases also. The Trade Winds then move on into Equatorial Latitudes with their moisture content and potential instability; the resulting cloud and rainfall both act to give a lower salinity to surface waters in the low latitudes. All of which underlines the fact that we can no more disregard atmospheric influences on the ocean than ignore oceanic effects on the atmosphere and on climatic conditions.

CHAPTER V

THE CLASSIFICATION OF CLIMATES

Climatic Regions

With the help of meteorological instruments we can read and record, at a given moment, various characteristics of the climatic elements described in the previous chapters; and, of course, we experience the weather resulting from the action and interaction of these elements in our locality. As night follows day, or as the weather conditions alter, as air masses supersede one another, bringing changes in wind direction, temperature, humidity, and precipitation, and as season follows season, we can follow and record these changes in terms of readings made at short intervals. After a number of years we will have amassed sufficient data to be able to recognise certain recurring climatic patterns; and certain values for the climatic elements may seem to be "normal" for that place. On the basis of mean climatic figures, we can now compare our particular climate, or various features of it, with those at other stations.

There are, of course, innumerable "local" climates, but even on a global basis we may find that whole areas, far removed from each other, have striking similarities in their climatic patterns; and that the data for certain climatic elements in each area are very similar over a given period. Thus we recognise similar "climatic regions".

The Hazards of defining "Climatic Regions"

To record the distribution of broadly similar types of climate we first need some basis for climatic classification. Rarely, if ever, do all the climatic elements have the same characteristics in different locations, no matter how similar their climates appear to be. The problem is to find the climatic feature or features on which to base our classification. We may find that two separate areas have *mean* rainfall amounts and *average* temperature figures which are very similar throughout the year; and yet the persistently high humidity and cloudiness of one, and the great extremes of temperature and intermittent storminess of the other, may have helped to create very different natural regions, with many dissimilar features of their landscapes and vegetation; and also their sensible climates (the "feel" of the climates to man) may be quite different. Therefore, to classify regions only on the basis of mean temperature and rainfall figures is not necessarily a good system: and it soon becomes evident that most systems of classification have particular merits yet include anomalies. Defining a climatic region by whatever methods are chosen is bound to be hazardous and run the risk of over-simplification, seldom is there a sharp climatic divide in nature, and transitional zones are usually found between the heart of one recognisable climatic region and that of another.

It is possible to give detailed climatic descriptions of the various parts of the earth's surface without making use of a classification at all. W. G. Kendrew gives a very full coverage, continent by continent, in his *"Climates of the Continents"* without making an overall classification; though he draws parallels between certain parts of the world. Nevertheless, by grouping climates into types, certain general truths about similar areas may stand out more clearly; and we may be able to assess more easily the influences of those elements shared by similar regions. If a climatic grouping is too broad, generalisations are less likely to be valid; but, while sub-division makes for greater accuracy of description, there is always a practical limit to the number of sub-divisions; no two places have exactly the same climate. With these facts in mind, we will consider the bases on which various classifications are made, and then some of the systems of classification; remembering that nature always appears to resist straightforward categorical schemes.

Bases for Classification

Since the time of the ancient Greeks men have recognised a three-fold division of the earth's climates, distinguishing between zones which are *tropical* (or torrid), *middle latitude* (or temperate), and *polar* (or frigid). This simple zonal arrangement implies a decrease in temperatures from equator to poles: but, of course, the mean summer temperatures, and the maximum temperatures, in the arid sub-tropics are usually higher than any found in the low latitudes, and "temperate" is hardly an adequate description for continental interiors in the middle latitudes during the winter!

But temperature values combined with those for precipitation are widely used in defining the limits of climatic regions. Regional climatic characteristics are apt to be reflected by the vegetation; and so the numerical values for temperature and precipitation which allow particular plants or forms of vegetation to flourish are often chosen to define the limits for climatic types. The combination of precipitation and temperature is usually considered on a seasonal basis; for a certain quantity of rain received in a hot season is likely to be less effective for plant growth than the same amount received during a cooler season, when the rate of evaporation is less. Some classifications use a value for "precipitation effectiveness", obtained by determining ratios of precipitation to temperature, others take into consideration the actual values for evaporation over the given period (though the fact that measured evaporation figures are not available for many parts of the world is obviously a drawback). The use of accurate values for the loss of water from moist soil and plant surfaces would be of particular value for the purposes of classification if it could be measured regularly at many widespread stations. Even so one would have to tread cautiously, for the relationships between climate and vegetation are complicated by many factors; for instance, infertile soils, poor drainage conditions, and interference by man, fire, or animals, may result in vegetation whose form is certainly not a simple response to climate.

SYSTEMS OF CLASSIFICATION

Köppen's Classification

Dr W. Köppen published a classification in 1918, which he later modified from time to time: in this he considered precipitation effectiveness for plant growth as the major factor, and chose appropriate seasonal values of temperatures and precipitation in order to determine the limits of his climatic groupings. He carefully observed the conditions of growth required by various groups of plants, ranging from the megatherms, which favour warm habitats, through the intermediate mesotherms, to microtherms which thrive in a colder environment; by relating these to various temperature limits he defined certain main climatic groups. His other main groups are the arid and semi-arid lands, with sub-groups on a temperature basis, and those with long winters and short summers—the polar and near-polar regions, mostly beyond the limits of tree-growth—but also defined by a mean temperature figure.

Main Groups

Köppen used groups of letters symbolically to designate and describe each climatic type. The five main groups are therefore:

A. Tropical Rainy: a hot climate with no cool season: the average temperature of each month is over 18° C.

B. Dry: evaporation exceeds precipitation.

C. Humid Mesothermal: the warmest month has a mean temperature above 10° C. the coldest month has a mean temperature between – 3° C. and 18° C.

D. Humid Microthermal: the warmest month has a mean temperature above 10° C. the coldest month has a mean temperature below – 3° C.

E. Polar: a polar type with no month averaging over 10° C.

The temperature value for the *D* Type, for example, recognises that a 10° C average for the warmest month coincides *roughly* with the poleward limits of forest; and that the – 3° C mean for the coldest month is near the equatorwards limit of frozen ground and where snow remains on the surface for at least a month.

Sub-groups

A second, small, letter is used to describe the rainfall distribution. In *A* climatic regions "*f*" indicates that no month has a mean rainfall of less than 60 mm; "*w*" that at least one month has under this amount. The values for the *Af* tropical rainy climate are those which Köppen believed would support a tall tropical rainforest. Other small letters are used, such as "*m*" for a monsoon region which supports rainforest despite a short dry season.

The *B* climates (dry ones) are also sub-divided into a *BW*, arid, type (*W* = Wüste, desert) and *BS*, semi-arid, or steppe, type. The *BS/BW* limits are identified from formulae, using different constants combined with the rainfall and temperature values for each sub-type. Other small letters are used as third symbols to aid description: thus *BWh* and *BWk* (*h* = heiss, *k* = kalt) represent deserts where mean annual temperatures are over and under 18° C respectively. Various minor characteristics of the *C*, *D*, and

E climates are also shown by means of additional symbols. Later we will consider G. T. Trewartha's modification of the Köppen classification within the framework of the five major groups, and examine the use of symbols in more detail.

Limitations

It must be stressed that in Köppen's form of empirical classification no attempt is made to take account of the *causes* of the climate described, nor of the relations between the location of the climatic region and those of pressure zones, air mass source regions, or other features. Trewartha stresses the need of supplementing empirical classifications with some description of the mode of origin of the climatic features used to define the boundaries (see p. 99–101).

Thornthwaite's Classification

During the early nineteen thirties, C. W. Thornthwaite put forward, and modified, a system of classification which also looks upon plants as "meteorological instruments". He derived a measure of the *effectiveness of precipitation*—a P/E Index—by dividing the total monthly precipitation (P) by the total monthly evaporation (E), and then adding the twelve values for each month. The main drawback, again, is that the actual evaporation data are not available for many parts of the world. To overcome this, Thornthwaite used observations, from various stations in the southwest U.S.A., of temperature and precipitation, and obtained a formula which served to give the P/E Index: this formula was then used for other parts of the world. With these P/E values available he distinguishes five "humidity provinces", each with characteristic vegetation.

Humidity Province		Vegetation	P/E Index
A.	wet	rainforest	128 and above
B.	humid	forest	64—127
C.	sub-humid	grassland	32—63
D.	semi-arid	steppe	16—31
E.	arid	desert	under 16

Small letters are used for *seasonal concentration* of precipitation: r=abundant in all seasons; s=deficient in summer; w=deficient in winter; d=deficient in all seasons.

He also developed a formula to be used for calculating *thermal efficiency*—T/E Index—and, with values again grouped from

0 (F′) to 128 and over (A′), recognised six temperature provinces:

A′—tropical;   B′—mesothermal;   C′—microthermal;
D′—taiga;   E′—tundra;   F′—frost.

The climate is then described by presenting the groups together. Thus the climate of the savannahs of Northern Nigeria is shown as CA′w. 120 possible combinations can be distinguished; but,

AMERICAN CLIMATES : METHODS OF CLASSIFICATION

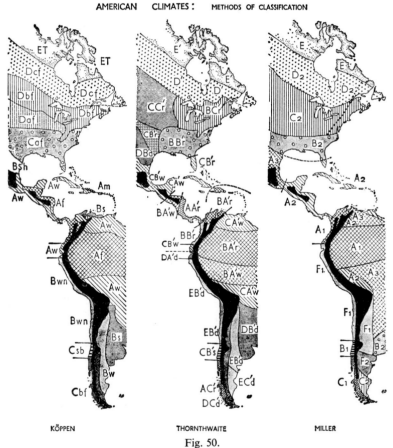

KÖPPEN   THORNTHWAITE   MILLER

Fig. 50.
A comparison of the climatic divisions of parts of the Americas according to the systems of classification used by Köppen, Thornthwaite, and Miller.

in making a world map of climatic regions, Thornthwaite chose 32 of these. Examples from a number of different regions are:

Amazon Lowlands	BA′r	Sicily	CB′s
Eastern São Paulo	BB′r	Aquitaine	BB′r
Northern Chile	EB′d	Western Britain	BC′r
Southern Chile	AC′r	East Anglia	CC′r

In 1948 Thornthwaite put forward a classification which considers the losses of water by evaporation from soil and plant cover as "evapo-transpiration". Regarding the plant as "the machinery of evaporation", he uses a formula to find the loss by evaporation and transpiration which would occur if water were always available to the roots. The loss is, however, calculated as a function of the temperature.

The potential evapo-transpiration is then compared with the precipitation, and climatic boundaries defined on that basis. Again, the drawback is the difficulty of obtaining values for loss of moisture to the atmosphere; hence the need for the calculation in terms of temperature. The chief use of the potential evapo-transpiration values, however, has been for single stations: curves drawn for monthly values can be compared with curves of precipitation, so that periods of water surplus or water deficiency can be gauged.

A. A. Miller's Classification

Miller's classification uses *temperature zones:*

A—hot; with mean annual temperature above 21° C.

B—warm temperate; with no month below 6° C.

C—cool temperate; with one to five months below 6° C.

D—cold; with six months or more below 6° C.

E—Arctic; with no month above 10° C.

To these are added F—desert climates; G—mountain climates.

Sub-divisions are then given on the basis of *seasonal* precipitation: "rain at all seasons", "winter maximum", "summer maximum", "constant drought", are examples. But this is, in some respects, a genetic type of classification; for the *causes* of rainfall are broadly considered by referring to "marine", or "continental", or "monsoon" types of climate. As seen above, some of the figures are chosen to show the relationships between plants and climate: as a generalisation, 6° C, is taken as the mean temperature below which continuous active growth ceases for many plants; for, even though sufficient moisture is present, most plants cannot make use of it below a certain temperature.

The examples given on pp. 96 and 97 (for Thornthwaite's classification) would be indicated on Miller's system as:

Northern Nigeria	A3	Tropical continental: summer rain.
Amazon Lowlands	A1	Equatorial: double maxima of rain.
Eastern São Paulo	A2	Tropical marine: no marked dry season.
Northern Chile	F1	Hot desert: no month below 6° C.
Southern Chile	C1	Cool Temperate marine: uniform precipitation or winter maximum.
Sicily	B1	Western Margin (Mediterranean winter rain.
Aquitaine	C1	Cool Temperate marine.
Western Britain	C1	Cool Temperate marine.
East Anglia	C1	Cool Temperate marine.

The basic scheme is a simple one, and broad regions stand out clearly; but additional description is necessary to indicate, for example, that the average temperatures are much lower in the deserts of Northern Chile than in mid-Sahara, for both are shown as F1. It would also be necessary to stress the variety to be found in those parts of the world shown as having a C1 climate: this becomes apparent even when a detailed regional study of Western Europe is made; and even more so when one considers that New Zealand's Canterbury Province and south-western Norway are also classified together as C1. This will, of course, be the drawback with any system; a great number of "sub-climates" will be found in any climatic region of sufficient size to be shown on a world map; and each locality will tend to have its own variations.

Many other ways of classifying climates have been put forward; but the examples quoted are sufficient to show that it is possible to group together an enormous number of local climates into general types with important characteristics in common, and so see recognisable patterns on a world scale. It should also be clear that the choice of one system rather than another will depend to some extent on the detail required and the purpose of classification, and that every system used will have a large number of drawbacks and over-simplifications.

CLIMATIC TYPES

Some of the chief characteristics of various types of climate are described in the next few chapters. For this purpose Trewartha's modification of Köppen's system is used. The climates are considered in groupings which are not entirely zonal; but neither are the patterns of the climates, soils, and vegetation over the earth's surface. A fairly simple two-letter grouping is used, but further detail is given in some cases by the use of a third-order symbol. The map of climatic regions based on this classification at the front of the book shows each of these groupings.

Trewartha's Modification of the Köppen System

Group A   *TROPICAL RAINY CLIMATES.* Temperature of the coolest month over 18° C.

    Af   *No dry season.* Driest month has over 60 mm. Intertropical convergence zone, with Tm (or Em) air masses.

    Am   *Short dry season,* but rainfall sufficient to support rainforest (wet monsoon type).

    Aw   *Dry during the period of low sun (winter).* Driest month under 60 mm. Dry Tc air in winter. *Wet during period of high sun,* when I.T.C. moves polewards and moist Tm air flows in.

Group B   *DRY CLIMATES.* Evaporation exceeds precipitation. *W*— arid; desert. *S*—semi-arid; steppe. The boundary between *BW/BS* is where formulae have the following values: winter precipitation maximum (r/t=1); summer maximum (r/t + 14 =1); or where, with precipitation evenly distributed, (r/t + 7 =1). In each case r=annual rainfall (cm), and t=mean annual temperature (°C).

    BWh   *Hot desert.* Mean annual temperature over 18° C. Source regions of Tc air: sub-tropical Highs. Dry Tc Trade Winds.

    BSh   *Tropical and sub-tropical semi-arid.* A short rainy season —Tc air for most of the year.

    BWk   *Middle latitude interior desert.* Tc air masses in summer and Pc air masses in winter. Large annual temperature range. Persistently dry.

BSk *Middle latitude semi-arid.* Dominated by dry Pc air in winter; mainly Tc air in summer; meagre rainfall, mostly in summer.

n (nebel) is used to show frequent fogs along coastlands with cool waters off-shore.

Group C *HUMID MESOTHERMAL* (Moist Temperate). Temperature of coldest month between 18° C and 0° C.

Cs *Sub-tropical, dry summers.* At least three times as much rain in wettest winter month as in driest summer month. Driest month less than 30 mm. Summers dominated by sub-tropical High (the *Cs* regions lie on stable eastern side of the Highs). Pm air in winter, with cyclonic storms and rain.

Csa *Hot Summers:* warmest month averages over 22° C.

Csb *Warm summers:* warmest month averages under 22° C.

Ca *Humid sub-tropical, hot summers.* Warmest month over 22° C. In summer moist Tm air from the unstable western side of the sub-tropical High over ocean. Winters with Pc air invading, and cyclonic storms developing.

Caf *No dry season.* Driest month over 30 mm.

Caw *Dry winters:* at least ten times the rain in the wettest summer month as in the driest winter month.

Cb *Marine climate, cool-warm summers.* Warmest month under 22° C. Mostly middle latitude west coasts which receive moist Pm air and series of depressions. Rain in all seasons.

Cbf *No dry season:* the most common *Cb* type (*Cbw* describes parts of south-east Africa).

Cc *Marine climate, short cool summers;* warmest month below 22° C; less than four months over 10° C, rain in all seasons.

Group D *HUMID MICROTHERMAL* (Rainy/Snowy, Cold). Temperature of coldest month under 0° C, and warmest month over 10° C.

Da *Humid continental, warm summers.* Warmest month over 22° C. Precipitation in all seasons, accent on summer maximum; winter snow cover. Zone of frequent clashes between polar air and tropical air. Variable weather.

Db *Humid continental, cool summers.* Warmest month under 22° C. As for *Da*, but long winter snow cover.

Dc *Sub-Arctic climate.* Warmest month below 22° C, and less than four months over 10° C. Winters are cold, and air stable under Pc air mass. Pm air sometimes gives cyclonic storms, especially in summer; but precipitation is light. Evaporation is small in winter, hence moisture remains.

Dd *Sub-Arctic with very cold winters.* Coldest month below −38° C. Very light precipitation.

For the *C* and *D* groups: *f*—no dry season; *w*—dry winter.

Group E   *POLAR.* Temperature of the warmest month less than 10° C.

ET *Tundra.* Mean temperature of warmest month above 0° C. Pm, Pc, and Arctic air masses interact, and cyclonic storms occur, with light precipitation, mostly in summer.

EF *Ice Cap. Perpetual frost;* no month with mean temperature over 0° C. Source regions for Arctic and Antarctic air masses.

Besides these groupings the system uses H for undifferentiated *highland climates,* and on maps adds stippling to certain tropical and sub-tropical uplands of moderate elevation (as for the plateaux of central Africa and south-eastern Brazil).

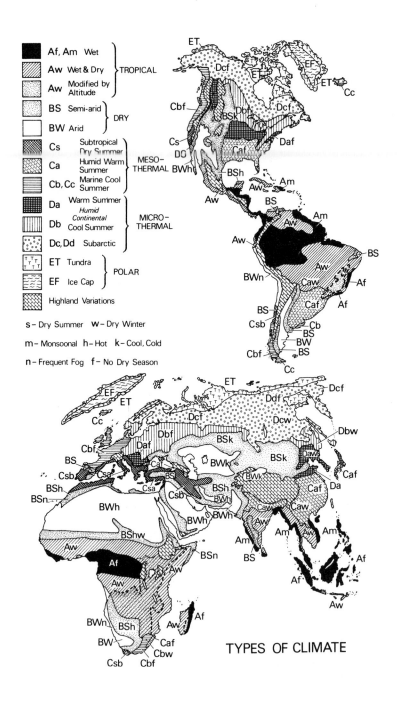

Af, Am Wet
Aw Wet & Dry } TROPICAL
Aw Modified by Altitude

BS Semi-arid } DRY
BW Arid

Cs Subtropical Dry Summer
Ca Humid Warm Summer } MESO-THERMAL
Cb, Cc Marine Cool Summer

Da Warm Summer *Humid Continental*
Db Cool Summer } MICRO-THERMAL

Dc, Dd Subarctic

ET Tundra } POLAR
EF Ice Cap

Highland Variations

s – Dry Summer   w – Dry Winter
m – Monsoonal   h – Hot   k – Cool, Cold
n – Frequent Fog   f – No Dry Season

TYPES OF CLIMATE

CHAPTER VI
TYPES OF CLIMATE (I): IN LOW LATITUDES

The descriptions of these climates are set out in a pattern which is broadly followed by the grouping of types of soils and vegetation in the later chapters. But, as we shall see, the nature of the soils and vegetation depend on many factors, of which the present climate is but one, and not always the dominant one.

Tropical Rainy Climate *Af*

This type occurs in lowlands within 5°-10° of the equator; though it may extend to higher latitudes on windward sides of the continents, where unstable air moves from sub-tropical highs over warm ocean currents. Above 1 000 m or so, low latitude highlands and hill slopes are too cool to be placed in this category, and do not support the typical form of lowland rainforest.

The noonday sun is never far from the zenith and there is little variation in the hours of daylight; but the high humidity, and large amounts of cloud keep the temperatures from soaring; maximum temperatures are usually well below those of the hot season in the dry outer tropics. There is little seasonal change in temperature: the occasional dry spells, with clearer skies, are usually the hottest periods. Mean monthly temperatures vary little and are generally of the order of 26°-27° C. The daily temperature range tends to be several times greater than the mean annual range; but, even so, temperatures seldom fall below 18° C at night; rising by day to between 30°-35° C. The result is a monotonous similarity of temperature, which, combined with high humidity, can be oppressive and wearing when experienced for any length of time.

The mean annual rainfall is high, especially over the oceans, where it contributes to the relative freshness of the water in these latitudes. The rate of evaporation, though high, tends to be less here than in the outer, sunnier, windier tropics; which also makes for a comparatively lower surface salinity in the oceans. The uplifting of warm, unstable air, caused by the convergence of tropical air masses, and aided by convection or orographic rising, allows towering cumulus clouds to build up: heavy rainstorms, often accompanied by thunder, are common in the late afternoon, at the time of maximum convection.

103

The daily regime tends to follow a regular pattern, especially during wetter spells. The somewhat cooler nights result in dew deposition from air of high humidity, though skies remain clear. Morning haze, or low mist over swampy land, clears rapidly; but

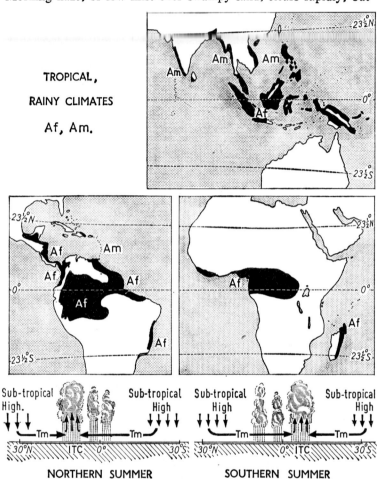

TROPICAL,

RAINY CLIMATES

Af, Am.

NORTHERN SUMMER   SOUTHERN SUMMER

Fig. 51.

The section, showing idealised conditions for May and October (with converging maritime air), indicates why, theoretically, there should be the double maxima of rainfall (as stressed in Miller's classification—A1 Type). But other factors, such as monsoonal air flows, tend to disrupt this simple pattern. The moist "Trade Wind coasts" of Brazil and Malagasy have quite different rainfall regimes, within the framework of the *Af* sub-group.

by mid-morning cumulus cloud develops, increasing in size and density until, during the heat of the afternoon, heavy downpours occur. Later, the skies clear once more.

Some days are much cloudier than others, however, and slow-moving shallow troughs and weak cyclonic systems sometimes develop in these latitudes of otherwise small pressure gradients, giving longer periods of rain. On the other hand, in some places, as in the eastern Amazon basin, parts of the year are noticeably drier than others, and there may be considerable variations in rainfall totals from year to year. The amount of rainfall tends to be greatest at places well within the zone of convergence. Theoretically there should be two periods during the year, shortly after the time of overhead sun, which are wetter than average; but, in fact, the readings from many lowland stations show no such maxima.

Here are low latitude rainforests (p. 206). Soils are usually heavily leached and ferallitic, with accumulations of residual insoluble minerals containing iron, aluminium, and manganese (p. 179).

TABLE 1

UAUPES.		0° 08′ S.				83 m				Amazon Lowlands.		
	J.	F.	M.	A.	M.	J.	J.	A.	S.	O.	N.	D.	Total
° C	26	27	26	26	26	26	25	26	27	27	27	26	—
ins	10·3	7·7	10·0	10·6	12·0	9·2	8·8	7·2	5·1	6·9	7·2	10·4	105·4
mm	262	196	254	269	305	234	223	183	132	175	183	264	2 677

ABSOLUTE TEMP.	MEAN DAILY (YEAR)	MEAN REL. HUMIDITY
Max. 38° C	Max. 31° C	05.30 hrs—97
Min. 11° C	Min. 22° C	12.30 hrs—74

SINGAPORE.		1° 18. N.				10 m				South-east Asia.		
	J.	F.	M.	A.	M.	J.	J.	A.	S.	O.	N.	D.	Total
° C	26	27	27	27	28	27	27	27	27	27	27	27	—
ins	9·9	6·8	7·6	7·4	6·8	6·8	6·7	7·7	7·0	8·2	10·0	10·1	95·0
mm	252	172	193	188	172	172	170	196	178	208	254	257	2 413

ABSOLUTE TEMP.	MEAN DAILY (YEAR)	MEAN REL. HUMIDITY
Max. 36° C	Max. 31° C	09.00 hrs—79
Min. 19° C	Min. 23° C	15.00 hrs—73

KISANGANI					0° 26′ N.				417 m			Zaïre Basin.
	J.	F.	M.	A.	M.	J.	J.	A.	S.	O.	N.	D.	Total
°C	26	26	26	26	26	25	24	24	24	25	24	25	—
ins	2·1	3·3	7·0	6·2	5·4	4·5	5·2	6·5	7·2	8·6	7·8	3·3	67·1
mm	54	84	178	157	137	107	132	165	183	218	198	84	1 705

ABSOLUTE TEMP.	MEAN DAILY (YEAR)	MEAN REL. HUMIDITY
Max. 36° C	Max. 30° C	05.30 hrs—97
Min. 16° C	Min. 21° C	11.30 hrs—68

Trade Wind Coasts with a modified *Af* climate

Fig. 46 shows parts of the tropical east coasts of Brazil, central
America, and Malagasy which have a rather similar type of climate
to that described above, though their temperature or rainfall regimes
vary in certain respects. As moist unstable air moves on-shore,
they receive a high annual rainfall. Rainy periods are often prolonged, and the various cyclonic disturbances are apt to be more
severe than those of lower latitudes, with occasional hurricanes.
Convection adds to the intensity of the rainstorms.

The mean annual temperature range is small, though rather
greater than in equatorial regions: the maritime air is a moderating
influence. The warm, wet coastlands support rainforest vegetation
very similar to that of lowlands nearer the equator.

TABLE 2

SALVADOR.					13° 00′ S.				47 m			Eastern Brazil.
	J.	F.	M.	A.	M.	J.	J.	A.	S.	O.	N.	D.	Total
° C	23	23	23	23	22	22	21	21	21	22	22	23	—
ins	2·6	5·3	6·1	11·2	10·8	9·4	7·2	4·8	3·3	4·0	4·5	5·6	74·8
mm	66	135	155	284	274	239	183	122	84	102	115	142	1 900

ABSOLUTE TEMP.	MEAN DAILY (YEAR)	MEAN REL. HUMIDITY
Max. 35° C	Max. 28° C	07.00 hrs—87
Min. 17° C	Min. 22° C	14.30 hrs—75

TAMATAVE.		18° 07′ S.				6 m				Eastern Malagasy.		
	J.	F.	M.	A.	M.	J.	J.	A.	S.	O.	N.	D.	Total
° C	27	27	26	25	24	22	21	21	22	23	25	26	—
ins	14·4	14·8	17·8	15·7	10·4	11·1	11·9	8·0	5·2	3·9	4·6	10·3	128·2
mm	366	376	452	400	264	280	302	203	132	99	117	261	3 256

ABSOLUTE TEMP.	MEAN DAILY (YEAR)	MEAN REL. HUMIDITY
Max. 37° C	Max. 27° C	07.30 hrs—90
Min. 17° C	Min. 21° C	13.30 hrs—75

Salvador (Table 2) has an untypically heavy autumn and winter rainfall, when frontal disturbances are caused by surges of air from the south interacting with the unstable tropical maritime air.

Tropical Wet Monsoon Climates *Am*

These climates, described in detail on pp. 83-8, are intermediate between *Af* and *Aw* types; for though they have high temperatures with a fairly small annual range, long periods with high humidity, and heavy rainfall, there is a marked dry season. During summer the Tm or Em air brings an exceptionally large rainfall to hills or mountains facing the main air streams, which as Figs. 51 and 89 show, are able to support rainforest. But though the slopes near Bombay are closely forested, the rainfall regime (Table 3) suggests an *Aw* classification. Dry Tc air is dominant during the winter months. Notice how the temperature rises to a maximum before the monsoon "bursts" but falls somewhat in the cloudy, muggy, wet period, despite the high altitude of the noonday sun.

In Miller's classification the Indonesian islands, Malaysia, and parts of New Guinea are shown as monsoon sub-types of the hot equatorial lands. The addition of "m" points to marked seasonal changes in the direction of air flow, and remarkable rain-shadow effects. Northern slopes have their lowest rainfall from May to September when air flows northwards into Asia; the southern slopes are well-watered during these months, but exceptionally dry from December to March when air moves towards northern Australia. Other low latitude locations show seasonal rainfall deficiencies; in the Amazon basin, stations south of the Guiana Highlands show a well-marked dry period, but can hardly be distinguished as a "monsoonal" sub-type.

TABLE 3

CHITTAGONG.			22° 21′ N.					26 m				Bangladesh.
	J.	F.	M.	A.	M.	J.	J.	A.	S.	O.	N.	D.	Total
° C	19	21	25	27	28	28	27	27	27	27	23	20	—
ins	0·2	1·1	2·5	5·9	10·4	21·0	23·5	20·4	12·6	7·1	2·2	0·6	107·5
mm	5	26	64	150	264	533	597	518	320	181	56	15	2 831

ABSOLUTE MAX./MIN.	MEAN DAILY MAX./MIN.	MEAN REL. HUMIDITY
39° C (April)	31° C/25° C (June)	08.00 hrs—87 (June), 81 (Jan.)
7° C (Jan.)	26° C/13° C (Jan.)	17.30 hrs—83 (June), 58 (Jan.)

BOMBAY.			18° 54′ N.					11 m				Western India.
	J.	F.	M.	A.	M.	J.	J.	A.	S.	O.	N.	D.	Total
° C	23	23	26	28	30	29	27	27	27	28	27	26	—
ins	0·1	0·1	0·1	0·1	0·7	19·1	24·3	13·4	10·4	2·5	0·5	0·1	71·2
mm	2	2	2	2	18	486	618	340	264	64	13	2	1 808

ABSOLUTE MAX./MIN.	MEAN DAILY MAX./MIN.	MEAN REL. HUMIDITY
38° C (Mar.)	33° C/27° C (May)	08.00 hrs—83 (July), 70 (Jan.)
12° C (Jan.)	28° C/19° C (Jan.)	16.00 hrs—83 (July), 61 (Jan.)

Tropical Climates with Wet and Dry Seasons *Aw*

Poleward of *Af* climates there is often a gradual transition to
an *Aw* type as the dry season becomes longer and longer, with
increasing latitude, until the climate is best described as "arid".
In fact, a transition of this sort takes place chiefly on the western
sides and in the interior of the land masses; for the eastern parts,
less affected by dry air from the sub-tropical highs persisting over
the oceans, experience moist on-shore winds and humid climates.

Movements of the I.T.C. Zone

During the somewhat cooler times of the year the outer parts
of the tropics come under the influence of the dry, subsiding air
of the sub-tropical highs. This air moves equatorwards, causing
drought conditions in the lands affected by it. But in the hot

season, as the altitude of the mid-day sun approaches the zenith, and air temperatures rise towards their maxima, air pressures fall over these outer tropics so that they receive converging tropical air flows, and thus lie in the I.T.C. zone. Moist air is brought

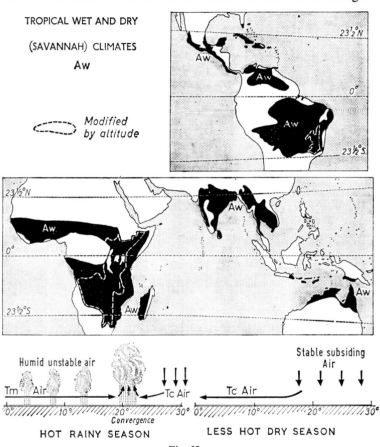

Fig. 52.
The section emphasises the change from humid summer conditions to dry winter ones, when the Tc air is dominant once more.
(*w* indicates winter dry season.)

in, and clouds build up in hitherto clear skies. Periods of heavy rain and thunderstorms occur. Mean temperatures in the cloudy, rainy part of the hot season become somewhat lower than immediately before the onset of the rains, despite the higher altitude of the sun. As the main I.T.C. zone retreats once more to lower latitudes the rains gradually cease, and the flow of dry air from the sub-tropical high is re-established.

Rainfall and Temperature Regimes

The rainfall amounts, length of dry season, and, of course, natural vegetation, vary considerably between the low-latitude *Af/ Aw* transition zone with only a short dry period, and the borders of the *Aw/BS* climates of the dry outer tropics, where rain occurs only in one or two months. In wetter parts the annual rainfall is of the order of 1 000-1 500 mm; but on the borders of the semi-arid lands less than 500 mm may fall in a year, a small total for plant growth where the summer temperatures are high and evapora-tion rapid. The annual amounts vary a great deal from year to year; and rainfall is much less reliable than in low latitude rainy climates. But it is the *seasonal distribution* which is so important to vegetation, and where the dry periods are long many plants exhibit xercphytic characteristics (pp. 192 and 220).

Convection, of course, leads to cloud formation, and affects the rainfall intensity, but it must be remembered that it is not neces-sarily a cause of rainfall in itself. Convection is a particularly active force in the hot season, and heavy rain falls from moist unstable air given a strong upward impulse. But the cooler season is in fact "less hot" rather than "cool", so that strong convection still occurs on sunny days (with temperatures much higher than the average summer day in Western Europe); yet rain does not occur in the drier air under these more stable conditions, although swirling "dust devils" may form during the dry months.

In the hottest part of the year the day temperatures may rise to well over 40° C. Even in the less hot seasons it may be 25°-30° C in the afternoons, though night temperatures fall to 15° C or below. There is, therefore, a fairly small mean annual range, which depends on location, but is of the order of 5-10 C.°

The Term "Savannah"—A Word of Warning

This regime is typical of the so-called "savannah-lands"; the name "savannah" describing the tropical grasses which form the dominant element of the vegetation. The actual vegetation varies, from the thorn scrub and coarse tussocky grasses of the regions with lengthy droughts, through the park-like grasslands with numerous, but scattered, trees and bushes of the "mid-savannahs", to the closer woodlands and tall elephant grass where the dry period is of short duration. The vegetation and its seasonal changes are described on p. 213. There are, however, several reasons why the name "savannah" must be used with care; especially as it is, unfortunately, apt to be used as a climatic term. While it is true that the nature of the vegetation reflects the change from frequent rains to lengthy droughts, the plant population in a particular place is affected by factors other than climatic, by soils in particular. Also the climate of many of the existing areas of grassy savannah seems capable of supporting woodland, and may well have done so in the past. The nature of the present forms of vegetation may be due not only to the climate and soils (which themselves have acquired characteristics due to climates past and present), but in part to the effects of clearance by man, or grazing by animals, or fires; all of which can prevent the regeneration of woodland. Hence it is unwise to relate tropical savannah grassland solely to a "savannah climate" or "tropical grassland climate"—terms which are sometimes used and which may be misleading.

The Distribution of Aw Climates—including Monsoon Lands

Fig. 52 shows that large parts of Africa, northern Australia, South and Central America, India, Burma, and South-east Asia experience such climatic conditions: in some of these countries, however, extensive upland areas are at altitudes where the average temperatures fall below those of the typical *Aw* climate.

In India, South-east Asia, and northern Australia the alternation of rainy and drought periods are part of monsoon systems (though, again, these involve a poleward migration of the I.T.C. during the hot season, and are fundamentally similar regimes). The rains set in with the arrival of moist Tm or Em air, though their onset tends to be sudden; dry subsiding air from mid-latitude high pressures predominates in the cooler season. This is classified by some as a Tropical Monsoon, Wet and Dry climate; but it is fundamentally similar to those of other *Aw* regions.

TABLE 4

KADUNA.		10° 35′ N.				643 m						Central Nigeria.
	J.	F.	M.	A.	M.	J.	J.	A.	S.	O.	N.	D.	Total
°C	23	24	27	28	27	25	24	23	24	25	24	23	—
ins	—	0·1	0·5	2·5	5·9	7·1	8·5	11·9	10·6	2·9	0·1	—	50·1
mm	—	2	13	64	150	180	216	302	269	74	2	—	1 272

ABSOLUTE MAX./MIN.	MEAN DAILY MAX./MIN.	MEAN REL. HUMIDITY
41° C (April)	35° C/22° C (April)	06.30 hrs—95 (Aug.), 35 (Jan.)
8° C (Dec.)	32° C/14° C (Dec.)	15.30 hrs—75 (Aug.), 14 (Jan.)

SOKOTO. 13° 01' N. 350 m **Northern Nigeria.**

	J.	F.	M.	A.	M.	J.	J.	A.	S.	O.	N.	D.	Total
° C	24	26	31	33	33	30	28	26	27	29	27	25	—
ins	—	—	0·1	0·4	1·7	3·7	6·0	9·6	5·2	0·5	—	—	27·2
mm	—	—	2	10	43	94	152	244	132	13	—	—	691

ABSOLUTE MAX./MIN.	MEAN DAILY MAX./MIN.	MEAN REL. HUMIDITY
47° C (April)	41° C/26° C (April)	06.30 hrs—87 (Aug.), 23 (Mar.)
7° C (Jan.)	33° C/16° C (Dec.)	12.30 hrs—64 (Aug.), 11 (Mar.)

GOIAS. 15° 58' S. 536 m **Central Brazilian Plateau.**

	J.	F.	M.	A.	M.	J.	J.	A.	S.	O.	N.	D.	Total
° C	23	24	24	25	24	22	22	24	26	26	24	23	—
ins	12·5	9·9	10·2	4·6	0·4	0·3	—	0·3	2·3	5·3	9·4	9·5	64·8
mm	318	252	259	117	10	8	—	8	59	135	239	242	1 646

ABSOLUTE MAX./MIN.	MEAN DAILY MAX./MIN.	MEAN REL. HUMIDITY
40° C (Sept.)	34° C/18° C (Sept.)	06.30 hrs—90 (Dec.), 64 (Aug.)
5° C (July)	32° C/13° C (June)	13.30 hrs—73 (Dec.), 40 (Aug.)

Semi-Arid Climates—Bordering the *Aw* Climates *(BShw)*

This type of climate, sometimes referred to as "low latitude steppe climate", occurs on the equatorial sides of the sub-tropical high pressure zones. It resembles the *Aw* type, with a long dry season under the influence of dry air from the zone of subsidence in the outer tropics (*w* = winter drought), and a short rainy season when the I.T.C. is displaced polewards during summer. As rain occurs in the hottest months, when evaporation is at a maximum, it is less effective for plant growth. In fact the total rainfall varies considerably from year to year, but is usually under 500 mm.

This is a transitional region between the *Aw* climates and those of the really arid, hot deserts on the poleward side. Temperatures are often very high during the summer, like those of the deserts. Such conditions are found south of the Sahara, in northern Australia, south-west Africa, and parts of the Mexican plateaux, with a curious enclave of this type in the "dry shoulder" of eastern Brazil For features of their xerophytic vegetation see p. 219.

TABLE 5

HALL'S CREEK.			18° 13' S.				366 m					North-west Australia.
	J.	F.	M.	A.	M.	J.	J.	A.	·S.	O.	N.	D.	Total
° C	30	29	28	26	21	19	18	21	24	28	31	31	—
ins	5·4	4·2	2·8	0·5	0·2	0·2	0·2	0·1	0·1	0·5	1·4	3·1	18·7
mm	137	107	71	13	5	5	5	2	2	13	35	79	460

ABSOLUTE MAX./MIN.	MEAN DAILY MAX./MIN.	MEAN REL. HUMIDITY
44° C (Jan.)	38° C/23° C (Nov.)	09.30 hrs—51 (Jan.), 29 (Sept.)
−1° C (July)	27° C/9° C (July)	15.30 hrs—36 (Jan.), 24 (Sept.)

Tropical and Sub-Tropical Dry Climates (The Hot Deserts) *BWh*

The Influence of Dry, Subsiding Air

These climates prevail on the westerly sides of the land masses between latitudes 20°-25°, and extend for some degrees north and south of this in the lands most strongly affected by subsiding air masses of the sub-tropics. The dry, subsiding air, of great stability, is able to exert a blanketing effect on air rising through convection, even during the great heat of summer. The air over the deserts may contain a considerable amount of moisture, especially during summer; but while the absolute humidity may be high, the relative humidity at low levels remains low, and the rate of evaporation is usually great. Only occasionally does the stable, subsiding air allow strong updraughts to rise to sufficient height for water vapour to condense. Just occasionally dark thunder clouds build up. Sometimes these yield rain which evaporates in the relatively dry air before it reaches the ground; but now and then local torrential downpours cause flash floods to course down dry channels, before soaking into broad depressions. Such waters erode bare unprotected desert surfaces, and even in deserts water vapour in the air is an important agent in weathering rocks.

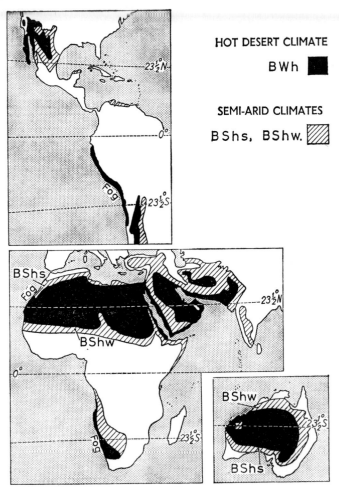

Fig. 53.

Notice the use of the symbols *s* (= summer drought) and *w* (= winter drought) used for the semi-arid regions bordering, respectively, the "Mediterranean" regions and the *Aw* climatic zones.

On the poleward sides of the deserts, rain belts associated with the middle latitude depressions are apt to affect the borders of the arid regions during winter, bringing occasional heavy storms. The outer limits of the deserts are difficult to define on a rainfall basis. Large areas of the deserts have a mean rainfall of less than 100 mm; but average figures mean little, for years may pass with absolute drought conditions, while a sudden torrential storm may bring hundreds of millimetres of rain in an hour or so.

The Effects of Rapid Gain and Loss of Radiation

In the dry air few clouds develop; so that with abundant sunshine, there is strong surface heating by day. During summer, shade temperatures of 50°-55° C may be reached, and 58° C (*136·4° F*) has been recorded in the southern Sahara, south of Tripoli. By night, radiation losses through a cloudless atmosphere cause air temperatures to drop considerably, though they remain high in summer (usually about 20°-24° C); daily ranges are thus of the order of 30 C°. During winter, even with the relatively low angle of the noonday sun, daily shade readings rise to 15° or 20° C, often higher. At night temperatures drop sharply, with minimums of 5°-10° C fairly usual: surface temperatures occasionally fall below freezing point. Such cooling is apt to produce heavy dew. By contrast to mid-day conditions, the nights often feel unpleasantly cold.

The Effects of Cool Offshore Currents

The western margins of the tropical and sub-tropical deserts are flanked by cool ocean currents and upwelling water, which help to emphasise the aridity (p. 89) and to extend desert conditions polewards, as in Peru and southern Ecuador. Fog or low cloud, with markedly lower temperatures on the coastlands, are features of these western regions, which may be classified as *BWn* climates. The desert coastlands of south-west Africa experience frequent fogs, which extend only a short way inland. In central and southern Peru low cloud is apt to produce a steady persistent drizzle during the winter months, yet the rainfall averages less than 50 mm a year. Where the cloud meets the Andean hillsides, the moisture may be sufficient to enable quick-growing plants to form the type of vegetation known as "loma"; this is sometimes plentiful enough to support winter grazing.

The eastern sides of the continents in these latitudes are generally affected by less stable air from the weaker western extensions of the sub-tropical highs; consequently they have humid, rather than arid, conditions. In north-east Africa, however, the air in summer tends to move parallel to the coast, and desert conditions extend into low latitudes.

Despite an overall lack of vegetation a surprising number of xerophytic plants are able to survive (p. 221), and seeds of others can lie dormant for a very long time under dry conditions.

TABLE 6

In Salah.	27° 12′ N.					280 m					Southern Algeria.	
	J.	F.	M.	A.	M.	J.	J.	A.	S.	O.	N.	D.	Total
° C	13	16	20	25	29	35	37	36	33	27	19	14	—
ins	0·1	0·1	*	*	*	*	—	0·1	*	*	0·1	0·2	0·6
mm	2·	3	*	*	*	*	—	2	*	*	3	5	15

* Less than 2 mm

Absolute Max./Min.	Mean Daily Max./Min.	Mean Rel. Humidity
50° C (July)	45° C/28° C (July)	07.00 hrs—65 (Dec.), 29 (July)
−3° C (Jan.)	21° C/6° C (Jan.)	13.00 hrs—38 (Dec.), 16 (July)

TABLE 7

Death Valley.	36° 28′ N.					−54 m					Eastern California.	
	J.	F.	M.	A.	M.	J.	J.	A.	S.	O.	N.	D.	Total
° C	11	13	19	24	29	34	38	37	32	24	16	11	—
ins	0·1	*	0·1	0·1	0·2	0·1	0·3	0·3	0·2	*	0·1	*	1·6
mm	2	*	2	3	5	3	8	8	5	*	3	*	40

* Less than 2 mm

Absolute Max./Min.	Mean Daily Max./Min.
57° C (July)	47° C/31° C (July)
−9° C (Jan.)	19° C/3° C (Jan.)

Semi-Arid Climates: poleward of the Hot Deserts *(BShs)*

Poleward of the hot deserts are areas where the annual rainfall is fairly low and variable, but where depressions, which affect the warm temperate west coast regions in the winter months, may bring occasional storms. At this cooler time of the year the rainfall is more effective for plant growth, so that coarse grasses and xerophytic plants can thrive in sufficient quantity to support a limited number of grazing animals on the move. Such conditions occur over large tracts of southern Australia, northern Arabia, Syria, and Iraq; in equivalent latitudes in northern Mexico and neighbouring parts of the U.S.A., semi-arid country tends to show more *BShw* characteristics, with summer rainfall maxima. In the typical *BShs* regions, however, the summer months remain dry and very hot, under the influence of the dry, sinking air masses of the sub-tropics (*s* = summer drought).

TABLE 8

MOSUL.			36° 19′ N.				222 m				**Northern Iraq.**	
	J.	F.	M.	A.	M.	J.	J.	A.	S.	O.	N.	D.	Total
° C	7	9	13	19	23	29	32	32	27	21	15	9	—
ins	2·8	3·1	2·1	1·9	0·7	*	*	*	*	0·2	1·9	2·4	15·1
mm	71	78	54	48	18	*	*	*	*	5	48	61	384

* Less than 2·5 mm

ABSOLUTE MAX./MIN.	MEAN DAILY MAX./MIN.	MEAN REL. HUMIDITY
51° C (July)	43° C/22° C (July)	06.00 hrs—92 (Jan.), 46 (Aug.)
−11° C (Jan.)	12° C/2° C (Jan.)	15.00 hrs—64 (Jan.), 13 (Aug.)

CHAPTER VII

TYPES OF CLIMATE (II): IN MIDDLE LATITUDES

Warm Temperate Dry Summer Climate (Mediterranean Type) Cs

These regions lie on the western sides of the continents, centred about latitude 35°. In summer they come under the influence of the subsiding, dry air of the eastern part of the sub-tropical high pressure zone. But in winter, when the source of this Tc air lies further south, the regions also receive air of Pm or Pc origin, and are visited by polar front depressions from the west. As these "Mediterranean" lands are meeting places for Pm, Tm, Tc, and in the northern hemisphere Pc air, so, occasionally, depressions form locally—more particularly in the Mediterranean region itself.

The broad climatic pattern is one of very warm to hot summers, with abundant sunshine and little rain, and mild winters with moderate rainfall. The mid-summer temperatures vary with location, but mean monthly values of 20°-25° C are usual. Mid-winter averages tend to be between 7°-13° C. As Table 8 shows, however, the temperatures of stations in cool, marine locations differ considerably from those near the borders of the arid regions or in sheltered localities; thus underlining the necessity for distinguishing the sub-types Csa or Csb (Fig. 54).

There is a fairly high daily range in summer, especially in the hotter parts of the regions. But for the many fruit farmers in this type of climatic region the winter temperatures cause more concern; for while there are generally pleasantly mild conditions, night temperatures may fall to near freezing point, and occasionally below; also the variable winter weather may bring unusually cold spells. Crops sensitive to cold, especially when blossoming, must, therefore, be sited to avoid places which are apt to collect cold air or suffer from an influx of cold air under certain meteorological conditions. Precautions against frost are usual in fruit-growing districts.

Annual rainfall amounts vary a great deal from wetter marine sites to sheltered inland locations: 500-1000 mm is a very rough average figure for this type of region. Rain mostly comes from fronts and quick-moving depressions, so that during the winter there are usually long sunny periods, favouring plant growth;

especially as rates of evaporation are much less than in the summer months. The mild growing season, followed by long periods of drought, results in a characteristic vegetation in which, *to-day,* the *chaparral* and *maquis* types described on p. 225 are distinctive; though mixed evergreen woodlands are climatically suited to many parts of these regions. In Europe, the distribution of the olive tree closely corresponds to the extent of this type of climate.

Variations in the Types of Cs Climates

About the Mediterranean itself this dry summer climate extends eastwards from the Atlantic seaboard to south-west Asia.   But

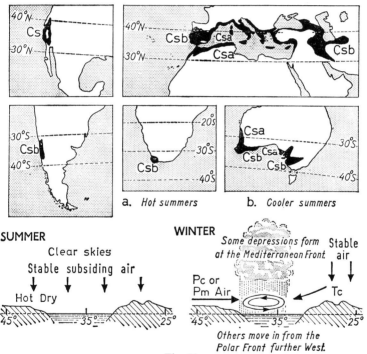

Fig. 54.

During the winter months all these regions may be affected from time to time by the passage of fronts associated with eastward-moving depressions: Depressions occasionally form at the so-called "Mediterranean Front" over, or close to the Mediterranean Sea itself. In the *a* regions the hottest month has a mean temperature exceeding 22° C : in the *b* regions 22° C or below.

there are notable differences between the marine sub-type of climate in southern Portugal, with cooler summers (*Csb*), and that of the eastern Mediterranean, with its lower rainfall and greater extremities of temperature (*Csa*).   In Chile and California the western coastlands are affected by air over cool waters off-shore; the coastal fogs of San Francisco are notorious; each country has a central valley parallel with the coast, much sunnier than the coastlands and with a lower rainfall; the eastern limits are set by the high mountains.   In coastal south-west Africa and south-western Australia the cooling effect of currents is less marked, but still evident.

We should note that, in Europe, countries bordering the Mediterranean include certain regions which do not experience this type of climate.   The Meseta of Spain has much colder winters than the coastlands, and the droughts of its hot summers are apt to be broken by violent thunderstorms, though the annual precipitation is small and the vegetation a steppe type.   The plains of northern Italy have a climate closer to a humid sub-tropical type, for the summers are too rainy and the annual precipitation unusually high for a *Cs* climate.

TABLE 9

NICOSIA.		35° 09′ N.						218 m				CYPRUS.
	J.	F.	M.	A.	M.	J.	J.	A.	S.	O.	N.	D.	Total
° C	10	10	12	17	22	26	28	28	26	21	16	12	—
ins	2·9	2·0	1·3	0·8	1·1	0·4	*	*	0·2	0·9	1·7	3·0	14·6
mm	74	51	33	20	27	10	*	*	5	23	43	76	364

* Less than 2·5 mm

ABSOLUTE MAX./MIN.	MEAN DAILY MAX./MIN.	MEAN REL. HUMIDITY
47° C (July)	36° C/21° C (July)	08.00 hrs —85 (Jan.), 49 (July)
−5° C (Feb.)	14° C/6° C (Jan.)	14.00 hrs —65 (Jan.), 29 (July)

LISBON.		38° 43′ N.						95 m				Portugal.
	J.	F.	M.	A.	M.	J.	J.	A.	S.	O.	N.	D.	Total
° C	11	11	13	14	17	20	22	22	21	17	14	11	—
ins	3·3	3·2	3·1	2·4	1·7	0·7	0·2	0·2	1·4	3·1	4·2	3·6	27·0
mm	84	81	79	61	43	18	5	5	35	79	107	91	686

ABSOLUTE MAX./MIN.	MEAN DAILY MAX./MIN.	MEAN REL. HUMIDITY
39° C (July)	27° C/18° C (Aug.)	09.00 hrs—83 (Jan.), 61 (July)
− 2° C (Feb.)	13° C/8° C (Jan.)	15.00 hrs—72 (Jan.), 46 (July)

STATIONS IN DIFFERENT Cs REGIONS			* MEAN DAILY MAX./MIN. ° C.		MEAN ANNUAL RAINFALL	
			Mid-Summer	Mid-Winter	(ins)	(mm)
San Francisco	38° N.	16 m	18/12	13/7	22·1	510
Fresno	*37° N.*	*101 m*	*37/18*	*12/3*	*9·1*	*231*
Valparaiso	33° S.	41 m	22/13	16/18	19·9	506
Santiago	*33° S.*	*510 m*	*29/12*	*15/3*	*14·1*	*358*
Cape Town	34° S.	17 m	26/16	17/7	20·0	508
Perth	32° S.	60 m	29/17	17/9	34·7	882

Italics—Inland Station. * Figures for Jan./July.

Middle Latitude Desert Climate *(BWk)*

In the heart of the northern continents, especially in central Asia, are lands which receive little moist air, particularly where high ranges block any maritime influences; they therefore have slight and irregular rainfall. The humidity of the dry, clear, winter air may be as low as 20 per cent. in central Asia.

These dry lands differ from the low latitude deserts in having a cold season: in many areas a bitterly cold winter. Summers are very warm to hot, and very hot in low enclosed basins. Both the annual and diurnal temperature ranges are large. But it is difficult to generalise about the temperatures; for both in Asia and North America middle latitude arid and semi-arid climates occur through some 20° of latitude, while topography varies from high plateaux, with outstanding ranges, to low inland basins. In the highlands, especially, the dry, clear, thin air allows excessive radiation transfer, and while the direct sunlight gives great heat at the surface, shade temperatures are low by contrast. Table 10 shows how the mean temperatures vary between different parts of the mid-latitude interiors.

In the continental interiors during winter the thermal high pressures dominate the climate. Some snow may fall, but the precipitation is generally very little. In summer the indrawn air, moonsoonal by nature, increases the humidity at low levels; but precipitation is only slight in the heart of the continents, and in basins, particularly, descending air becomes relatively drier still. Nevertheless, infrequent as storms are, there is a marked summer maximum deep in the continents. But in the more westerly parts

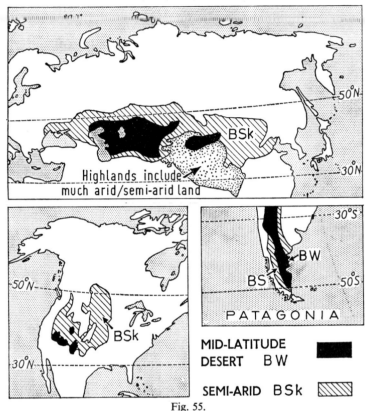

Fig. 55.

The temperature conditions vary a great deal according to the latitude and altitude of these dry lands; but the annual range is generally large, except in the case of Patagonia.

the continental highs are not so well established in winter, and allow the occasional ingress of maritime air.

Even if summer convection brings little rain, it may, during the heat of the day, set in motion strong, searingly dry, and often dusty, winds, which can be a great discomfort to travellers in these arid lands.

Middle Latitude Semi-Arid Climate (Dry Steppe) *BSk*

Between the truly desert lands and the humid climates lie transitional areas having many of the characteristics of the deserts; again, there are enormous tracts of this dry, steppe country in central Asia and North America. They have more rainfall than the heart of the arid lands, but their annual totals are variable and the rainfall unreliable. Evaporation exceeds precipitation by a considerable amount, especially in the lower latitudes. Precipitation is of the order of 250-300 mm, sometimes higher, but its effectiveness for plant growth obviously depends on the rate of evaporation. Thus the summer rain, due to influxes of moist air and strong convection, often comes as heavy, thundery downpours, of brief duration, but drying rapidly. The annual temperature range is again great, especially in high latitudes, where winters may be very cold indeed.

Grassy dominants of the steppe vegetation usually grow in clumps, bare soil between. Extensive grazing is possible, but rash attempts at agricultural developments without irrigation have often led to serious soil erosion under these climatic conditions.

TABLE 10

AKMOLINSK.		51° 12′ N.					405 m				Kasak, S.S.R.	
	J.	F.	M.	A.	M.	J.	J.	A.	S.	O.	N.	D.	Total
° C	−19	−18	−12	0	6	17	19	17	11	1	−8	−15	—
ins	0·7	0·5	0·5	0·6	1·1	1·7	1·6	1·5	1·0	1·1	0·7	0·6	11·7
mm	18	13	13	15	28	43	40	38	25	28	18	15	297

ABSOLUTE MAX./MIN.	MEAN DAILY MAX./MIN.	MEAN REL. HUMIDITY
35° C (July)	26° C/13° C (July)	07.00 hrs—86 (Jan.), 67 (July)
−36° C (Jan.)	−16° C/−22° C (Jan.)	13.00 hrs—83 (Jan.), 44 (July)

ASHKHABAD.		37° 57′ N.					226 m				Turkmen, S.S.R.	
	J.	F.	M.	A.	M.	J.	J.	A.	S.	O.	N.	D.	Total
° C	−1	7	8	15	19	26	29	24	22	15	8	4	—
ins	1·0	0·8	1·9	1·4	1·2	0·3	0·1	0·1	0·1	0·5	0·8	0·7	8·9
mm	25	20	48	35	30	8	3	3	3	13	20	18	226

ABSOLUTE MAX./MIN.	MEAN DAILY MAX./MIN.	MEAN REL. HUMIDITY
45° C (July)	36° C/22° C (July)	07.00 hrs—87 (Jan.), 54 (July)
−26° C (Jan.)	3° C/−4° C (Jan.)	13.00 hrs—69 (Jan.), 28 (July)

MEDICINE HAT.		50° 01' N.					653 m				Alberta, Canada.	
	J.	F.	M.	A.	M.	J.	J.	A.	S.	O.	N.	D.	Total
° C	−11	−10	−2	7	13	17	21	19	13	7	−2	−7	—
ins	0·6	0·6	0·6	0·8	1·6	2·4	1·7	1·4	1·1	0·6	0·7	0·7	12·8
mm	15	15	15	20	40	61	45	35	28	15	18	18	325

ABSOLUTE MAX./MIN.	MEAN DAILY MAX./MIN.	MEAN REL. HUMIDITY
42° C (July)	29° C/13° C (July)	05.00 hrs—87 (Jan.), 78 (July)
−43° C (Jan.)	−6° C/−19° C (Jan.)	11.00 hrs—77 (Jan.), 45 (July)

WINNEMUCCA.		40° 58' N.					1 324 m				Nevada, U.S.A.	
	J.	F.	M.	A.	M.	J.	J.	A.	S.	O.	N.	D.	Total
° C	−2	1	7	8	13	17	22	21	15	9	3	−1	—
ins	1·1	0·9	1·0	0·8	0·8	0·6	0·2	0·2	0·4	0·6	0·8	1·0	8·4
mm	28	23	25	20	20	15	5	5	10	15	20	25	213

ABSOLUTE MAX./MIN.	MEAN DAILY MAX./MIN.	MEAN REL. HUMIDITY
42° C (July)	32° C/12° C (July)	05.00 hrs—83 (Jan.), 47 (July)
−38° C (Jan.)	4° C/−8° C (Jan.)	12.00 hrs—62 (Jan.), 19 (July)

Patagonia—A Dry Climate in an Unusual Location

In Argentine Patagonia dry climates extend to the east coast of this narrow land mass; most receives under 250 mm of rainfall a year. Here, in the rain-shadow of the Andes, air from the west becomes warmer and relatively drier on descent to the low eastern plateaux. Mean monthly temperatures are, naturally, higher in the north, but even in the south do not fall below 0° C, despite the cold Falkland Current off-shore. This current helps maintain the aridity; for though fogs are frequent over the cold eastern waters, the easterlies which blow from the sea in the rear of the occasional northward-moving depression have a low absolute humidity. The winds are frequently strong, which adds to their drying effect. Tussocky grassland covers much of the region.

In the extreme south the rainfall is higher, and the climate becomes a cool one with marine influences. Apart from this, Patagonia as a whole, as far west as the moister Andean foothills, must be classed as an arid or semi-arid land; but it is hardly a cold-winter middle latitude desert of the type described above.

TABLE 11

SARMIENTO.				45° 36′ S.				268 m				Patagonia.
	J.	F.	M.	A.	M.	J.	J.	A.	S.	O.	N.	D.	Total
° C	18	18	14	11	7	3	3	6	8	12	14	16	—
ins	0·2	0·3	0·3	0·4	0·8	0·8	0·6	0·5	0·5	0·4	0·2	0·3	5·1
mm	5	8	8	10	20	20	15	13	13	10	5	8	140

ABSOLUTE MAX./MIN.	MEAN DAILY MAX./MIN.	MEAN REL. HUMIDITY
37° C (Jan.)	26° C/11° C (Jan.)	07.30 hrs—77 (July), 52 (Jan.)
−11° C (June)	7°C/−2° C (July)	13.30 hrs—59 (July), 29 (Jan.)

Sub-Tropical Humid Climate *Ca*

No distinct Dry Season (Caf)

These climates are found mainly in the eastern parts of continents in the sub-tropics and lower middle latitudes. Rain falls at times throughout the year, though there is usually a summer maximum. The sub-tropical high pressures are weaker in the western parts of the oceans, so that tropical maritime air moves onto the land areas, especially during the summer months when the interiors become hot. In Asia such movements occur as part of the well established monsoon systems, described on p. 83. The warm, moist, unstable air gives oppressive summer weather, with high humidity, and mean temperatures of the order of 25°-30° C. Rainfall is plentiful, though the annual total varies between 800-1 800 mm, according to location; in general, the regions gradually become drier towards the interior of the land masses. Summer convection causes many tropical downpours and thunderstorms are common. Cyclonic storms may also bring rain throughout the year; and, because of this, rather untypically, many parts of the south-eastern U.S.A., west of the Mississippi, have a slight winter maximum. Tropical hurricanes are most frequent in early autumn, affecting the near-tropical eastern seaboards most severely.

In China, air moving from the cold Asiatic interior brings winter temperatures well below those of east-coast locations of comparable

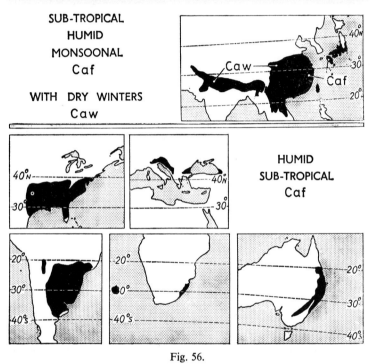

SUB-TROPICAL
HUMID
MONSOONAL
Caf

WITH DRY WINTERS
Caw

HUMID
SUB-TROPICAL
Caf

Fig. 56.

Regions with the warmest summer month averaging over 22° C (f = no dry season; w = dry winter).

latitude in Australia, Argentina, and South Africa, which have no adjoining broad land areas in higher latitudes to create a frequent flow of cold air. Shanghai's January mean of 3° C compares with July averages of 10° C in Buenos Aires, and 11° C in Sydney. In south-east Argentina and Australia winters are warm and mild, with occasional frontal rain belts. Many parts of south-eastern U.S.A. have generally mild winters, but with really cold spells, and thus rather lower winter averages than corresponding southern hemisphere locations, though higher than those of eastern Asia: Colombia, South Carolina, averages 8° C in January, and Little Rock, Arkansas, 6° C.

In all these regions there is greater stability in winter; for when maritime air encroaches it does so over the now cooler land surfaces, and convection is, of course, less intense. In the U.S.A., however, much rain does fall in this season, mostly when surges of cold polar air conflict with tropical air masses, and periods of steady frontal rain occur. In eastern Australia the south-central coastlands receive a well distributed rainfall, for depressions are experienced in all seasons; but severe cyclones are apt to occur in late summer, causing torrential rain as they move in from lower latitudes on to sub-tropical coastlands. Further north the summer rainfall maximum is well marked; for during winter the easterly winds bring more stable air on-shore, giving a much drier season.

Small parts of southern Europe have climatic characteristics which place them in the *Caf* category: among them the plains of northern Italy and the lower Danube Basin, which receive precipitation throughout the year, with a maximum in the summer.

Dry Winter (Caw)

In China winter is the driest season, and the south-central interior, like northern India, has a *Caw* climate. Air masses clash over and near the Chinese coastlands (p. 88). The southern and central parts are more truly *Caf* climates.

Caf areas in the sub-tropics with plentiful, well-distributed rainfall support broad-leafed forests, or conifers on permeable, well-leached soils (p. 170). Towards the interiors where the rainfall is less, forests tend to give way to grassland, though soils greatly influence the nature and distribution of the vegetation. The South American pampas are exceptional, for grassland predominates and extends to the east coast, possibly because the alluvial and loess soils are very porous; nevertheless, trees and shrubs may once have been widespread, and clearing, burning, and grazing responsible for the subsequent dominance of grasses.

It is worth emphasising again the notable differences in the temperature and rainfall values within the humid sub-tropics; the average figures in Tables 12-14 show something of the variations between one region and another. Even in a single country, China, or the U.S.A., there are wide differences between one part of the climatic region and another: but for all the *Caf* regions the rainfall is all-year-round, and generally reliable.

TABLE 12

Caf Types

NANKING.		32° 03′ N.					16 m				Eastern China.	
	J.	F.	M.	A.	M.	J.	J.	A.	S.	O.	N.	D.	Total
° C	2	4	9	14	20	24	28	27	22	18	11	4	—
ins	1·6	2·0	3·0	4·0	3·2	7·2	8·1	4·6	3·7	2·0	1·6	1·2	42·2
mm	40	51	76	102	81	183	206	117	94	51	40	30	1 072

ABSOLUTE MAX./MIN.	MEAN DAILY MAX./MIN.	MEAN REL. HUMIDITY
40° C (July)	31° C/24° C (July)	06.00 hrs—43 (Jan.), 88 (July)
−13° C (Jan.)	6° C/−2° C (Jan.)	14.00 hrs—29 (Jan.), 75 (July)

PORT MACQUARIE.		31° 38′ S.					19 m				Eastern New South Wales.	
	J.	F.	M.	A.	M.	J.	J.	A.	S.	O.	N.	D.	Total
° C	22	22	21	18	16	13	12	13	15	17	19	21	—
ins	5·5	7·0	6·4	6·5	5·6	4·7	4·3	3·3	3·8	3·5	3·7	5·0	59·3
mm	140	178	162	165	142	120	110	84	96	89	94	127	1 507

ABSOLUTE MAX./MIN.	MEAN DAILY MAX./MIN.	MEAN REL. HUMIDITY
41° C (Feb.)	26° C/18° C (Jan.)	09.00 hrs—75 (Aug.), 75 (Jan.)
−1° C (June)	18° C/7° C (July)	15.00 hrs—65 (Aug.), 75 (Jan.)

CHARLESTON.		32° 47′ N.					3 m				South Carolina, U.S.A.	
	J.	F.	M.	A.	M.	J.	J.	A.	S.	O.	N.	D.	Total
° C	10	11	14	18	23	26	27	27	25	20	14	11	—
ins	2·9	3·3	3·4	2·8	3·2	4·7	7·3	6·6	5·1	3·2	2·3	2·8	47·6
mm	74	84	86	71	81	120	186	167	130	81	59	71	1 205

ABSOLUTE MAX./MIN.	MEAN DAILY MAX./MIN.	MEAN REL. HUMIDITY
40° C (July)	31° C/24° C (July)	07.30 hrs—79 (July), 81 (Jan.)
−14° C (Feb.)	14° C/6° C (Jan.)	12.00 hrs—67 (July), 64 (Jan.)

TABLE 13

STATIONS IN DIFFERENT Caf REGIONS		MEAN DAILY MAX./MIN.		MEAN ANNUAL RAINFALL	
		*MID-WINTER °C	MID-SUMMER °C	(ins)	(mm)
Canton (China)	23° N.	17/9	33/26	64·7	1 644
Rockhampton (Aus.)	23° S.	23/10	32/22	39·1	993
Santos (Brazil)	24° S.	23/16	29/22	88·1	2 238
Mobile (Alabama)	31° N.	16/7	32/33	62·1	1 577
Durban (S. Africa)	31° S.	23/11	27/21	39·7	1 009
Osaka (Japan)	35° N.	8/0	31/23	52·6	1 336
Buenos Aires (Arg.)	35° S.	14/5	29/17	37 4	950
Springfield (Missouri)	37° N.	6/—4	31/20	42·1	1 069

* Figures for January or July according to the hemisphere.
Notice the contrast in winter temperatures between the northern and southern Caf regions.

TABLE 14
Caw Types

NEW DELHI.			28° 35′ N.					218 m			Northern India.	
	J.	F.	M.	A.	M.	J.	J.	A.	S.	O.	N.	D.	Total
°C	14	17	22	28	33	33	31	30	29	26	20	15	—
ins	0·9	0·7	0·5	0·3	0·5	2·9	7·1	6·8	4·6	0·4	0·1	0·4	25·2
mm	23	18	13	8	13	74	181	172	117	10	2	10	640

ABSOLUTE MAX./MIN.	MEAN DAILY MAX./MIN.	MEAN REL. HUMIDITY
46° C (May)	41°C/27°C (May)	08.00 hrs—80 (Aug.), 51 (Nov.)
−1° C (Jan.)	21° C/7° C (Jan.)	16.30 hrs—64 (Aug.), 31 (Nov.)

CHUNKING.			29° 33′ N.					230 m			Central China.	
	J.	F.	M.	A.	M.	J.	J.	A.	S.	O.	N.	D.	Total
°C	7	10	15	19	23	26	29	30	25	19	14	10	—
ins	0·6	0·8	1·5	3·9	5·6	7·1	5·6	4·8	5·9	4·4	1·9	0·8	43·0
mm	15	20	38	99	142	181	142	122	142	112	48	20	1 032

ABSOLUTE MAX./MIN.	MEAN DAILY MAX./MIN.	MEAN REL. HUMIDITY
44° C (Aug.)	35° C/25° C (Aug.)	average—all hours: 91 (Nov.), 76 (Aug.)
−2° C (Jan.)	9° C/5° C (Jan.)	

Cool Temperate Humid (Maritime) Climates *Cb Cc*

This type of climate is typical of the western parts of the continents in the middle latitudes, where eastward-moving air and depressions bring temperature and humidity characteristics derived from the oceans over the land areas. Marine controls modify latitudinal controls, and in winter tend to overshadow them, as the

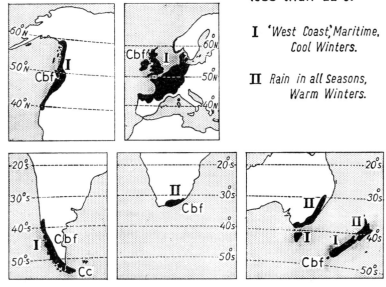

COOL TEMPERATE HUMID CLIMATES   Cbf, Cc.

Rain at all seasons. Warmest months average less than 22°C.

I 'West Coast', Maritime, Cool Winters.

II Rain in all Seasons, Warm Winters.

Fig. 57.

Here the *Cbf* regions include a considerable diversity of winter conditions (and, incidentally, of vegetation): a further sub-division is made, distinguishing between areas with very warm winters (II) ("warm temperate" rather than "cool temperate") and those with much cooler winters (I).

isotherms in Fig. 21 clearly show. They affect lands from about lat. 40° to lat. 60° and over.

The extent of penetration of marine influences into the land areas depends largely on relief. In north-central Europe oceanic influences are carried far inland across the extensive lowlands; whereas in western Canada and southern Chile high mountains restrict this type of climate to the narrow coastlands. The converse is true also: continental influences are more apparent in western European countries than in other west coast regions of this type.

The weather is noted for its changeability, due mainly to the eastward procession of lows and their associated fronts and consequent ridges and troughs. The summers are warm to very warm. July averages are of the order of 13°-18° C, but vary with distance from the ocean and with latitude. Oceanic effects are cooling in summer, so the mean temperatures are usually several degrees below the latitudinal mean. Long drought periods are rare, though in western Europe and western North America northward extensions of sub-tropical high pressure occasionally persist long enough to bring spells of unusual heat, and even droughts.

Winters are mild and so the mean annual temperature range is fairly small. The maritime influences are strong in winter. In Europe, air heated by passage over the relatively warm Atlantic waters keeps the temperatures of western coasts well above those of the interior: thus, being about 15 C° warmer than the average for the latitude, the ports of northern Norway remain open to shipping; even those well within the Arctic Circle. Changeability is, however, a major characteristic: for although continental high pressures may extend their influence westwards from time to time in midwinter, causing severe cold, this may change in a few hours to warm, damp conditions as westerlies re-establish themselves or as a warm front arrives. Continental influences increase away from the west coasts, as is clearly shown in Table 14. This is even noticeable in so narrow and westerly a country as Britain.

There is rain at times throughout the year; but precipitation amounts vary a great deal from place to place, depending very much on relief. In Europe, western hill country may receive 5 000 mm a year, while rain-shadow areas a short distance inland have as little as 500 mm. The precipitation is chiefly associated with fronts which cross the land areas; but high relief, causing additional uplift, tends to increase the amount that falls. Western parts also tend to have a winter maximum, often with high rainfall in autumn. Away from the west it is the summer months that have most: not because there are more rainy days in summer, but because conditions are more favourable for turbulence, and individual storms generally give much heavier rainfall, and are sometimes of a thundery nature. Depressions are less numerous in summer, but pass more easily towards the low pressures over the continent, where rainfall is markedly greater at this time of year. During winter, depressions are more frequent; but high pressure to the east may slow down their passage across the western regions, so that cloudy skies and periods of steady, light rain or drizzle, may persist for a long time. Snow does not usually last long in the lowlands, compared with the duration of snow in the continental interiors in these latitudes.

Anticyclonic conditions may bring hot, sunny spells in summer, yet in winter cause long periods of frost or persistent fog (p. 49). But in some of these regions there is little likelihood of such a pressure build-up, especially in the southern hemisphere where the narrow land masses in these latitudes hardly interrupt the air flows over the expanses of ocean. Southern Chile experiences a very regular succession of eastward-moving depressions throughout the year, with strong westerlies a common feature. New Zealand's South Island seldom has long anticyclonic spells or lengthy periods of frontal rain; as depressions move rapidly eastward, short rainy periods are followed by clear bright conditions, with much unbroken sunshine. The North Island is also visited in summer by occasional cyclonic storms of tropical origin.

The natural vegetation is forest. In Europe this is usually deciduous or mixed forest on lowlands in lower latitudes, with coniferous trees on highlands and in the poleward parts of the regions. But in temperate regions parent soil material has considerable influence on the plant cover. In Western Europe little *natural* forest remains. In some countries the abundant rainfall and mildness allows dense tree growth. There is a variety which indicates that climate alone does not determine the form of vegetation (p. 190). In north-western U.S.A. huge conifers flourish: in Chile there are broad-leafed evergreens and conifers: Tasmania has eucalypts, and dense, almost impenetrable, saxifrage: while southern New Zealand's very mild and moist west coast has thick forests of native rimu and rata, with tall shrubs and tree ferns, close stands of evergreen beech forests in the south, and tussock grassland east of the mountains.

TABLE 15

SHANNON.			52° 41′ N.				2m						Western Ireland.
	J.	F.	M.	A.	M.	J.	J.	A.	S.	O.	N.	D.	Total
° C	5	6	7	9	11	14	15	16	14	11	8	6	—
ins	3·8	3·0	2·0	2·2	2·4	2·1	3·1	3·0	3·0	3·4	4·2	4·3	36·5
mm	96	76	51	56	61	54	79	76	76	86	107	110	927

ABSOLUTE MAX./MIN.	MEAN DAILY MAX./MIN.	MEAN REL. HUMIDITY
31° C (July)	20° C/12° C (Aug.)	06.30 hrs—91 (Aug.), 89 (Jan.)
−11° C (Jan.)	8° C/2° C (Jan.)	17.30 hrs—77 (Aug.), 88 (Jan.)

BERLIN.   52° 27′ N.   57 m   **Germany.**

	J.	F.	M.	A.	M.	J.	J.	A.	S.	O.	N.	D.	Total
° C	−1	0	4	8	13	16	18	17	14	9	4	1	—
ins	1·9	1·3	1·5	1·7	1·9	2·3	3·1	2·2	1·9	1·7	1·7	1·9	23·1
mm	48	33	38	43	48	59	79	56	48	43	43	48	609

ABSOLUTE MAX./MIN.	MEAN DAILY MAX./MIN.	MEAN REL. HUMIDITY
36° C (July)	23° C/13° C (July)	07.00 hrs—79 (July), 89 (Jan.)
−26° C (Feb.)	2° C/−3° C (Jan.)	14.00 hrs—55 (July), 81 (Jan.)

TABLE 16

PRINCE RUPERT.   54° 17′ N.   52 m   **British Columbia.**

	J.	F.	M.	A.	M.	J.	J.	A.	S.	O.	N.	D.	Total
° C	1	2	4	6	9	12	13	14	12	9	5	2	—
ins	9·8	7·6	8·4	6·7	5·3	4·1	4·8	5·1	7·7	12·2	12·3	11·3	95·3
mm	249	193	213	170	135	105	122	130	196	310	313	287	2 421

ABSOLUTE MAX./MIN.	MEAN DAILY MAX./MIN.	MEAN REL. HUMIDITY
31° C (June)	18° C/11° C (Aug.)	04.00 hrs—96 (Aug.), 83 (Jan.)
−19° C (Jan.)	4° C/−1° C (Jan.)	16.00 hrs—77 (Aug.), 78 (Jan.)

CABO RAPER.   46° 50′ S.   40 m   **Southern Chile.**

	J.	F.	M.	A.	M.	J.	J.	A.	S.	O.	N.	D.	Total
° C	11	11	10	9	8	7	6	6	7	8	9	10	—
ins	7·8	5·8	7·1	7·7	7·5	7·9	9·5	7·5	5·6	7·0	6·7	7·0	87·1
mm	198	147	181	196	191	201	242	191	142	178	170	178	2 212

ABSOLUTE MAX./MIN.	MEAN DAILY MAX./MIN.	MEAN REL. HUMIDITY
22° C (Mar.)	14° C/8° C (Jan.)	07.00 hrs—85 (Jan.), 83 (July)
−2° C (June)	8° C/3° C (July)	14.00 hrs—83 (Jan.), 82 (July)

INVERCARGILL.	46° 26' S.		4 m						South Island, New Zealand.			
	J.	F.	M.	A.	M.	J.	J.	A.	S.	O.	N.	D.	Total
° C	14	14	13	11	8	6	5	7	9	11	12	13	—
ins	4·2	3·3	4·0	4·1	4·4	3·6	3·2	3·2	3·2	4·1	4·2	4·0	45·5
mm	107	84	102	105	112	91	81	81	81	105	107	102	1155

ABSOLUTE MAX./MIN.	MEAN DAILY MAX./MIN.	MEAN REL. HUMIDITY
32° C (Jan.)	19° C/9° C (Jan.)	08.30 hrs—76 (Jan.), 83 (July)
−7° C (July)	9° C/1° C (July)	

TABLE 17

Stations with relatively high summer temperatures.

MEAN DAILY MAX./MIN. (°C)*

	SANTANDER (Spain)	PORTLAND (West U.S.A.)	MELBOURNE (Australia)	PORT ELIZABETH (South Africa)
Lat.	43° N.	45° N.	38° S.	34° S.
Mid-Summer	23/17	25/13	26/14	26/16
Mid-Winter	12/7	7/1	13/6	19/7

* For January and July.

Continental Humid (Cold Winter) Climates Da, Db

There is no broad land area in the southern hemisphere south of lat. 40°, other than Antarctica, so these climates are found only in northern land masses. They occur in continental interiors, mainly between 35°-55° N. (further north in eastern Europe), and in eastern coastal lands between about 38°-50° N. They include the interior of North America from Nebraska to the southern parts of the prairie provinces, most of the Middle West, and eastern America from Maryland to the St Lawrence mouth.

In eastern Europe and central Asia, various enclosed European lowlands, including parts of the Danube Basin, and a great stretch of country from Poland to central Russia, north of the steppes, have this general type of climate. Eastern Asia, Manchuria, south-east Siberia, northern China, and northern Japan are also in this broad category. Because of this great spread, the symbols *Da* are used

HUMID CONTINENTAL WITH COLD WINTERS

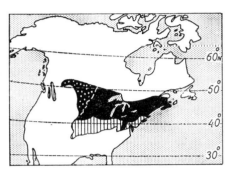

Da *Warm summers*

Db *Cool summers*

Precipitation
10−20 ins p.a.

Remainder of shaded area over 20 ins p.a.

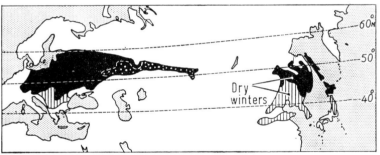

Fig. 58.

These parts of eastern Asia experience much greater differences between summer and winter precipitation than the American regions (see Table 19).

to indicate warm summers, and *Db* shorter and cooler summers (but with the advantage of a longer daily period of insolation).

Winter Conditions

Most characteristic is the cold winter. In the Euro-Asia land mass, this is most marked in lands affected by a persistent flow of cold air from the thermal high pressures of central Asia. In eastern

Asia winter precipitation is small. From the somewhat moister eastern Europe it decreases to a small amount in central Asia. Precipitation occurs where the cold Pc air meets maritime air. In North America, waves of cold Pc air move southwards and eastwards from time to time, displacing Tm air and causing a sharp fall in temperature. The more northerly parts, especially in the interior, experience long cold spells. But winter weather in the rest of the American *Da* and *Db* regions is changeable; for here polar and tropical air may meet, and local depressions are apt to form in the central and eastern parts of these North American climatic regions. Such lows mostly move eastwards and bring fairly rapid changes in temperature, wind direction, and precipitation. Snow is often heavy in winter, and lies for long periods, especially in the northern interior: here it helps to lower temperatures by reflecting insolation. However, a snow cover helps to prevent deep freezing of the ground.

Summer Conditions

Summer temperatures are high for the latitudes, and there is less difference in temperature between the various parts of these climatic regions than in winter. In both America and Euro-Asia there is generally greater precipitation in summer; for then the land surfaces heat rapidly, convection is at a maximum, and moist unstable air moves more freely into the land mass (though moist air from eastern oceans moves against the general air flow in these latitudes). Thundery storms develop in the humid Tm air, giving short, but heavy downpours. Depressions also bring rainfall in summer, especially in North America, but are less frequent than in winter. Autumn and spring seasons are short, with tendencies towards rain in spring and dry, clear weather in autumn.

Variations within the Da regions

The overall climatic differences between the various parts of these *Da, Db* regions are great. In general, precipitation decreases towards the interior and also polewards. North America does not experience the great differences between winter and summer precipitation found in eastern Asia, though the drier interiors do have a more pronounced summer maximum. More southerly and more maritime locations have milder winters, and summer temperatures are much higher in the southern than in the northern parts of the interior, which border on the sub-arctic regions (Table 18). Distinctions between *Da* and *Db* climates are necessary, and valid overall, but no clear boundary exists on the ground; neither are direct comparisons of climatic conditions between parts of one land mass and parts of another of real value, for they vary so greatly in extent, relief, and intensity of their thermal highs and lows.

The vegetation types associated with these regions consequently vary a great deal from place to place. Deep in the continents are prairie grasses, with deciduous trees along streams and rivers. Towards the sources of humid air, the tree cover increases, and more humid parts have a variety of forest types: deciduous hardwoods occur mostly in southern parts, giving way polewards to mixed forests and then coniferous softwoods. But these are broad generalisations, modified by the effects of local relief and soils.

TABLE 18

East Coast Climates—Very Warm to Hot Summers (*Da*)

BOSTON.		42° 22′ N.				38 m						Massachusetts, U.S.A.	
	J.	F.	M.	A.	M.	J.	J.	A.	S.	O.	N.	D.	Total
° C	−2	−2	2	8	14	19	22	21	17	12	6	−1	—
ins	3·6	3·3	3·8	3·5	3·1	3·2	3·3	3·6	3·2	3·3	3·6	3·4	40·8
mm	71	84	96	89	79	81	84	71	81	84	71	86	1 036

ABSOLUTE MAX./MIN.	MEAN DAILY MAX./MIN.	MEAN REL. HUMIDITY
40° C (July)	27° C/17° C (July)	08.00 hrs—71 (July), 72 (Jan.)
−28° C (Feb.)	2° C/−7° C (Jan.)	12.00 hrs—66 (July), 63 (Jan.)

INCHON.		37° 29′ N.				70 m						Korea.	
	J.	F.	M.	A.	M.	J.	J.	A.	S.	O.	N.	D.	Total
° C	−3	−2	6	11	16	19	24	25	20	14	6	2	—
ins	0·8	0·7	1·2	2·6	3·3	3·9	10·9	8·8	4·3	1·6	1·6	1·1	40·8
mm	20	18	30	66	84	99	277	223	110	40	40	28	1 036

ABSOLUTE MAX./MIN.	MEAN DAILY MAX./MIN.	MEAN REL. HUMIDITY
37° C (Aug.)	29° C/22° C (Aug.)	05.30 hrs—95 (July), 73 (Jan.)
−21° C (Jan.)	1° C/−7°C (Jan.)	13.30 hrs—76 (July), 57 (Jan.)

TABLE 19

Db Climates

MINSK.	53° 54′ N.	27° 33′ E.								230 m			White Russian S.S.R.
	J.	F.	M.	A.	M.	J.	J.	A.	S.	O.	N.	D.	Total
° C	−8	−7	−2	4	12	15	17	16	11	5	−1	−6	—
ins	1·4	1·5	1·3	1·5	2·0	2·8	3·0	3·1	1·6	1·5	1·5	1·7	22·9
mm	35	38	33	38	51	71	76	79	40	38	38	43	582

ABSOLUTE MAX./MIN.	MEAN DAILY MAX./MIN.	MEAN REL. HUMIDITY
33° C (July)	21° C/12° C (July)	07.00 hrs—76 (June), 91 (Jan.)
−33° C (Jan.)	−6° C/−11° C (Jan.)	13.00 hrs—58 (June), 86 (Jan.)

KAZAN.	55° 47′ N.	49° 08′ E.								80 m			R.S.F.S.R.
	J.	F.	M.	A.	M.	J.	J.	A.	S.	O.	N.	D.	Total
° C	−15	−13	−7	3	12	16	19	11	7	1	−6	−10	—
ins	0·8	0·6	0·7	0·8	1·3	2·4	2·3	2·0	1·7	1·6	1·2	0·9	16·3
mm	20	15	18	20	33	61	59	51	43	40	30	23	414

ABSOLUTE MAX./MIN.	MEAN DAILY MAX./MIN.	MEAN REL. HUMIDITY
38° C (July)	24° C/14° C (July)	07.00 hrs—75 (July), 88 (Jan.)
−43° C (Jan.)	−13° C/−18° C (Jan.)	13.00 hrs—49 (July), 85 (Jan.)

REGINA.	50° 26′ N.						570 m					Saskatchewan, Canada.
	J.	F.	M.	A.	M.	J.	J.	A.	S.	O.	N.	D.	Total
° C	−18	−17	−9	3	11	16	18	17	11	4	−6	−14	—
ins	0·5	0·3	0·7	0·7	1·8	3·3	2·4	1·8	1·3	0·9	0·6	0·4	14·7
mm	13	8	18	18	45	84	61	45	33	23	15	10	374

ABSOLUTE MAX./MIN.	MEAN DAILY MAX./MIN.	MEAN REL. HUMIDITY
42° C (July)	26° C/11° C (July)	05.30 hrs—88 (July), 91 (Jan.)
−49° C (Jan.)	−12° C/−24° C (Jan.)	12.00 hrs—54 (July), 86 (Jan.)

CHAPTER VIII

TYPES OF CLIMATE (III): SUB-ARCTIC AND ARCTIC

Sub-Arctic Climates *Dc, Dd*

These climates lie poleward of the middle latitude continental climates, and their more northerly parts, especially, are characterised by long, extremely cold winters, short summers, and large annual temperature ranges. For the *Dd* climates the temperature of the coldest month is below − 38° C. Their own poleward limit is

NORTHERN POLAR LANDS

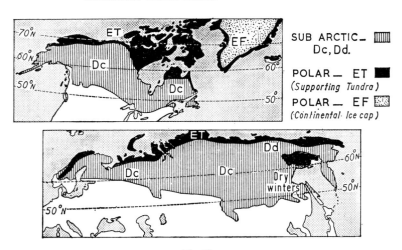

Fig. 59.
The mean temperature of the coldest month is below 0° C. For the *E* Group that of the warmest month is under 10° C.

taken as the 10° C isotherm for the warmest month; below this temperature tree growth is inhibited, and tundra is the chief form of vegetation, instead of the extensive softwood coniferous forest (taiga) which is typical of the *Dc* climatic region.

During the long winters, the very few hours of low intensity insolation cannot match the loss of heat by radiation, so that in the centre of the continents, where the absolute humidity is low, temperatures fall to below − 50° C; the lowest temperature recorded in this

139

region being − 68° C, in Siberia, near Verkhoyansk. Cold dense air masses build up intense thermal high pressures, from which air surges at times into lower latitudes and towards the coasts. Central Siberia is excessively cold in winter; but though other areas with this type of climate have very cold winters, they do not normally experience such extremely low temperatures. Churchill, in Canada, has recorded − 50° C, but its mean January temperature is − 27°C, when much of the North-west Territories averages about − 30° C. In southern Siberia, and many places along the trans-Siberian railway, the mean figure is nearer − 20° C to − 25° C; so that the subdivision *Dd*, with extremely cold winters, applies only to the far north-east of Siberia.

By contrast, during the short summers the temperature climbs rapidly: and though the altitude of the noon-day sun is not great, there are many hours of insolation. Monthly mean temperatures rise to over 16° C, and mid-day readings may approach 30° C. Again, the actual figures vary with location, though for all places in this climatic region at least one month must have a mean temperature of 10° C or over.

The precipitation of the *Dc* region is some 250-500 mm a year in the interior; rather greater in eastern Canada and north-western Europe; the *Dd* area has under 250 mm. Most precipitation falls in summer; but even a light winter snowfall may lie for long periods with little melting or evaporation loss, and snow gradually accumulates through the winter, until the spring melt. Falls are very light indeed in the heart of Siberia, though sufficient moisture may be retained to allow tree growth. The vegetation of these regions is described on p. 241.

TABLE 20

CHURCHILL.			58° 47′ N.				13 m				Manitoba, Canada.	
	J.	F.	M.	A.	M.	J.	J.	A.	S.	O.	N.	D.	Total
° C	−28	−26	−21	−10	−1	6	12	11	5	3	−15	−24	—
ins	0·5	0·6	0·9	0·9	0·9	1·9	2·2	2·7	2·3	1·4	1·0	0·7	16·0
mm	13	15	23	23	23	48	56	69	59	35	25	18	406

ABSOLUTE MAX./MIN.	MEAN MONTHLY MAX./MIN.	MEAN REL. HUMIDITY
36° C (July)	18° C/6° C (July)	06.00 hrs—88 (July), 97 (Dec.)
− 50° C (Jan.)	− 24° C/− 33° C (Jan.)	12.00 hrs—71 (July), 93 (Dec.)

GÄLLIVARE.		67° 08′ N.					365 m				**Sweden.**	
	J.	F.	M.	A.	M.	J.	J.	A.	S.	O.	N.	D.	Total
° C	−11	−12	−8	−2	6	11	15	12	6	−1	−1	−10	—
ins	1·7	1·1	1·0	1·2	1·5	2·3	3·0	2·9	2·1	2·3	1·8	1·5	22·4
mm	43	28	25	33	38	59	76	74	54	59	45	38	569

ABSOLUTE MAX./MIN.	MEAN MONTHLY MAX./MIN.	MEAN REL. HUMIDITY
34° C (July)	21° C/9° C (July)	08.30 hrs—68 (July), 84 (Jan.)
−42° C (Jan.)	−7° C/−16° C (Jan.)	14.30 hrs—52 (July), 83 (Jan.)

BOGOLOVSK.		59° 45′ N.	59° 01′ E.				192 m				**R.S.F.S.R.**	
	J.	F.	M.	A.	M.	J.	J.	A.	S.	O.	N.	D.	Total
°C	−21	−16	−9	−3	7	13	16	14	8	−1	−12	−19	—
ins	0·6	0·7	0·7	1·0	1·8	2·7	3·3	3·3	1·7	0·9	0·9	0·8	18·4
mm	15	18	18	25	45	69	84	84	43	23	23	20	467

ABSOLUTE MAX./MIN.	MEAN MONTHLY MAX./MIN.	MEAN REL. HUMIDITY
34° C (July)	21° C/12° C (July)	07.00 hrs—77 (July), 85 (Jan.)
−42° C (Jan.)	−17° C/−24° C (Jan.)	13.00 hrs—59 (July), 79 (Jan.)

VERKHOYANSK.		67° 34′ N.	133° 51′ E.				100 m				**R.S.F.S.R.**	
	J.	F.	M.	A.	M.	J.	J.	A.	S.	O.	N.	D.	Total
° C	−51	−45	−32	−15	0	12	14	9	2	−13	−38	−47	—
ins	0·2	0·2	0·1	0·2	0·3	0·9	1·1	1·0	0·5	0·3	0·3	0·2	5·3
mm	5	5	3	5	8	23	28	25	13	8	8	5	135

ABSOLUTE MAX./MIN.	MEAN MONTHLY MAX./MIN.	MEAN REL. HUMIDITY
37° C (July)	19° C/8° C (July)	07.00 hrs—62 (June), 70 (Jan.)
−68° C (Feb.)	−48° C/−53° C (Jan.)	13.00 hrs—45 (June), 70 (Jan.)

Polar Climate—Supporting Tundra *ET*

This lies between the zone of permanent frost with its cover of
ice and snow, the ice-cap type of climate where no vegetation grows,

and the poleward limits of the sub-Arctic climates described above. Here no month has a mean temperature of more than 10° C.

The summers are cool and short: for only 2-4 months are the average temperatures above freezing point; but the sun is above the horizon for most of the twenty-four hours, so that the diurnal range is small. Many days are pleasantly warm, some very warm. In winter, with no insolation to counteract continuous radiation losses for months on end, temperatures fall rapidly, and continue to fall, so that bitterly cold conditions prevail. The snow cover remains until May when melt-water, unable to drain through the permanently frozen sub-soil, tends to produce swampy conditions. Most precipitation comes during the summer months.

In continental locations the annual precipitation seldom exceeds 250 mm; and under the anticyclonic conditions of winter the snow is usually dry and powdery in texture.

Some tundra regions receive maritime influences, notably those relatively near the coasts of north-western Europe. Average temperatures are much higher there than in interior tundra lands; also summer precipitation tends to be higher in Western Europe and the Labrador Peninsula.

The life cycle of many plants runs its course in a few months; the carpet of flowers of early summer gives way to bright berries before the short autumn. The nature and relative abundance of vegetation again varies with location (p. 244): there is usually a mat of plants, including stunted trees and heaths in the warmer parts, but often only mosses and lichens on rocks bordering the ice-caps. Such extremes create characteristic soils (pp. 167-9).

TABLE 21

Ruskoye Ust'ye.		71° 01′ N.		149° 29′ E.					6 m		R.S.F.S.R.	
	J.	F.	M.	A.	M.	J.	J.	A.	S.	O.	N.	D.	Total
° C	−39	−38	−32	−24	−8	4	9	7	0	−14	−27	−35	—
ins	0·2	0·2	0·2	0·1	0·4	0·8	1·1	1·1	0·7	0·3	0·3	0·3	5·7
mm	5	5	5	3	10	20	28	28	18	8	8	8	146

Absolute Max./Min.	Mean Monthly Max./Min.	Mean Rel. Humidity
32° C (July)	13° C/6°C (July)	07.00 hrs—79 (July), 81 (Jan.)
−52° C (Jan.)	−37° C/−40° C (Jan.)	13.00 hrs—71 (July), 82 (Jan.)

GODTHAAB.		64° 11′ N.		51° 43′ E.			20 m			**South-west Greenland.**		
	J.	F.	M.	A.	M.	J.	J.	A.	S.	O.	N.	D.	Total
°C	−10	−10	−7	−4	1	7	7	6	4	−1	−5	−8	—
ins	1·4	1·7	1·6	1·2	1·7	1·4	2·2	3·1	3·3	2·5	1·9	1·5	23·5
mm	35	43	40	33	43	35	56	79	84	64	48	38	598

ABSOLUTE MAX./MIN.	MEAN MONTHLY MAX./MIN.	MEAN REL. HUMIDITY
24° C (July)	11° C/3° C (July)	(Average all hours) 92 (June), 85 (Jan.)
−29° C (Jan.)	−7° C/−12° C (Jan.)	

HEBRON.		58° 12′ N.		62° 21′ W.			15 m			**North-east Canada.**		
	J	F.	M.	A.	M.	J.	J.	A.	S.	O.	N.	D.	Total
°C	−21	−21	−14	−8	0	4	8	9	5	−1	−7	−16	—
ins	0·9	0·7	0·9	1·1	1·6	2·1	2·7	2·7	3·3	1·6	1·1	0·6	19·3
mm	23	18	23	28	40	54	69	69	84	40	28	15	491

ABSOLUTE MAX./MIN.	MEAN MONTHLY MAX./MIN.	MEAN REL. HUMIDITY
31° C (July)	13° C/4° C (Aug.)	(Average all hours) 85 (July), 82 (Jan.)
−41° C (Jan.)	−17° C/−24° C (Jan.)	

Polar Climate—Ice Caps *EF*

Energy Gained and Lost. Here no month has a mean temperature above freezing point; here are the lowest temperatures of any of the global climates. During those winter months with no gain from insolation there is continuous loss of radiant energy. During summer, there is continuous insolation, but the oblique rays provide relatively little energy. Snow and ice surfaces reflect back about four-fifths of the solar radiation received. In clear weather radiation losses through the dry air are particularly great. Precipitation is low, most of it as small, hard, snow particles.

The Arctic and Antarctic ice-caps differ in certain important respects. The Arctic is an ocean region with only a perimeter of land; while the Antarctic is mostly land with bordering oceans; as a climatic region, it covers about three times the area of the Arctic

EF type.   In summer the land surfaces around the Arctic contribute more energy to the atmosphere than the water surfaces surrounding the Antarctic.   Also, the Arctic air holds more water vapour than that of the Antarctic, and so the loss of long-wave radiation tends to be less.   However, the earth is nearest the sun during the Antarctic summer: as a result about 7 per cent. more solar energy is received by the Antarctic atmosphere in midsummer than by the Arctic atmosphere in the northern midsummer.   Again, the Antarctic surface is at such an altitude that solar radiation has to pass through only about two-thirds of the mass of air which covers the surface at the North Pole.   But these latter advantages to the Antarctic, in

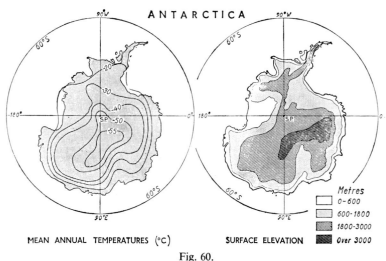

MEAN ANNUAL TEMPERATURES (°C)   SURFACE ELEVATION

Metres
0–600
600–1800
1800–3000
Over 3000

Fig. 60.
The Mean Annual Temperatures vary with both latitude and altitude.

energy gained, are offset by the fact that in the Arctic heat from the underlying ocean passes through the ice and helps to warm the atmosphere; which is not the case in the Antarctic.

Surface temperatures in various parts of the Antarctic depend both on latitude and altitude.   Mean annual temperatures at the Soviet base of Vostock, which stands 3 300 m above sea-level, are – 56° C, compared with – 51° C at the Pole, a thousand miles further south but with surface altitude 600 m less.   For three successive years Vostok recorded minimum temperatures of – 87° C, – 86° C, and – 88° C (– *127*° *F*).   In winter, temperature inversion occurs in the air above the cold surfaces. Strong down-slope winds develop, usually up to a hundred metres or so in depth. When they reach a certain velocity, gustiness sets in, causing intense local blizzards. Mean annual temperatures on the Greenland ice-cap are of the order of -30° C to -35° C, and about -20° C to -25° C over the surface of the Arctic Ocean.

Latent Heat and the Balance of Energy. Both Arctic and Ant-arctic regions play a large part in maintaining the world's heat resources in balance. An inward gain of heat energy occurs only during a brief summer period; at all other times the polar regions radiate more heat energy than they receive. Yet inflow and outflow of energy must be nearly balanced each year, otherwise the polar regions would become progressively colder. The source of extra energy arrives by advection, that is by a horizontal movement of warm air and water vapour, which helps to balance the loss by radiation. More is becoming known of the total heat value of air flowing into the Antarctic now that a network of stations exists around the borders of the land mass. Vertical readings of wind speeds and air temperatures enable the "sensible" heat to be calculated. Besides this, an estimate of the total annual precipitation within the Antarctic provides the basis for the calculation of the vast amount of latent heat released when the water vapour condenses to drops and the drops solidify into ice; vapour carried into Antarctica releases a large quantity of heat. The average precipitation over Antarctica is thought to be equivalent to 150-200 mm of water, though only about 50 mm falls near the South Pole.

Air Circulation—At the Surface and in the Upper Atmosphere. The general pattern of atmospheric circulation over and around the two polar regions is briefly described on pp. 15 and 75. In winter in the southern hemisphere strong westerlies in the lower atmos-phere form a zonal belt in the higher middle latitudes; and although there are occasional surges of polar air into lower latitudes there is less exchange of air along the meridians than there is in the northern hemisphere. There are also fewer incursions of warm air into the Antarctic; largely because continental masses do not extend from tropical to polar regions in the southern hemisphere. However, eastward-travelling cyclonic storms do move in from time to time, causing heavier snowfall. Small cyclonic storms also form round the continental edge, but few move over the central region.

In winter, in the upper air, far above the cold, dense air masses over the Antarctic plateau and the South Pole, there is a low pressure vortex, with regions of high pressure over the perimeter of the continent and low over the centre; but, again, the strong zonal winds do not readily allow an exchange of air from lower latitudes.

During summer, in the stratosphere, this winter low is replaced by a high. At low levels the occasional large cyclonic storms are now able to bring heat and moisture into the continent.

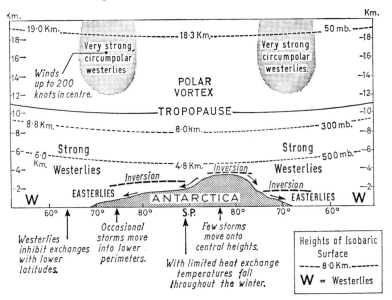

Fig. 61.

Winter conditions affecting the Antarctic Continent. Strong zonal air movements (*i.e.* air moving rapidly along the parallels) tend to prevent an influx of heat from lower latitudes. Notice, near the surface, the polar easterlies, and the strong westerlies of the higher middle latitudes.

The Arctic climate varies much more. With land and sea areas alternating, considerable differences occur between various polar regions; the zonal westerlies are interrupted more frequently as cold air surges southwards. In summer, the heating of the adjoining land masses makes for more climatic variations. Even over the Greenland ice-cap, cyclones move in fairly frequently, bringing cloud and snow. In summer, the north polar regions are not nearly as cold as those near the South Pole; also the margins of Antarctica, though much warmer in summer than in the interior, do not have the relatively high summer temperatures of the marginal *Dc* regions in the northern hemisphere.

TABLE 22

EISMITTE.		70° 53′ N.		40° 42′ W.				3 000 m		**Central Greenland.**		
	J.	F.	M.	A.	M.	J.	J.	A.	S.	O.	N.	D.	Total
°C	−36	−47	−40	−31	−21	−17	−12	−18	−22	−36	−43	−38	—
ins	0·6	0·2	0·3	0·2	0·1	0·1	0·1	0·4	0·3	0·5	0·5	1·0	4·3
mm	15	5	8	5	3	2	3	10	8	13	13	25	110

ABSOLUTE MAX./MIN.	MEAN MONTHLY MAX./MIN.	MEAN REL. HUMIDITY
−3° C (July)	−7° C/−17° C (July)	(Average all hours)
−65° C (Mar.)	−41° C/−53° C (Feb.)	86 (July), 77 (Feb.)

LITTLE AMERICA.*		78° 34′ S.		163° 56′ W.				9 m.		**Ross Sea, Antarctica.**	
	J.	F.	M.	A.	M.	J.	J.	A.	S.	O.	N.	D.
°C	−7	−16	−21	−29	−31	−27	−38	−36	−40	−26	−19	−7

ABSOLUTE MAX./MIN.	MEAN MONTHLY MAX./MIN.	MEAN REL. HUMIDITY
6° C (Dec.)	−4° C/−9° C (Jan.)	(Average all hours)
−59° C (Sept.)	−34° C/−46° C (Sept.)	76 (Mar.), 88 (June)

SOUTH POLE.*				2 956 m						**Antarctic Continent.**	
	J.	F.	M.	A.	M.	J.	J.	A.	S.	O.	N.	D.
°C	−41	−49	−57	−57	−56	−58	−62	−59	−55	−45	−35	−39

Absolute Minimum at VOSTOK (78° S.): −88·3° C (1960).

* (Readings for 3-5 consecutive years).

CHAPTER IX

SOILS

Soil Components

Soil is a material consisting of mineral and organic matter in the form of solids, liquids, and gases. Here the term is taken to include both the top earthy layers, in which most of the plant roots are growing, and the sub-soil beneath, which includes material weathered from the parent rock, and which is usually considerably deeper than the surface earth. Inorganic particles derived from the break-up of rocks make up the bulk of most soils, though a peaty soil may have a greater proportion of organic matter. The organic content consists of the decaying plant and animal matter and the results of that decomposition, which may, like some of the inorganic substances, dissolve and form part of the soil liquid content. Living organisms, insects, worms, and bacteria among them, affect the composition of the soil in a number of ways.

The size of the material varies from large stones and gravels, through small sand grains, to minute particles of silt and clay, some less than ten-thousandth of an inch across. Spaces between the particles are filled with gases; mostly those of the atmosphere, but including some produced by bacterial and chemical action.

Parent Material and Inorganic Contents

The parent rock is broken down by mechanical or chemical weathering into fragments of inorganic substances, which come to form a large part of the soil cover. In any place the inorganic matter may either have been derived from the local bed-rock or else transported from other sources, and so may be a mixture of materials of various origins.

Even when little transportation has occurred, the parent rock does not alone determine the nature of the soil. As we shall see, many processes are involved in creating a mature soil, and soil types may be virtually independent of the parent rock under certain circumstances. Also, the same bed-rock may have provided the inorganic materials for a number of different soils, formed under different conditions of climate, relief, or drainage.

Naturally, there is a great variety of substances, with varying physical and chemical properties, in a complex substance such as

soil. Among the commonest solids resulting from rock disintegration are silica, which in the form of quartz is very resistant to
chemical break-down, and various silicates: together these make up
over half the mass of the earth's crust. The elements present in
soil compounds are many, and of varying importance to plants.
Aluminium, iron, and potassium occur in oxides combined with
silica in complex molecules; compounds of calcium, and sodium
are numerous.

The Importance of Clay Minerals

Clays consist of extremely fine particles, formed by the alteration
of various parent materials. They are usually mainly composed of
distinctive "clay minerals" with tiny particles of other minerals.

The clay minerals are very important to soil formation, soil
properties, and to plant life. Their atoms of silica, aluminium and
oxygen, form lattice structures arranged in layers. The composition
of the lattice and the actual arrangement of the layers characterise an
individual clay mineral. However, the clay minerals change their
composition under various environmental conditions. For instance, under hot, wet conditions they tend to lose silica from their
structure. Fig. 62 shows a simplification of this process. Notice
that the layers are indicated, and not the internal structure of the
molecules.

One clay, *montmorillonite*, is seen to have a particular 2:1 layered
structure. Weathering, under the conditions described, involves a
loss of silica. Initially, this produces a 1:1 layered *kaolinite*; but
further weathering leaves the *aluminate*.

A parent rock, such as basalt, can thus produce montmorillonite,
in combination with hydrated iron oxides; then weather to form
kaolinite, with iron oxides; and finally alumina and iron oxides – as
in bauxite: all as a result of progressive desilification. It must be
stressed that though clays may break down through hydrolysis under
moist conditions, the end products of decomposition, and the retention or loss of these in the soil, vary with temperatures; and with
the acidity, or basicity, of soil solutions (p. 159).

Some soils contain only very small amounts of certain elements—
"trace elements"—which are nevertheless of great importance to the
growth and development of plants, even though only minute quantities need to be absorbed. The common elements of organic
decomposition—carbon, oxygen, hydrogen, and nitrogen—together
with sulphur and phosphorus are re-absorbed in soluble compounds

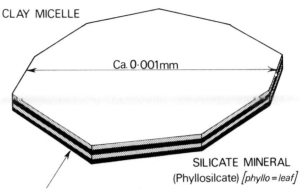

CLAY MICELLE

Ca. 0·001mm

SILICATE MINERAL
(Phyllosilcate) *[phyllo = leaf]*

Layers of silicate /aluminate (repeated)

DESILIFICATION

silicate layer

aluminate layer

weak bond

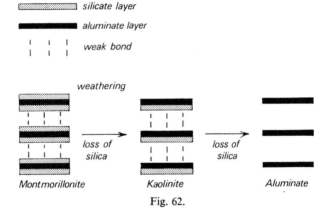

weathering

loss of silica

loss of silica

Montmorillonite   *Kaolinite*   *Aluminate*

Fig. 62.

through the membranes of the root hairs of plants. Nearly all plants receive the inorganic compounds they require in this way, by absorbing soil liquids; so that it is not sufficient for the elements required by plants merely to be present in the soil: they must be in a form which can be readily absorbed.

As we study soil contents we find that certain components play a special role in helping to hold, and preventing the loss of, nutrients required by plants. Other substances may not be absorbed by plants yet may be important because they affect the texture of the soil, and hence its aeration, drainage, or water-holding properties.

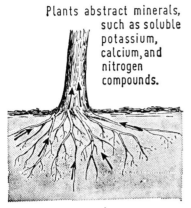

Plants abstract minerals, such as soluble potassium, calcium, and nitrogen compounds.

MINERAL NUTRIENTS

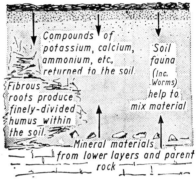

SOURCES
OF MINERAL NUTRIENTS

Rotting vegetable/animal matter.

Compounds of potassium, calcium, ammonium, etc., returned to the soil.

Fibrous roots produce finely-divided humus within the soil.

Mineral materials from lower layers and parent rock

Soil fauna (Inc. Worms) help to mix material

Fig. 63.

Organic Matter and its Decomposition

Plants, parts of plants, and animals which die and remain in the earth are important soil constituents; and so are certain living organisms. Earthworms spread and partly digest such remains, and fungi and bacteria, especially, cause the disintegration and decomposition of organic material into water, carbon dioxide, organic acids, and various soluble salts, including nitrates. Certain bacteria, which occur in nodules on the roots of leguminous plants, can assimilate gaseous nitrogen and convert it into protein, which is broken down by other bacteria into ammonia and nitrates. Nitrogen thus becomes available for the growth of plants capable of absorbing soluble nitrates from the soil. This is a vital cycle of events: for green plants can make direct use of carbon dioxide and water vapour from the air, and with energy from sunlight can synthesise sugars and build up cellulose and other structural matter, but they cannot acquire nitrogen directly. Nitrogen contained in soluble compounds, is absorbed via the roots, as are other necessary elements.

As the roots within the soil, and leaves and stems nearer the surface, decompose, an end product known as *humus* is formed. (This name is sometimes misapplied to surface layers of slowly rotting leaf-mould.) Humus which results from such decomposition is a complex colloidal mixture of substances, black in colour. A colloid, containing very fine material, can exist either as a mobile fluid or, at lower temperatures, as a "gel" or flexible solid. Thus it may be present in soil as minute particles or as a jelly coating the mineral grains. Usually about half of it is humic acid combined with various bases. The basic content of humus formed by some plants may be high enough to give an alkaline rather than an acid reaction, when it is known as *mild humus* or "mull", rather than *raw humus* or acidic "mor". Obviously there are also intermediate varieties. Humus plays a very important role in helping to retain in the soil certain elements which the plants can then use (p. 156).

The bacteria in the soil require oxygen, and are unable to act if waterlogging prevents the absorption of free oxygen. Excessive cold and drought conditions also limit their activity. In such cases the vegetable matter remains unaltered, or peaty in nature, and humus formation is checked.

The Texture of Soils

Size of Particles

The size of the particles affects the properties of soils in several ways. Water drains rapidly through open sandy soils, but is held in soils of very fine texture. In a clay soil, for instance, the particles are too small to allow adequate drainage. In some fine soils the water adheres so firmly to the particles as to restrict its availability to plants.

Material larger than 2 mm diameter is classed as *gravel* or *stones*. Below this size are *coarse sands* down to 0·2 mm, *fine sand* to 0·02 mm, and *silt* to 0·002 mm diameter. Still smaller are the *clay* particles. The sum of the surface areas of the vast number of minute particles which make up clay is so great that it enormously increases its power of adhesion to other substances; because of this, elements which may be of value to plant life are not so easily washed out. When mixed with humus the very fine particles form what is known as a *clay-humus complex*, a colloidal mass with valuable retentive properties.

Soils are broadly described as *sand* if they include about 80 per

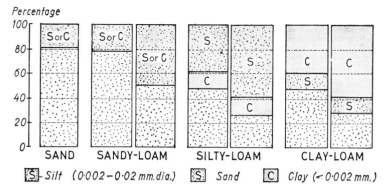

Fig. 64.

Soil composition in terms of the size of particles. Sand particles may vary from those in fine sands (down to 0·02 mm) to coarse sandy materials (0·2 mm-2 mm in diameter).

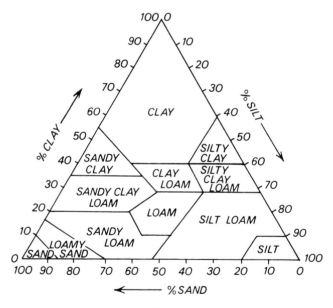

Fig. 65.

cent. sand to 20 per cent. or less silt or clay. A *sandy-loam* contains between 50-80 per cent. sand, and the rest silt or clay. Other
types of "loam" include 30-50 per cent. sand, with 30-50 per cent.
silt, and up to 20 per cent. clay. If silt predominates it is a *silty
loam*, if clay then a *clay loam*.
   A triangular graph of the type shown in Fig. 65 is a useful way of
expressing the texture of a soil. The latter can be established by
seiving through decreasing meshes, to separate grain sizes, or by
sedimentation techniques which compare settling rates of particles
in water—the rates being proportional to the diameters of the
particles.

Grain groupings
   The mineral particles in a soil tend to bind together as aggregates,
or *peds*. The ways in which grains are grouped together in a soil are
also important, because of their effects on the soil's porosity, and
therefore on its aeration and water content, and on the development
of plant organs within the soil. More directly, the grouping of soil
particles affects the ability of the soil to stand up to erosive agents.
Soils may be regularly granular; with a crumb structure; made up of
large, sharp-edged, irregular blocks (blocky); divided into vertical
columns or long prisms (prismatic); or they may have flat, thin
horizontal layers (platy soils). Organic substances formed by
plant decomposition affect the groupings of the particles Those
formed under grass, where numerous roots decay, seem to aid the
formation of regular crumbs. The growth of fine filaments of
micro-organisms tend to bind the particles together.

Hard Pans and Salt Layers
   Soil textures tend to vary with depth. Under certain conditions, the texture can change abruptly; as where compounds have
been deposited, or otherwise formed, as a hard layer within the soil
itself. One which occurs frequently in podsols (p. 169), is an "iron
pan"—a layer of compounds formed by precipitation not far
below the surface. This comes about because water containing
certain organic material can dissolve iron oxide (ferric oxide), which
is normally insoluble in water. This iron solution is washed down
into the soil; but where, lower down, the soil acidity falls below a
certain value, an iron compound is precipitated, and the iron pan
built up. Salt layers of different composition, concentrated by
upward movements of soil water, are sometimes formed within, or
near the surface of soils.

Above (*left*): Dense rainforest in tropical red soil above deep regolith formed on weathered granitic rock near Rio de Janeiro. (*D. C. Money*)

Above (*right*): Immature soils with organic horizons in porous material ejected from Mt. Ngaurohoe, New Zealand. Debris from more recent eruptions covers the lower darker layers formed beneath an earlier surface. (*D. C. Money*)

Below: Exfoliated masses, formed under hot moist conditions, overlook Leme beach, Rio de Janeiro. Thick forest establishes itself on surprisingly steep weathered slopes. (*D. C. Money*)

Above: Winter rainfall readily infiltrates the deep regolith and pervious bedrock of limestone near Khirokitia, Cyprus. The dry soil supports only low shrubs (*garrigue*). (*D. C. Money*)

Below (*left*): It is difficult for mature soils to develop on steep, mobile talus slopes, as here on the Pentadactylos, northern Cyprus. (*D. C. Money*)

Below (*right*): Residual particles left in solution hollows in Maltese karst limestone give pockets of red soil which support small xerophytic plants. (*D. C. Money*)

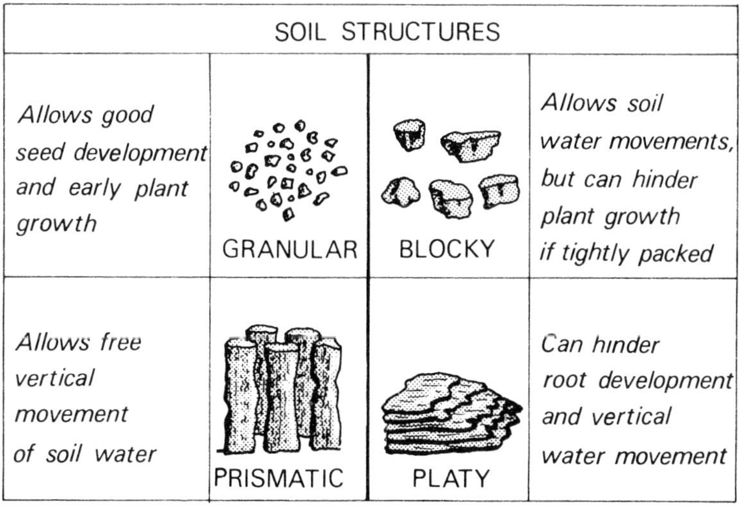

Fig. 66.

Changes in Texture

Continual cultivation is bound to affect soil texture. The normal agricultural practises of ploughing, harrowing, and rolling are used to break down aggregates to give a finer, more even surface structure. Ploughing breaks crusts and increases porosity; though this may not always be desirable. In hot countries with seasonal periods of potentially rapid evaporation, the efficient use of peasant hoes may be more effective than deep ploughing which allows upward movements and loss of soil moisture. Elsewhere, excessive tillage may lead to a complete breakdown, with the danger of erosion, especially in soils which are naturally silty or sandy.

The use of heavy machinery on wet soils may over-compact the surface, and even cause clay particles beneath the surface to be re-oriented and form a dense horizontal layer—a *ploughpan* which hinders water percolation, aeration, and root development.

The practice of "zero-tillage", seeding grains into narrow holes or slits, without ploughing, is sometimes used where there is a danger of deterioration through ploughing. But this usually calls for extra treatment to control weeds and pests, and some danger of surface compacting if the land is not ploughed at all.

Farmers may attempt to alter soil texture through addition. In areas of sandy soil it is not unusual to find a calcareous, silty clay (marl) used to increase the soil's clay content and basicity.

Colour

Soil colour may, or may not, be significant in indicating the composition of the soil. Very small amounts of a compound may produce an overall coloration no different from that of a soil which contains it in abundance: this is often so with iron salts. On the other hand colour difference can be significant: as where the red-brown of ferric iron compounds occurs in well-aerated soils, while bluish-grey colours are seen in waterlogged soils from exactly the same parent material. In the latter case the exclusion of oxygen makes for the presence of ferrous rather than ferric iron compounds.

Other colours may be due to substances which make for fertility. But one must beware of rash assumptions: the fertile czernozem soils of the prairie grasslands have a blackish appearance, for humus is well distributed throughout the profile (although the organic content is usually only of the order of 10 per cent., and indeed the soil may have only half that amount and appear black). The blackness of the Deccan volcanic soils, however, is partly due to the presence of titanium compounds. Again, black peaty soils may be mainly organic in nature, yet in this condition infertile. We should be cautious, therefore, in drawing inferences from soil coloration.

Plant Nutrients in Soils: Their Removal or Retention

We have seen that a plant requires certain nutrients from the soil, and that these are present in the soil as the result of the weathering of parent material, or transportation from some other locality, or by plant decay, decomposition, and bacterial action. Other factors help to determine whether or not the nutrients remain long enough to be available for plants, and these are highly important where soil fertility is concerned.

Clay-Humus Particles and the Retention of Bases

Many salts are soluble and could easily be removed by a heavy rain storm. Those of potassium, calcium, magnesium, and other metals, and also of the ammonium ion, which are all substances needed by the plants, could be washed out and so unavailable as nutrients. (We can regard an ion as an atom or group of atoms carrying an electric charge: the cations of metals, or "basic" ions, have positive charges, while "acidic" anions have negative ones; ions are separated when the salts dissolve in water.) Certain soil constituents can check the removal of bases, however. Both clay particles and humus, and the close combination of the two known as

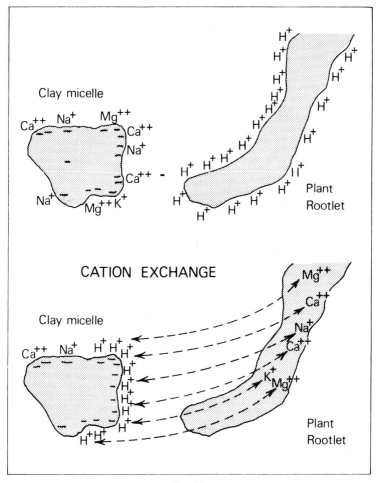

Fig. 67.

the "clay-humus complex", can form linkages with the basic ions. The potassium ions, for example, can be held so that they are not readily washed out. The presence of clay and humus can, therefore, help a soil retain its natural fertility, or hold elements from an added fertiliser, in a way which sandy soils cannot: water percolating through the latter can remove bases more easily. But though these nutrients are thus retained by clay-humus molecules, plant roots *are* able to remove them.

Hydrogen ions carried by the rootlet are exchanged for cations held by clay or humus, thus providing nutrients to be transported in solution through the xylem tissue to other plant organs. Humus has about twice the cation exchange capacity of pure clay. The cation exchange capacity of the clays varies with the surface area available for cation adsorption. Montmorillonite has a greater surface area than illite, for exchange purposes; both have a large area compared with kaolinite.

Leaching under Acid Conditions

As rain-water is dilute carbonic acid ($H^+H^+CO_3^=$), its hydrogen ions can be replaced by metallic ones; in this way it robs the clay-humus complex of its bases (which form carbonates and are washed downwards). Unless the parent material can keep on supplying bases, the clay-humus complex must become, and remain, acid. The removal of bases by percolating water is called *leaching*. Much

CLAY–HUMUS PARTICLES : ACTION IN SOILS

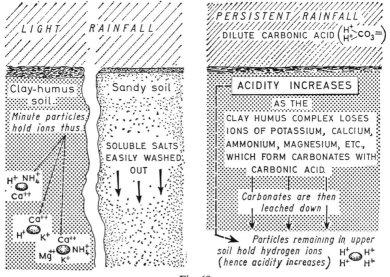

Fig. 68.

Under conditions of light rainfall clay-humus soils can retain basic ions, in contrast to coarse sandy soils: heavy leaching under acidic conditions tends to replace and remove these bases: carbonates and bicarbonates are formed and leached out.

humus may add to the acidity and speed the leaching action. Calcium carbonate, which is, of course, present in large quantities in soils derived from chalk and other limestones, is very easily removed by acid rain-water; but the parent material is often very thick and able to maintain a calcium supply. Calcium carbonate is present in many soils, and where it can be retained is a very important basic soil constituent.

Clays contain complex silicates (p. 149), in which silica (SiO_2) may be combined with varying numbers of molecules of iron and aluminium "sesquioxides" (compounds in which two metallic atoms are combined with three oxygen atoms—Fe_2O_3 and Al_2O_3). Where the soil is wet and acid, and there is a downward movement of acid water, the clay molecules break up, and the iron and aluminium oxides are carried downward as well as the strong bases, leaving the silica. In those parts of the low latitudes with high temperatures and much rainfall the clay molecules again decompose rapidly; but under *less acidic* conditions it is the silica which is washed downwards, or removed, and the iron and aluminium sesquioxides which remain.

WET, LEACHED SOILS

Temperate Conditions (Moderate Temperatures)	*Tropical Conditions* (High Temperatures)
Slow Decomposition: Acid Soils	Rapid Decomposition: Bases released quickly
*Clays break up: SILICA REMAINS	*Clays break up: †OXIDES OF IRON, ALUMINIUM REMAIN
†Oxides of iron, aluminium, and various mineral salts are leached down.	Silica and various mineral salts are leached down
↓ ↓	↓ ↓
Mineral redeposition where the soil is less acid.	Persistently wet conditions may remove minerals by percolation.
	Long dry period may draw up minerals (hard pans may form above).

* CLAY contains complex Silicates such as $xFe_2O_3.yAl_2O_3.zSiO_2$
Iron/Aluminium Silica Sesquioxides.
† The oxides are usually hydrated.

The Acidity of Soils

We have seen that acidity has an important bearing on the chemical composition of soils. Soils may become acid because the organic matter which decomposes contains few bases; or because of a lack of basic parent material; or because the presence of inorganic and organic acids cause the replacement and removal of basic ions. Such acidity may hinder the rate of absorption by the plant roots and also affect the rate of bacterial decomposition.

We have also seen that both acids and bases dissociate to give ions. It is possible to indicate soil acidity by measuring the concentration of hydrogen ions (which are provided by the acids). The symbol *p*H is used to show this concentration. *An acid soil* is represented by a *smaller* *p*H value than a basic one (because the logarithm of the reciprocal of the hydrogen ion concentration is used. Thus 1/10 000th part by weight = *p*H1; hence 1/100.000th part = *p*H2; 1/10 000 000 000 part = *p*H7. It is evident, therefore, that *p*H5 represents an acidity ten times as great as *p*H6, and so on).

*p*H values

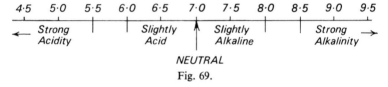

Fig. 69.

A soil which is neutral, neither acidic nor basic, has a *p*H value of 7. A soil with organic acids present, and clay-humus complex with hydrogen instead of metallic ions attached, may have a *p*H value of 3; whereas a soil containing bases from parent material such as calcium carbonate, and with the clay-humus complex holding basic ions, may have a *p*H value of 9. If, therefore, a particular soil is losing bases (and perhaps becoming less fertile on this account) the *p*H value will tend to decrease. But though the *p*H values show the balance between the acidic and basic contents, they do not necessarily give an indication of the *quantity* of bases retained in the soil.

Vertical Movements of Water—Effects on Soils

Pedalfer Formation

When precipitation received exceeds the loss by evaporation, excess water may be able to pass downwards through the soil and perhaps remove calcium carbonate and other bases and colloids from the upper levels. We have seen that in a cool climate leaching under acid conditions leaves silica behind; whereas in hotter regions leaching tends to leave hydrated oxides of aluminium (bauxite), iron (limonite), and manganese (manganite). Soils in which the clay particles are broken down by these processes are termed *pedalfers* (Al—aluminium, Fe—iron).

Pedocal Formation

When drying conditions persist for a sufficiently long period, water with salts in solution is drawn up by capillary action; evaporation takes place at, or near, the surface, so that solid salts are deposited. If evaporation exceeds precipitation for a very long time, various salts, such as calcium carbonate and calcium sulphate may be deposited in the upper parts of the soil, or even form a crust. Where dry and rainy periods alternate, the salts may be taken down again, and accumulate at a depth depending on the balance between these two processes—perhaps a metre beneath the surface, often much less. Under these conditions the clay-humus particles retain bases and are not broken down. Alkaline soils of this type, and those with lime accumulation in the form of nodules or layers of calcium carbonate, are known as *pedocals* (Ca—calcium).

Hard Pans and Concretions

We already have several examples of the deposition of minerals in layers within the soil: the iron compounds which tend to form a hard pan in podsols, and the concentrations of calcium carbonate deposited by a combination of capillary action and evaporation. A hard pan may have the disadvantages of accumulating infertile material, and may also interfere with vertical movements in the soil. On the other hand some accumulations may benefit both the texture and soil fertility, especially when deep ploughing mixes soil constituents. Iron pans, as described above, are apt to impede drainage and lead to waterlogging; whereas calcium carbonate in prairie czernozems (p. 175) helps to improve the structure of these fertile soils.

A Summary of Climatic Influences on the Soil

The quantity of precipitation and its seasonal distribution, and the changes in humidity and temperature of the air, all have con-

siderable bearing on the upward or downward movements of water
through the soil. A leaching process which removes bases and
colloids is known as *eluviation;* the reception of these materials by
a lower soil level is termed *illuviation.* Very heavy rainfall, as in
tropical storms, may physically remove soil material, which may
then be carried away by streams, often resulting in loss of fertility
or soil erosion.

High temperatures and a ready supply of oxygen favour bacterial
activity, and speed up many chemical processes; and in warm,
moist soils, plant decomposition may proceed rapidly. Very rapid
decomposition in tropical forests often means that, despite a frequent supply of plant material, the break-down into soluble compounds, followed by re-absorption or perhaps physical removal,
proceed in a rapid cycle, so that humus does not accumulate in
the way one might expect.

High temperatures may also increase evaporation, so that in
dry climates there may be insufficient moisture for plants, and the
soil may either cake or crumble. Low temperatures and excess
water, reducing the amount of oxygen available, tend to hinder bacterial activity. Carbon dioxide is more soluble at low than high
temperatures, and although rates of reaction fall with temperature,
chemical weathering by carbonic acid may increase.

The production of mineral matter from parent rock by weathering is obviously connected with climate, and break-up resulting
from expansion/contraction and freeze/thaw depends both on
temperature and moisture conditions. Winds also act physically by
removing, transporting, and depositing soil particles, which may lead
to the accumulation of fertile loess. They also increase evaporation
from the surface, which may lead to the removal of nutrients as dry
top-soil is blown away.

The Time Factor in Soil Formation

The rate at which a soil develops to a recognisably mature form
varies considerably with circumstances. Time is needed for a
balance to be achieved between the numerous physical, chemical,
and biological processes affecting it. One or more of these processes may become dominant, and act rapidly to influence the
composition of the soil: generally a mature balance is achieved
slowly, perhaps over hundreds, or even thousands, of years; and
then may remain almost constant for comparable periods of time.

Soils developing on material of recent accumulation, such as alluvium or glacial debris, are said to be "young" or "immature". But age is only relative, and equilibrium within the soil, and a balance between the processes affecting it, may be achieved slowly or rapidly. In any case, soil is a dynamic substance involving continuous activity within its body. Variations in the local environment can cause a rapid change in the make-up of soils which have long reached maturity.

The Effects of Relief on Soil Formation

In a broad area where there has been little general climatic change for a long time, and where the soils in general have acquired a certain maturity, and are thus fertile or infertile, as the case may be, there are often remarkable local differences in forms of vegetation. These may be due to local variations in the soils and in their moisture content. For instance, relief affects the rate of run-off, the removal of soil from slopes by soil creep or erosion, the accumulation at the foot of slopes, or in valley bottoms, and must therefore produce soil variations. Steep slopes are likely to have thinner soils than bottom lands, and, with more rapid drainage, may be less moist; and as they may support different plant communities from a flat lowland, so their soils will have different organic contents. Gently sloping land, if well drained, will generally prove most suitable for soil formation under favourable climatic conditions.

The mixing of soil contents due to soil creep or erosion, with a conseqent re-sorting of materials, may lead to the formation of better soils; where, for instance, the fertility of plateau soils has fallen with time, those developed by the erosion of scarp slopes of the plateau edge may prove more fertile; even though they are derived from the same parent rock and from the old soils of the upland.

Local topographic variations may also affect soils through the different forms of vegetation which have been able to maintain themselves on the various wind-swept, sheltered, shaded, sunny, steep, or gently sloping locations. The plants themselves provide different local environments, shade for instance, and return differing amounts of organic matter to the soil.

Soil Profiles

If we look at the vertical development of a soil we may find different materials, textures, consistencies, and colours occurring at various depths, down to the parent rock. Some, however, are remarkably uniform in these respects throughout their "profile";

in others, colours and textures may change gradually, though the soil near the surface may clearly differ from that several feet beneath.

In many soils definite layer-like *horizons* or "levels" can be recognised in profile, and soils may be described or broadly classified in terms of similarities in their various horizons. As stated, not all are clearly layered in this way; and even in related soils some may plainly show horizons, of the type described below, which are lacking in the others.

Characteristic letters are used to describe the horizons, with numbered sub-divisions according to the complexity of the soils and the need for detailed description (soil scientists use symbols to distinguish between features which need not concern us here). To demonstrate the horizontal arrangement in soils, we will consider one formed under temperate conditions with excess of precipitation over evaporation; a regular leaching has carried matter from the upper layers to those beneath; and there is a ready supply of plant matter.

Soil Horizons—An Example from a Moist Cool-Temperate Region

On the surface there is an accumulation of leaves and other fallen plant material; this is sometimes called the *Aoo* horizon. Below this, where bacteria and fungi are active, there is decomposed, and decomposing, organic matter, older leaves, decaying plant stems, roots, and insects, which form a dark coloured humus-producing *Ao* layer. The composition and depth of the *Ao* layer depends on the amount and nature of the organic matter, and the speed with which it decays and is removed; but it is often only 50-100 mm thick. Assuming a fairly regular downward movement of soil water, the soil beneath, which mainly contains inorganic materials, receives a solution of carbonic and organic acids, dark with humus, and so becomes stained to a brownish colour. However, in the example chosen, it is likely that below this the dark colour will give way to a lighter one; not only with increasing distance from the *Ao* horizon, but because the clay minerals immediately beneath the *Ao* layer are likely to lose metallic compounds (p. 156), including the coloured iron ones; so that pale, sandy soil results. The dark mineral layer of *eluviation* (downward loss of minerals and colloids) is the A_1 horizon, distinguished from the lighter A_2 one beneath, which is not stained to the same extent.

The salts and colloids are taken down to accumulate in lower levels, which are the *B* horizons of *illuviation*. These acquisitions usually make the B horizons darker than the A_2 level immediately above. Transitional layers may be distinguished in some soils: an A_3 horizon, darker than the A_2 but with A level characteristics, rather than B ones, gives way to a B_1 level more closely resembling

SOIL PROFILE (Idealised Podsolic Type)

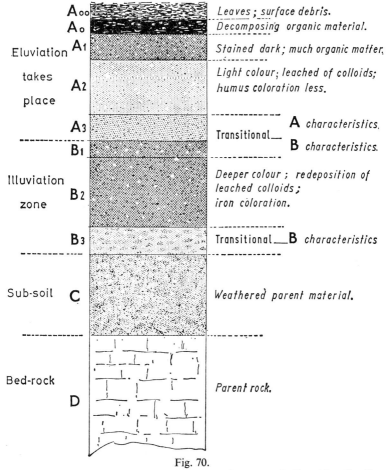

Fig. 70.

Here the layer-like "horizons" are shown diagrammatically. Not all soils are clearly layered in this way, and in many the colours and textures vary gradually. The depths of the soils and the depths of the horizons are also very variable—sometimes less than 100 mm, sometimes several metres.

the main, deeper coloured, B_2 horizon beneath; on the other hand these may not be distinguishable, even under the type of conditions we have described. There may also be a transitional B_3 horizon between the level of maximum accumulation and the C layer, which chiefly consists of material weathered from the parent rock, D, beneath.

This, then, illustrates the profile of a particular type of soil and the method of labelling the horizons. It is useful to distinguish between the A horizons of eluviation and the B ones of illuviation, and to be able to state in these terms where concentrations of plant nutrients, if any, are likely to be. Soils typical of certain zones on the earth's surface may be distinguished and recognised by their characteristic profiles. In many cases the parent rock from which the soil is derived is less important than the climatic conditions under which it has developed. But, again, it must be realised that in broad "soil zones" local factors may have acted to prevent, or delay, the development of a typical zonal soil.

The Pedon

This is a three-dimensional soil unit, with a minimum area of from 1 to 10 m². This is considered large enough to describe particular properties of horizons at a given place, and to study horizon shapes. It is used particularly in soil investigation and classification by U.S.A. soil scientists.

THREE DIMENSIONAL STUDY UNIT

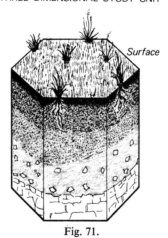

Fig. 71.

Soil Horizons exposed in a Pedon.

CHAPTER X

SOILS AND THEIR DEVELOPMENT

In the previous chapter we have seen that various natural processes combine to create certain recognisable soil groups. These processes are affected by local temperatures, precipitation, and rates of evaporation, all of which act directly on soil material and soil organisms. So it is not surprising that there are broad zones on the earth's surface where reasonably similar climatic conditions aid the development of similar soils. These broad soil groups can be classified, and their general distribution shown, as in Fig. 74. Here the classification used is based on that of the American C.F. Marbut (1928), who was influenced by earlier Russian soil schemes of genetic classification. But see also pages 188–9.

In soil formation, climate is not necessarily more important than the parent material, which in any case may affect soil forming processes. Also, it takes a very long time for a soil to acquire a mature form typical of a particular climatic environment: hence the climate under which any mature soil has developed may not be exactly that of its local climate to-day. Even a recognisable "soil type" may be undergoing modifications; and not only by climate, but by such physical actions as erosion, deposition, or changes in the general pattern of drainage. Thus soil material may be removed, added to, or affected by unusual dessication or leaching.

Nevertheless, the concept of zonal soils is a valuable one; even though, as we have seen with climates, numerous exceptions occur within the framework of any classification. To begin with it is as well to appreciate that certain soils of recognisably similar characeristics may occur in a number of different soil zones—in other words, they are *intra-zonal*. Among these are soils which have developed under waterlogged conditions; soils with a high saline content; and those formed on the same parent rock in different climatic zones, whose main characteristics are due to the nature of the rock rather than the climate (as in many limestone areas). Some soils are of very recent accumulation and thus "immature", like those of alluvial flats, screes, dunes, or lava flows which have had little time to weather or acquire characteristics due to the climate: such soils are *azonal*.

167

ZONAL SOILS IN THE HIGHER LATITUDES

Tundra Soils

Under climatic conditions of the *ET* type described on p. 133, the sub-soil remains permanently frozen. Precipitation is not heavy, but sufficient under these conditions for the soil to remain very moist. In summer, following the thaw, and when most precipitation occurs, much of the surface and top soil becomes waterlogged. Bacterial action is thus restricted; so beneath the low, but often close, vegetation of tiny shrubs, grasses, mosses, and lichens is a black mass of slowly decomposing plant matter with much acid humus. Beneath is a clayey mud, stained blue-grey by ferrous iron compounds which have not been oxidised to the familiar red-brown of ferric iron. This is known as a "gley" soil, and may be formed

TUNDRA GLEY SOILS

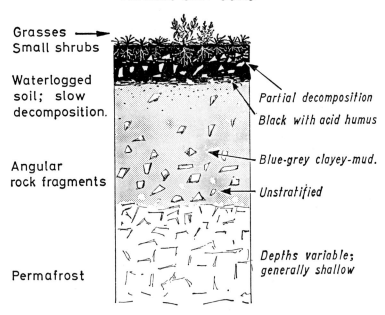

Grasses → Small shrubs

Waterlogged soil; slow decomposition.

Angular rock fragments

Permafrost

Partial decomposition

Black with acid humus

Blue-grey clayey-mud.

Unstratified

Depths variable; generally shallow

Fig. 72.

Gley soils are common in the badly drained tundras, but not all tundra soils are gley soils. In some locations, with better drainage, podsolic types are formed: in others there may be thin layers of sandy clay and humus.

under bog conditions in other zones. But in the tundra such soils generally contain numerous angular rock fragments, the products of weathering of the parent rock, and quite large rocky chunks may move through the soil, impelled by the seasonal freeze-thaw action. These soils are thus mixed vertically, and do not show the strata that characterise the forest and grassland soils of the temperate zones.

As the winter sets in, the water freezes in the upper layers and a general increase in volume takes place, with a "heaving" effect due to the expansion within the soil. The thaw causes a contraction, with quite extensive shrinkage. Stones held in the temporarily frozen zone may thus be stranded on the surface, and conglomerations of stones, some quite large, are a typical feature of the uneven surface of the ground. Movements by gravity, after upheaval, tend to sort the stones into irregular "rings" or polygons. Stones may be heaved upward within the mass when the soil water freezes and expands once more. The upward heaving is usually emphasised by the fact that the autumn freeze takes place first at the surface, holding the saturated soil in between two frozen layers.

Not all tundra soils are bog soils. Some are better drained for a while and so develop stratification of the podsol type described below. Some parent rocks exert their own influence, even here. Limestones, for instance, dissolve readily as the organic acids and carbonic acid act on them (carbon dioxide is more soluble in water at low temperatures). As they provide bases for the soils, the vegetation in turn is affected, and the typical peaty soil may not occur. Nevertheless, the majority of the tundra contains a great deal of ground that is either waterlogged or frozen during the course of the year, and gley soils are common.

True Podsols

These are found where precipitation occurs throughout the year, and where lengthy cool, or cold, winters check organic decomposition, so that plant matter and partly decomposed material remain near the surface, unchanged for many months. Here the extensive stands of conifers take little mineral material from the soil, and their debris is deficient in bases; hence the humus formed from the carpet of needle leaves is usually strongly acidic.

The annual precipitation is often low; but spring-melt suddenly releases water, which causes unusually strong leaching, and enables the organic acids to remove iron and aluminium oxides from the *A* layers, leaving a high silica content. The result is an upper zone of sandy soil, stained in its A_1 layer but ashy-grey in the A_2 horizon. This is the profile shown in an idealised form on p. 165. The *B* horizon is coloured brown, and has a tendency to a clayey consistency, largely due to the accumulating colloids. The oxides may have a cementing effect here, and iron sesquioxides often produce a "pan" sufficiently well developed to hold up water, and at times give rise to waterlogging and peaty conditions in the upper soil.

Because of the lack of bases in the *A* horizons, lime and other fertilisers are generally necessary before such soils can bear the types of crops which will flourish in these climates. In the true podsols the horizons are often clearly visible. There are few mixing agents, and the lack of earthworms, especially, helps to maintain the sharp divisions. Not all podsols have such clear profiles; there are others whose lower horizons are "blurred". Where trees other

PODSOLS

CONIFEROUS VEGETATION Few bases extracted or returned.

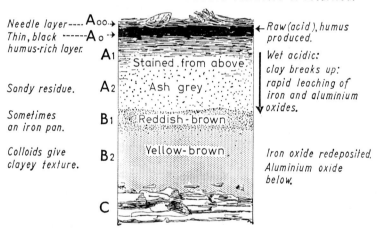

Needle layer---- A_{oo} →
Thin, black ------ A_o →
humus-rich layer. A_1
← *Raw (acid), humus produced.*

Stained from above

Wet acidic: clay breaks up: rapid leaching of iron and aluminium oxides.

Sandy residue. A_2 *Ash grey.*

Sometimes an iron pan. B_1 *Reddish-brown*

Colloids give clayey texture. B_2 *Yellow-brown.*

Iron oxide redeposited. Aluminium oxide below.

C

Fig. 73.

Podsols may be formed by leaching under vegetation other than coniferous forest: but with slighter acidity the horizons may not be so "sharp". The profile varies from less than 100 mm to a metre or more in depth.

than conifers occur under these climatic conditions the acidity of the humus may not be so pronounced, and the *A* and *B* layers less distinct.

MID-LATITUDE SOILS—CHANGES FROM PODSOLS TO PEDOCALS

The following groups of soils are found mainly in the higher-middle latitudes. That they have markedly different characteristics

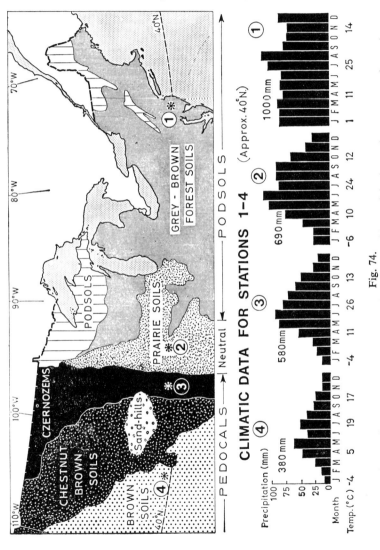

Fig. 74.

Broad soil groupings in northern U.S.A. with mean monthly precipitation and temperatures for stations ranging from the north-eastern seaboard, through the Middle West, to Montana and Wyoming.

is largely due to variations in the amount of precipitation received and in its seasonal distribution. The effects of the local vegetation in screening the surface and providing organic material for the soil are also significant. There are close inter-relations and interactions between the plant cover and the soils. For example, between the eastern parts of the U.S.A. and the extensive semi-arid interiors, the amount of precipitation received decreases, and there is a growing tendency towards a summer maximum; as the vegetation changes from dense mixed forests to dry grassland and semi-arid scrub, it is mirrored by a succession of recognisable soil groups. There are, of course, many variations within a zone characterised by a particular soil group; sometimes due to different parent materials, as in the Nebraska sandhills, sometimes to local relief and climates, as in mountain country. Very generally, the soils in the east are mainly pedalfers and those in the western interior, as far west as the Sierra Nevada and Cascade ranges, are pedocals (Fig. 74).

GREY-BROWN FOREST SOILS

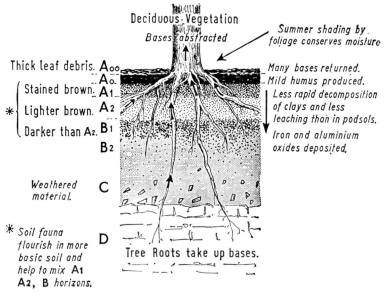

Fig. 75.

The total depth of the A and B horizons may be of the order of a metre.

Grey-Brown Forest Soils (Podsolic)

These occur where the rainfall amounts are of the order of 750-1 000 mm a year, and where higher temperatures allow the growth of broad-leaved deciduous forests. The thick leaf-debris of the deciduous forests returns many of the bases abstracted by the trees. Bacterial action is also relatively rapid. Thus the resulting humus is still acidic, but is "mild humus", much richer in plant foods than the "mor" beneath the conifers. As the soils are less acidic and less leached, so the *A* horizon is a browner colour than that of the true podsols, tending to become grey-brown with depth. Nevertheless, clay decomposition does occur; so that bases, and iron and aluminium sesquioxides, are carried down to a *B* horizon, which is darker than the lower parts of the *A* horizon.

Soil fauna are more plentiful under these conditions, so that earthworms and other organisms help to redistribute the soil contents. The tree roots often penetrate the bed-rock, or at least reach the sub-soil, and bring up bases, which leaf-fall eventually returns once more to the soil.

In the northern hemisphere these soils occur over much of north-eastern U.S.A., Western Europe, and European Russia; and also in Japan and northern China. The forests of these regions are by no means entirely deciduous: in the northern parts, particularly, stretches of coniferous forest intermingle with the broad-leaved woodlands. The interactions between plant cover and the soils give rise to a considerable variety of flora and soil types, and the parent rock is often a dominant factor in these latitudes. For instance, in north-west Europe porous conditions on outwash gravels and sands allow heaths and conifers to develop at the expense of other types of vegetation, and podsolisation is rapid and more complete there. But here, we are considering the principal types of zonal soils, and the grey-brown forest soils are widespread in the region mentioned, where they are used for rotation farming. They occur also under similar conditions in the southern hemisphere.

Prairie Soils (Transitional Podsolic/Pedocal)

In the U.S.A. these occur westward of the grey-brown forest soils, where annual precipitation falls from some 1 000 mm to about 600 mm; in Eastern Europe they are found to the east of the grey-brown earths. In each case the original vegetation and the soils themselves have been much disturbed by clearing and cultivation;

but the natural conditions under which the soils were formed seems to have favoured grassland rather than forest. Precipitation, especially during the heavy summer showers, is sufficient to carry calcium carbonate and some of the soluble salts deep into the soil; but the base-holding clay-humus particles are little affected. With long, hot periods, and persistent winds helping evaporation, the dry top soil favoured grassland rather than forest. The tall grasses provided much organic matter above and within the soil. Dark humus coloration is typical; and though decay is slow in the cold winters, decomposition in early summer gives the soil a deep brown colour, finely divided humus, and a crumby structure.

The soils, transitional between the pedocals and pedalfers, have not the calcium carbonate deposits of the czernozems (p. 176–7) nor are they heavily leached of their bases in the upper parts; hence clear *A* and *B* horizons are not distinguishable. With fairly humid

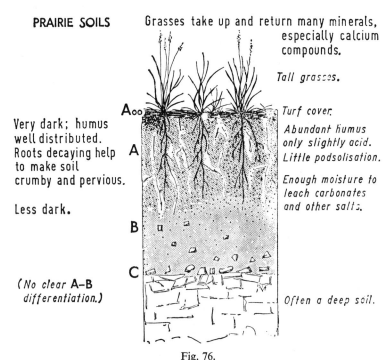

PRAIRIE SOILS

Grasses take up and return many minerals, especially calcium compounds.

Tall grasses.

A₀₀

Very dark; humus well distributed. Roots decaying help to make soil crumby and pervious.

A

Turf cover.

Abundant humus only slightly acid. Little podsolisation.

Enough moisture to leach carbonates and other salts.

Less dark.

B

C

(No clear A–B differentiation.)

Often a deep soil.

Fig. 76.
Prairie soils: transitional between the pedalfers and pedocals.

atmospheric conditions, these deep, nearly neutral, soils of good structure have proved particularly suitable for arable farming, and their fertility has been exploited over much of the Corn Belt of the U.S.A., and further south into Oklahoma and Texas.

Czernozems Black Earths (Pedocals)

We have seen that in the U.S.A. the prairie soils are transitional·

CZERNOZEMS

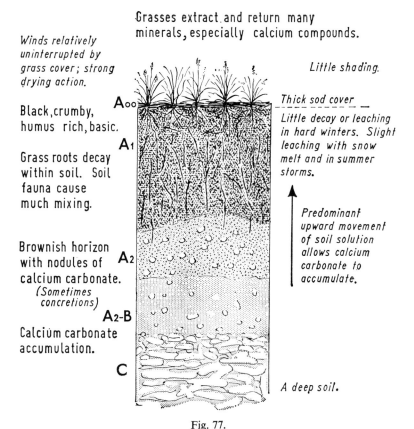

Grasses extract and return many minerals, especially calcium compounds.

Winds relatively uninterrupted by grass cover; strong drying action.

Little shading.

Black, crumby, humus rich, basic.

A₀₀

Thick sod cover

Little decay or leaching in hard winters. Slight leaching with snow melt and in summer storms.

A₁

Grass roots decay within soil. Soil fauna cause much mixing.

Brownish horizon with nodules of calcium carbonate. (Sometimes concretions)

A₂

Predominant upward movement of soil solution allows calcium carbonate to accumulate.

A₂-B

Calcium carbonate accumulation.

C

A deep soil.

Fig. 77.

Pedocal soils which lie beneath large stretches of the central prairies and steppes. The dark horizons may be a metre in depth, often more.

between the podsolic grey-brown forest earths and the pedocal soils which lie beneath the temperate grasslands of to-day. The close grass cover of the true prairies, which in America stretch in an arc from Saskatchewan and the south-central part of Alberta to the eastern-central parts of Texas, no longer survives in its original state: for this is a great agricultural region. These are drier lands than those in which the neutral prairie soils have been formed. Even so, the original grasses were fairly tall, and on dying down built up a dense sod cover. Within the soil their extensive root systems decayed, providing humus distributed through the upper few feet of the soil, and also producing a fine crumbly soil structure. Grasses extract many bases from the soil, especially calcium; but later they return them to the soil. During the hard winters there is little decay or leaching; and, though there is slight leaching with the snow-melt in spring, the summer rain-storms only occasionally interrupt the upward movement of soil moisture. With evaporation caused by high temperatures and drying winds, the sub-soil remains very dry. Heavy storms leach out some of the sodium and potassium salts; but subsequent upward movements cause calcium carbonate to accumulate as nodules, often most concentrated a metre or so down. The soils thus remain basic, and the clay content does not break up. They differ, therefore, from podsols in that a dark, nearly homogeneous A_1 layer forms, about a metre thick, but sometimes much more; and beneath this a brownish A_2 layer with calcium carbonate nodules merges into what can hardly be called a B horizon, but which has received some bases and colloids: for as there is very little leaching, and carbonate concretions form, this A_2—B horizon is not well defined; it gives way to the light, weathered parent-material below, sometimes with a well-marked junction, sometimes not.

Black earths of this kind are also found in rather different climatic conditions, under grasslands developed on limestone soils, often as extensive "oases" in otherwise forested country; such is the black soil belt in Alabama. Czernozems also develop in middle latitudes where tracts of loess have acquired a suitable texture and a high lime content. These are fertile soils and give reasonably good yields for long periods when under plough. They retain water well; and ploughing mixes still further their basic mineral content, humus, and calcium carbonate particles. Another extensive area of agricultural development on these soils lies in the U.S.S.R., to the west, north, and north-east of the Black Sea, stretching away eastward beneath the meadow and tussock steppes.

The Rio Grande, New Mexico flows through a sub-tropical *BSh* region. But local vegetation responds to relief, soil materials, soil depth and water content, and 'micro-climates', rather than to average *BSh* characteristics: compare (*above*) the vegetation (and lack of it) on slopes, rockfalls, screes, waterside, and valley flats. Neither does potentially fertile soil pre-determine close vegetation or productivity. At altitudes of 2–3 000 m in Central Peru (*below*), the hillsides have long been cleared of natural vegetation. Field terraces fail to prevent drastic erosion. The trees in the Vilcanota valley are introduced eucalypts. (*Above: Paul Popper Ltd*) (*Below: D. C. Money.*)

Above (*left*): Profile of a czernozem soil—deep, rich in humus, but prevented from being acidic by the upward movement of bases. Calcium carbonate nodules appear in the upper profile; there is no clear distinction between **A** and **B** profiles. (*Conzett and Huber, Zurich*)

Above (*right*): Shallow-rooted coconuts grow in red-yellow soil developed on gneiss in southwest Sri Lanka. A thick whitish zone of kaolin clay with quartz grains is formed beneath. (*D. C. Money*)

Below: Terra rossa accumulations provide fertile soils for grains and horticulture near Asteromeritis, Cyprus. (*D. C. Money*)

But under the short grass steppes and the drier tussocky grasslands, czernozems give way to chestnut-brown soils.

Chestnut-Brown Soils and Brown Soils (Pedocals)

In the belts of country on the drier margins of the true prairies there is a slower rate of growth. The grasses are shorter, or occur in separate tussocky clumps, and provide less organic matter. With less humus, the *A* level is a chestnut-brown rather than black, and there is sufficient calcium carbonate in the upper layers to give the soil a prismatic structure and to make it friable. The depth of the soil decreases with aridity; while the layer of calcium carbonate accumulation is relatively thicker. Men have been tempted to

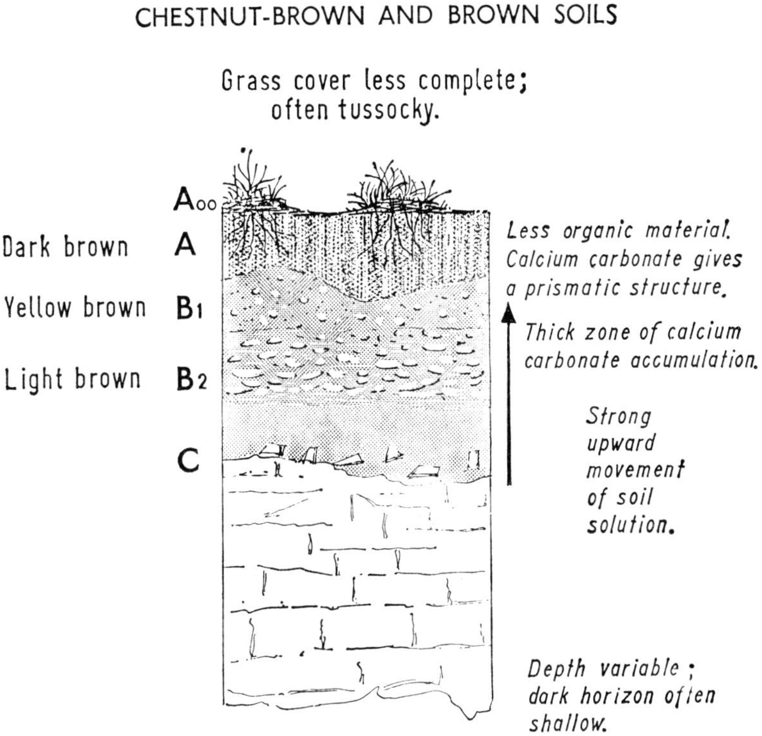

CHESTNUT-BROWN AND BROWN SOILS

Grass cover less complete; often tussocky.

Dark brown   A   *Less organic material. Calcium carbonate gives a prismatic structure.*

Yellow brown   B1

Light brown   B2   *Thick zone of calcium carbonate accumulation.*

C   *Strong upward movement of soil solution.*

Depth variable ; dark horizon often shallow.

Fig. 78.

Pedocal soils found mainly beneath the short grassland or tussock grass country of the drier margins of the prairies and steppes.

use these soils for grain growing. But without irrigation or careful
moisture conservation they have rapidly deteriorated: erosion has
been severe in this soil belt in the American west. In some areas
dry farming methods, and cultivation with irrigation, have been
successful; but, on the whole, such country serves as grazing land.
Even grazing can be a danger if annual grasses are consumed before
seeding, for species can thus be eliminated from grazing lands in
a remarkably short time. Still drier conditions support only patchy
grassland or sage brush, which provide even less humus for the
soil. The lighter coloured brown soils formed under these conditions have a high basic content.

Grey Desert Soils (Sierozems) and Desert Red Soils

In the semi-arid inner basins and plateaux of the western U.S.A.,
and to the south and east of the chestnut-brown soil belt in Euro-
Asia, are grey "sierozems", with very little humus and thick deposits
of "caliche" (calcium carbonate or calcium sulphate) at shallow
depth. In hotter regions, Desert Red Soils stained with iron compounds are found. Nevertheless, as neither type has been leached
of plant food, those of fine texture may become fertile with irrigation and humus building. The saline soils of the dry steppes or
deserts are considered on pp. 182–3.

TRANSITIONAL TEMPERATE—TROPICAL SOILS
Sub-Tropical Red/Yellow Soils (Podsolic)

These occur in regions of abundant rainfall, but have developed
under warmer conditions than the grey-brown podsols. In the
U.S.A., for instance, they are found south of the grey-brown forest
soils in the warm, moist south-eastern parts. These too, are
podsolic. But, despite a heavy leaf-fall from the dense forest
cover, the humus content is low, for bacterial decomposition is rapid
during the hot moist summers and mild winters. Under these conditions iron and aluminium oxides tend to remain in the upper part
of the soils, even though most bases and colloids are washed downward to form a darker B horizon beneath the light-coloured A_2
layer. The remaining iron compounds give the upper parts of the
soil a typical red coloration; though in really strongly leached soils,
on sandy belts for instance, the soils are yellow rather than red.
Various pines grow well on these podsols and form natural forests,

SUB-TROPICAL RED SOILS

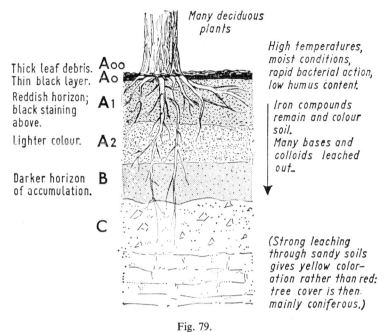

Many deciduous plants

Thick leaf debris. **Aoo**
Thin black layer. **Ao**

Reddish horizon; **A₁**
black staining above.

Lighter colour. **A₂**

Darker horizon **B**
of accumulation.

C

High temperatures, moist conditions, rapid bacterial action, low humus content.

Iron compounds remain and colour soil.
Many bases and colloids leached out.

(Strong leaching through sandy soils gives yellow coloration rather than red: tree cover is then mainly coniferous.)

Fig. 79.

Soils formed in the moist sub-tropics; transitional between the temperate podsols and the tropical latosols.

especially on the yellow soils.

Similar soils occur in south-eastern China and other moist tropical locations.

TROPICAL SOILS

Ferralitic Soils

In the humid tropics the clay-rich material weathered from parent rock may be strongly leached, and podsolisation may occur —especially on acidic rocks. But with high temperatures, plant remains are rapidly broken down, so that, despite a plentiful supply of forest debris, little organic matter accumulates. The process is continuous, and, with bases so readily available, the upper layers of the soil may scarcely become acidic at all, particularly, of course, on basic rocks. Under these conditions the clay minerals break down rapidly; but as they decompose the silica contents may now be removed to lower levels of the soil or carried away in solution; whereas the oxides of iron and aluminium remain. These silica-leached reddish, or red-brown, soils are now generally termed *ferralitic*. In wet conditions much of the iron is in hydrated form, so that soils may be yellowish in colour.

As the parent rocks break down rapidly, the soils may become deep if they are formed on an almost level surface; on anything but gentle slopes they are easily eroded away, particularly when the vegetation is cleared. The balance between the vegetation cover and the soils is a delicate one. Despite the luxuriant appearance of tropical forests the idea that all tropical soils have great natural fertility is false. Clearance for cultivation means that the rapid exchange of bases between plant cover and soil is interrupted, and the ground is exposed to alternate spells of hot sun and torrential rains; organic matter is quickly removed, vegetation is difficult to regenerate, and serious erosion may occur.

When wet, such soils tend to have a sticky, plastic consistency; but on drying out they become crumbly. However, this is a generalisation, for many different forms of tropical red soils exist. Under alternate wet and dry conditions the sesquioxides may bind together to form a thick layer near the surface, which, when the silica contents have been washed out, is left as a porous red rock. This concentrated iron-rich zone may harden, and has often been used for building purposes and hence known as *laterite* [*later*—a brick (Latin)]. In some tropical locations hard laterite layers occur at the surface where they have formed; in others surface erosion has exposed the hard infertile layers beneath.

In some soils the iron compounds form concretions in nodular form, known as "laterite gravel". Tropical peneplains with alternating wet and dry seasons may have extensive lateritic crusts several metres thick; but it is quite likely that many laterite crusts now found in dry locations are relics of those formed in earlier, wetter periods. Tropical red soils formed in regions of heavy seasonal rainfall may rapidly harden when vegetation is removed. In some parts, deep red crumbly soils, still containing silica, may cover gently sloping surfaces; these are not laterites. Indeed tropical soils vary with slopes, weathering and drainage.

Tropical Podsols

It is evident that many tropical soils are neither truly ferralitic nor lateritic. Even where climatic conditions should support

TROPICAL RED/YELLOW SOILS

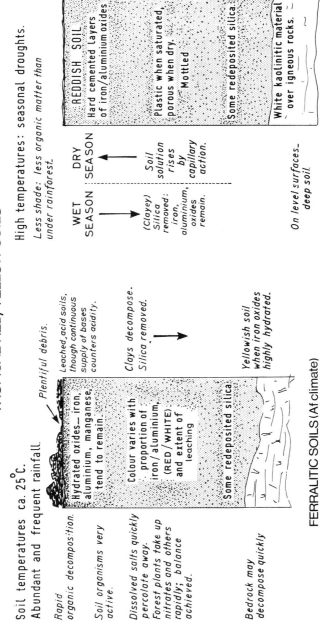

Soil temperatures ca. 25°C.
Abundant and frequent rainfall.

High temperatures: seasonal droughts.

Less shade: less organic matter than under rainforest.

Plentiful debris.

Rapid organic decomposition.

Leached, acid soils, though continuous supply of bases counters acidity.

Soil organisms very active.

Hydrated oxides – iron, aluminium, manganese, tend to remain.

Colour varies with proportion of iron/aluminium, (RED/WHITE) and extent of leaching

Dissolved salts quickly percolate away. Forest plants take up nitrates and others rapidly; balance achieved.

Clays decompose. Silica removed.

Some redeposited silica.

Bedrock may decompose quickly

Yellowish soil when iron oxides highly hydrated.

FERRALITIC SOILS (Af climate)

WET SEASON

DRY SEASON

(Clayey) Silica removed: iron, aluminium, oxides remain.

Soil solution rises by capillary action.

On level surfaces_ deep soil.

REDDISH SOIL

Hard cemented layers of iron/aluminium oxides

Plastic when saturated, porous when dry.
Mottled

Some redeposited silica.

White kaolinitic material over igneous rocks.

FERRUGINOUS SOIL, perhaps with LATERITE (Aw/Am climate)

rainforest, a parent material, such as a coarse sandstone, may be poor in bases; thus, if the soil drains very freely, its acidity may be sufficiently high to enable a tropical podsol to be formed. Indeed, these have been found over wide areas in the Guiana Highlands and in parts of south-east Asia, where they support a scrub-forest or heath forest.

Tropical Black Earths

In some tropical grasslands with seasonal droughts, deep black soils have been formed which contain much calcium carbonate in their lower levels. These freely-drained soils resemble the temperate czernozems; this is especially so in soils formed beneath the interior grasslands in the central-southern parts of the Great Australian Basin; somewhat similar soils are also found in Rhodesia.

While these soils resemble czernozems in the way they have been formed, other black soils of the tropics are found beneath both grasslands and forests, usually where the basic parent materials gives them a high *p*H value. Some tropical black earths have a high humus content, while other fertile black soils do not. The black cotton soils of the Deccan often have very little humus, and owe their black coloration to titanium salts derived from basalt. These soils are deeply cracked in the dry season, and often crumble when the hard surface is broken by ploughing. In the wet season they acquire a sticky, plastic consistency, and the cracks close as the soils swell out. Calcium carbonate often occurs in these soils below the lower limit of the surface-cracks.

INTRAZONAL SOILS

Some types of soil are of widespread occurrence and owe their characteristics to conditions which are common to quite different parts of the world, such as rapid evaporation and consequent aridity, waterlogged or swampy ground, or a parent rock with a dominant influence on soils: these and other common conditions produce typical soils which are not confined to one zone—they are intrazonal.

Saline Soils

We have seen how in semi-arid conditions a thick layer of calcium carbonate is sometimes built up very close to the surface, as in the light-brown pedocals. Sometimes a thick calcareous layer, containing mainly calcium carbonate or calcium sulphate, is found at the surface, as in the grey sierozems and the "tosca" areas southeast of the Argentine pampas. Soils of the dry interiors of the land masses may also become impregnated with sodium chloride (common salt) and so become saline rather than calcareous.

Saline soils are often formed in inland drainage areas, for sodium chloride is much more soluble than the calcium salts. Thus, even if streams or flood water only wash over, or through, small deposits of rock-salt, they may gain a sufficient concentration of sodium chloride to be redeposited, and so accumulate, in an inland drainage basin. Some inland basins were formerly covered with sea water and the soils have remained saline. Much salt reaches the interior, rather surprisingly, in the form of minute particles left when salt water evaporates over oceans; these are carried inland in the atmosphere and slowly accumulate over long periods of time.

Where strong evaporation brings salt solutions to the surface, a greyish saline crust may be formed. Soils with this type of accumulation are called *solonchak*. If periodically there is heavy rainfall, the salt may be washed down from the upper part of the soil, and form a highly saline accumulation in the *B* zone; the soil above remains structureless and infertile, but sticky when wet and hard when dry: this is known as a *solonetz* soil.

Waterlogged Soils (Bog Soils, Peat Soils, Meadow Soils)

The tundra soils, described above, have characteristics common to all waterlogged soils, but also certain features found only in *ET* climatic regions. In general, waterlogging results in a deprivation of oxygen and hindrance of bacterial action, so that plant decay is retarded. Partly decomposed plants form a peaty layer perhaps a metre or so thick. Under such chemical "reduction" conditions ammonia, methane, and various sulphides are formed, rather than the nitrates, carbon dioxide, and sulphates which are produced in the presence of abundant oxygen. Beneath the peaty layer is the sticky mass of bluish-grey clay of the gley horizon, stained with ferrous iron salts rather than ferric compounds.

Meadow soils form on the flood plains of streams, where the drainage is poor, but where vegetation nevertheless flourishes (usually meadow in the middle latitudes). Thus a dark humus layer overlies the gley horizon.

On high moist moorland areas where the drainage is also poor,

MEADOW SOIL

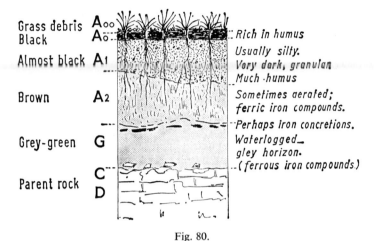

Grass debris A₀₀
Black   A₀̄   :: Rich in humus
Almost black A₁   Usually silty.
                   Very dark, granular
                   Much ·humus
Brown   A₂   Sometimes aerated;
                   ferric iron compounds.
                   ·Perhaps iron concretions.
Grey-green G   Waterlogged_
                   gley horizon.
Parent rock C   ·(ferrous iron compounds.)
            D

Fig. 80.

A soil formed where the drainage is poor, and including a gley horizon, see Fig. 72.

and parent rocks supply few bases, a bog peat develops, which slowly breaks down to a highly acid raw humus. On the other hand, some low-lying boglands receive water with a high calcium content, and here the peat is mild in nature and, as in true English Fens, breaks down when drained and ploughed into a rich soil for agriculture.

Soils formed on Limestone

Unlike many parent rocks limestones have certain characteristics which make them intrazonal, for their influence on soil formation and the nature of the soils is often more important than local climatic influences. The soils derived from limestones are basic in character; and even in moist regions, where podsolisation is of general occurrence, they do not usually become acid in character. Calcium carbonate, which makes up their bulk, is soluble in the slightly acid rain-water. Thus any insoluble parts of clay, silica, or other compounds which may be present as impurities in limestone or occur within the limestone mass, are left as residues when the calcium carbonate dissolves. The *clay-with-flints* which often lies directly on chalk has usually been formed in this way; and so has the *terra rossa* developed on limestones in Mediterranean

LIMESTONES WITH RESIDUAL SOILS

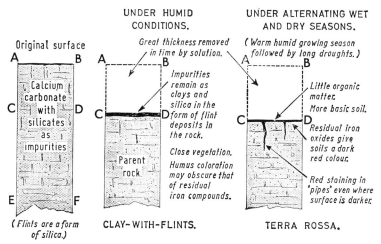

Fig. 81.

The rates of removal of calcium carbonate vary a great deal, and even under humid conditions can be very slow. There may, therefore, be considerable fluctuations in local climates during this time. Under present humid conditions, any iron coloration may be masked by humus staining; but on limestones in regions with Mediterranean climates the iron-red colour is often the dominant one (though periodic humid conditions are essential for decalcification).

regions. In the latter case, and on limestones in certain hot semi-arid areas, the calcium carbonate dissolves during rainy periods; but the downward percolating basic soil water may cause a concentration of iron oxide in the residual clay particles. The rate of decalcification, which leaves this as a residue, varies. But it is generally a long, slow process, involving, according to some authorities, the loss of some 400 metres of limestone to produce a metre thickness of terra rossa. As there is little humus in such regions, the iron-red colour is often the dominant one.

In temperate conditions which would normally favour podsolisation, and lead to the formation of brown soils under grass, or mixed grass and forest, a parent limestone is usually covered by a soil known as *rendzina*. This, like many limestone soils, tends to be thin, but has a brown or black, friable *A* level, rich in humus and calcium. This lies above a grey or yellowish material with many limestone fragments.

AZONAL SOILS

Many recently formed soils have not had time to acquire the characteristics of a mature soil, and have no clear profile. Some may be thin, or skeletal, like those found on hill slopes. Others are deep, and of various textures, such as the sand, silt, and clay mixture of alluvial or marine deposits, the glacial drifts with their variety of components, and the re-sorted sands and gravels of outwash materials. A "skeletal" nature implies that, even though the minerals present in the soil are sufficient for plant growth, the organic content is lacking; such is the case with many newly formed soils, like screes.

Also azonal are recent volcanic soils, and loess. Loess tracts and the limon of northern France are fine, mixed, deposits, which are strictly "rocks" in the geological sense, but which quickly form potentially fertile, easily worked soil. In Europe they usually range in texture from fine sand to clay, and are often calcareous. In a typical loess the mineral particles have been transported by wind: and although some so-called loess in northern Europe has been resorted by water, most of it consists of material borne by the wind from extensive morainic deposits during dry conditions following the last Glacial Period.

Mountain Soils

It is impossible to generalise satisfactorily about soils in mountain country. We can only consider factors which are most likely to affect soil formation, and then notice the effects of soil-forming processes in specific mountain areas.

The climate at a particular altitude must tend to assert its own set of influences on the soil there. As in high mountains there are many vertical climatic "zones", it is reasonable to suppose that there will be corresponding changes in soil groups with altitude. In the humid tropics one might expect ferralitic soils at lower altitudes to give way to temperate podsolic soils in the higher parts. That regular soil zones are not so easily distinguishable, except in a broad sense, is due to facts which are not primarily climatic.

The slopes themselves are apt to lose material through the effects of "creep", or perhaps "downhill wash". These movements may be rapid on slopes with sparse vegetation, although this again depends on the parent rock; but even on slopes covered by vegetation, mineral material moves downwards. Particles may accumulate at the base of slopes, lie as hillside scree, or be washed outwards as an alluvial fan, or thin alluvial sheet. Soil water may bring down *colloids* and bases leached from higher up, so developing an azonal soil.

Where mountain soils are not disturbed in this way, especially on level, or nearly level, surfaces such as mountain plateaux, they may develop into mature soils with characteristic profiles. Later, the dissection of such country by erosive agents may produce a number of different soil types in a much altered landscape. These soils will have developed on the debris-covered valley slopes, or on flatter valley floors, and so are likely to be very different from those of the old plateau. Not only will the mineral contents differ as a result of the breakdown of the old profile, but their water-holding properties will almost certainly vary: thus, relics of the level upland may have an impervious layer near the surface which impedes drainage; while the slopes are freely drained. In further contrast, valley soils may be liable to saturation for long periods. Consequently striking soil variations are encountered even in a broad upland area of moderate relief with a more or less uniform climate.

The Catena

In mountainous country, the soils, as we have seen, are often closely related to the relief; so that in a single climatic region very different types of soil occur beneath high plateaux, hill slopes, and valley floors. At any given time such adjacent soils are each likely to have a different moisture content; so it is not surprising that they bear different types of vegetation. On the Brazilian highlands, for instance, in what is generally an *Aw* climatic region, the ancient level plateau surfaces bear forms of grassy savannah-with-trees, while adjacent plateau-edge slopes are apt to be covered with close, dry forest, the outwash areas with woodland savannah, and valley floors with a forest which has many tropical lowland evergreen species. This pattern is repeated in many parts of eastern Brazil.

In other parts of the world there are recognisable sequences of soils and vegetation related to certain altitudes, slopes, and parent materials: Fig. 101 illustrates variations found in a moist part of Britain on a countryside which includes a high moorland and its adjacent valley.

The term *Catena* is used to describe any *regular* repetition of soil sequences down a slope due, directly or indirectly, to topography, or to changes in parent material. The component parts may be shown by a vertical section, or may be mapped to show their

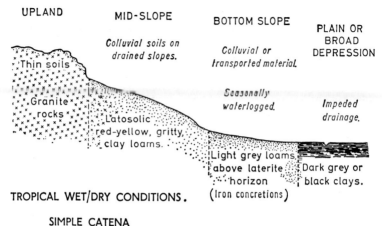

Fig. 82.
A simplified diagrammatic representation of the sequence of soil types which is repeated in many parts of the East African tablelands, under broadly similar climatic conditions. (There is no attempt here to show soil profiles, and in practice horizontal boundaries are seldom clear-cut.)

area distribution.   Fig. 82 shows a simplified sequence of soils found in many parts of the East African plateau.   Sometimes the term is used to indicate a characteristic sequence of different soils from the same parent material, but which vary with relief and drainage.

Soil Classifications

The terms used for the zonal soils are broadly based on Marbut's scheme, a simple genetic classification which is useful for an introduction to pedology.   But the conditions under which these soil horizons are assumed to develop imply that the soil remains in a virgin state, whereas more and more of the earth's surface responds directly or indirectly to human interference.

The US Dept. of Agriculture Soil Survey's 7th Approximation (1960) is a classification which is widely used.   This seventh attempt to formulate an ideal classification is based on specifically diagnosed soil properties.   It is a highly complex scheme based on a number of orders which refer to various characteristic properties.   The orders are then each sub-divided into soil groups—with new, and somewhat alarming, names.

The different soil conditions, and the very varied arrangements of soil horizons, which are found in practice has led to a trend of classifying soils by their actual horizon characteristics, instead of the results of regular genetic processes.

The whole is too complex to put forward here, but it is as well to look at the main orders of the 7th Approximation and briefly comment on their characteristics.

1 *Entisols*: recently developed, generally azonal, soils.

2 *Vertisols*: clayey soils with deep cracks which open and close, and allow surface materials to be transferred into their mass.

3 *Inceptisols*: moderately developed young soils, where leaching is active, but only beginning to develop horizons.

4 *Aridisols*: dry soils, with light surface horizons, low in organic material.   They have a wide variety of sub-surface forms, including various salt enrichments.

5 *Mollisols*: with many bases, especially calcium, and a soft, dark A horizon, with decomposed organic matter; as beneath the temperate grasslands.

6 *Spodosols*: virtually podsols.

7 *Alfisols*: soils with moderate to high base content, where gentle leaching has created a clay horizon by downward migration.

8 *Ultisols*: deep weathering; a lower base content; with a lower, closely packed clay horizon.

9 *Oxisols*: high mineral alteration; generally in the humid tropics, with clays of kaolinite and sesquioxides of iron and aluminium.

10 *Histosols*: organic soils, such as peat.

CHAPTER XI

VEGETATION

To understand the nature of various forms of vegetation we must first know something about plant life and the characteristics and behaviour of plants. Student geographers probably know little about the characteristics of the majority of the individual plant species which make up the vegetation of the regions they study; but they should certainly aim to recognise the more dominant of them, and try to appreciate what enables them to thrive, and what prevents others thriving, in a particular environment.

The composition of the vegetation depends on the interaction of the various elements of the environment in which it lives (its "habitat"). We have seen that climatic conditions are extremely important, and so are those of relief, soils, and other "natural" phenomena. But not all the vital elements affecting plant distribution can be regarded as "natural" in this sense. Man has been using and clearing vegetation for his own purposes for a very long time, and in the more closely inhabited parts of the world little remains of the original vegetation as man first came upon it. Even in many of the less populated regions of the savannah and rain-forests it is evident that long periods of grazing, burning, or periodic clearing have produced what is really a secondary vegetation, and have wrought changes in the soil structure. However, some of these huge areas affected by man's activities have acquired a vegetation which has remained unchanged for sufficiently long to be regarded, for the purposes of study and classification, as a recognisable "type" with characteristic plant associations—part of the global pattern of vegetation at the present time.

THE PLANT

Plant Organs

The higher flowering plants, in the evolutionary sense, have certain characteristics in common. Roots help to hold the plant in the soil, and absorb soil water, with its soluble nutrients. Stems hold up the leaves and reproductive parts. The leaves absorb the carbon dioxide and water-vapour which, with the help of light energy, are converted to carbohydrates, and aid the release of energy in the plant by taking in oxygen for respiration. The flowers develop seeds for reproduction.

Plant organs increase in length as their cells divide to form more cells at the growing points, near the tips of the stems and roots, and in buds at certain times of the year. Other cells divide to add to the girth of stems and roots. Various stimuli, like light energy, can act to affect the process of cell division, so that plant growth may take place in a particular direction, and so cause organs to bend. Other circumstances, such as the availability of moisture and oxygen, can determine whether branching takes place or not.

Many cells in the plant have different shapes and structures, appropriate to their different functions. Some have developed in a way which enables a plant to survive or flourish in a particular environment: by providing, for instance, a thick bark or a waxy surface, and so guarding against the excessive loss of water by transpiration.

Responses to Environment: Competition: Colonisation

Plants tend to thrive only where conditions are suitable for their particular species; such "conditions" include physical and biotic influences, and also the facts of competition with other plants. Many different elements of the environment act on the plants, directly and indirectly, and one or more of them can determine whether or not a plant species will survive or flourish in that environment. The inter-relation of these elements is very important. A simple instance is that plants need water to survive, and sufficient water for their need may be present in the soil yet unavailable for a considerable period because the temperature is too low for their roots to be able to absorb it.

We will first consider, briefly, some of the environmental factors which are likely to be important for plant growth; then some of the inherited characteristics of plants, which enable them to withstand apparently adverse physical conditions and also competition in a particular environment. These are dealt with separately; but, naturally, it is the *interaction* of many features of the temperature, humidity, relief, soils, animal life, and the competition between the plants themselves, which result in various distinctive plant associations and types of vegetation. Even then, the history of colonisation must come into it; for, under suitable conditions, species may survive from past forms of vegetation; others suited to the environment may not be present in a certain part of the world because the means of their transportation has been lacking. There must be the seeds, spores, or plant organs available for development if a particular association of plants is to become established, whatever the other environmental factors.

ELEMENTS OF THE ENVIRONMENT

Water

Plants must have sufficient water to live, grow, and reproduce. The rate of absorption of water by the roots, the distribution of water within the plant itself, and the ease of passage through the stomata (pores) of the leaves are affected by the surrounding temperature and humidity (which may not be the same for the different organs of a plant).

The nature and amount of precipitation, and its seasonal distribution, are all important for plant growth. A large amount of rain falling in one season followed by a long, dry period may favour certain plants adapted to survive lengthy droughts; while the same annual rainfall total received at short intervals throughout the year may allow quite different species to become dominant. Much of the rainfall may not be available for plants, as soil water, due to rapid run-off or evaporation; while in other places soils may retain sufficient water for plants to use over ensuing periods of drought; much depends on the water-retaining properties of soils. Precipitation in the form of snow may blanket the ground and protect plants against excessive cold, and also provide a store of water for release in spring-time.

An excess of water, leading to waterlogging or aquatic conditions, will obviously favour those plants adapted to receive sufficient aeration in such an environment; among the many varieties of higher plants, for instance, is the water hyacinth, which floats freely, buoyed up by the bulbous nature of its modified leaf-stalks.

Plants which live satisfactorily in a truly watery environment are termed *hydrophytes,* and those in wet, marshy conditions *hygrophytes.* Those which live where there is neither excess nor deficiency of water are known as *mesophytes*; while those of the dry regions, with organs adapted to enable them to obtain and conserve water, are called *xerophytes.*

Temperature

For each plant there are certain maximum and minimum temperature limits for normal growth, and also limits beyond which the plant cannot survive. Within these limits lies a further range of temperatures most favourable for plant growth. Once again we find that it is the *combination* of other factors with high or low temperatures which particularly affect a given plant: perhaps the accompanying intensity of light, or the air humidity. During the bitter winter of 1962-3 olive trees in southern Italy survived periods of dry cold; yet shortly afterwards a cold, damp spell, with no lower temperatures, caused considerable damage to the trees.

We should consider not only the plant as a whole, but the various parts of a plant, which may be harmed by quite different temperatures; the seeds, for instance, are usually much more tolerant than the shoots. A given temperature may also have different effects on a plant according to its state of development: whether it is the blossom or fruit that is exposed to those conditions, for example.

A plant's response to night temperatures may also have considerable bearing on its geographical location or distribution. Many plants can only flower, and therefore perpetuate themselves, when night temperatures are sufficiently low in relation to day temperatures; they may not be able to reproduce successfully when temperatures are persistently high. The English daisy is an example of this; if the day temperature reaches 26° C the night temperature should fall below 10° C. Thus the distribution of varieties and strains of plants may be governed by quite small variations from the necessary night temperatures.

We have already seen that some of the indirect effects of temperature may be extremely important to plants: affecting, for instance, the rate of evaporation of near-surface water, or the rate of absorption of soil water by roots.

Light

Light energy is required for photosynthesis of the carbohydrates required by plants, and it is thus another important environmental factor. The amount and intensity of light vary from place to place, and from time to time, in accordance with the latitude, season, local relief, climatic factors (such as cloud cover), and with the proximity of other plants. Leafy layers may occur in vegetation at various heights: for some full-grown plants a certain height above the ground may meet their light requirements, which may be quite different for plants above and beneath them. Climbing plants may twine about other sturdier, taller ones as they seek the light.

Air Movements

These affect the rate of evaporation and the temperature of plants, depending on the strength of such movements and the relative humidity and temperature of the air itself. In some plant organs which experience rapid transpiration, processes may take place which cause growth to occur more strongly on their lee-side: on the other hand, growth may be inhibited by too rapid transpiration. Wind can also have an indirect effect on vegetation by drying out soils, so leading to a lack of available soil water, and perhaps to

FACTORS OF PLANT ENVIRONMENT

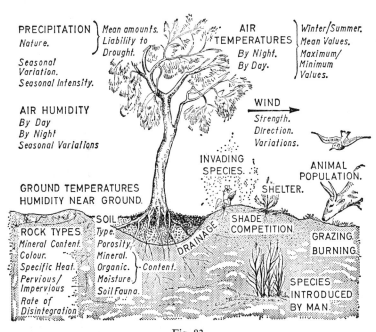

Fig. 83.

A diagrammatic representation of the many factors which may act and interact to affect plant life in a given locality. Even this simple summary will stress how inadequate is the quotation of mean temperature and rainfall figures as an account of plants' habitat, or as a description of the environment of a type of vegetation.

erosion. Its force may also move vegetation or break stems. Air movement can also act positively by assisting the spread of vegetation and is an important agent of seed dispersal.

Structure and Relief

These have very many direct and indirect influences on plant life. Considering only a few, we see that relief can help to create certain conditions of moisture and temperature by acting as a barrier to winds, by presenting slopes to direct insolation, or to the wind, and by virtue of altitude. In areas of strong relief, with a variety of local climates, there will most likely be many different types of plants and various forms of vegetation. Slopes influence the depth and texture of the soil and the drainage. Gravitational movements of soil materials, under favourable climatic conditions, may create a sequence of different soil types, and so further affect the pattern of the vegetation.

Soil (Edaphic) Conditions

These are obviously of very great significance to plants, and their main characteristics are considered on p. 148 *et seq.* The balance between forms of vegetation and soils is a delicate one. The amount of organic matter present and the inorganic contents are each vitally important in natural soils. The death of plants, or parts of plants, followed by the accumulation of organic matter in the soil helps to maintain the life cycle. The moisture and chemical contents of the soil help to remove, or make available, food of organic origin for the new plants, aided by the action of various living organisms. Deficiencies of certain soil elements may have a considerable effect on plant organs: so that the nature and condition of particular organs, the leaves perhaps, may indicate the presence or absence of certain minerals in the soils.

Biotic Factors

The micro-organisms in the soil are among the most lowly of the living forms affecting plant life (p. 151). A multitude of other animals is usually associated, in some way or another, with the numerous plants forming the vegetation. They may live with them in a balanced community, or may help to bring about fundamental changes in the nature of that vegetation. There are innumerable interactions between the animals themselves; and these, too, ultimately affect the plant cover. Birds of prey and large animals keep down the numbers of smaller birds and animals which, acting as seed carriers or insect consumers, are linked with the plant world. Diseases affecting animals may bring changes in the vegetation, in the way that myxamatosis, by destroying innumerable rabbits, had an almost immediate effect on grass growth and crop yields, and on the establishment of plant seedlings.

Obviously there are endless examples of biotic influences on vegetation: from the insect world of locusts and caterpillars, and the animals which feed on them, to man and the remarkable changes wrought by his systematic burning and clearing of natural vegetation, his use of grazing animals, which prevent the re-establishment of shrubs and trees, and his powers of control over the growth and activities of fungi, insects, animals, and plants themselves.

ADAPTATIONS AND INTERRELATIONS OF PLANTS

Adaptations

If we inspect those plants which are the dominant ones in the vegetation over a certain part of the earth's surface, we see that they possess inherited characteristics which allow them to flourish in that particular environment. In arid locations, for instance, plant organs are modified to obtain, store, or prevent the loss of water. Deep taproots reach water far below the surface, elongating themselves as long as they remain in dry aerated conditions, so that thirty feet is not an unusual root length for a large plant. Succulents like the cacti store water in cells in the stem or leaves; other plants have roots spread over the surface to absorb as much moisture as possible during humid or wet periods. The thickening of tissues, the development of a waxy surface, means of contracting or protecting stomata, small leaves, or leaves reduced to spikes, and deciduous behaviour, all help to prevent the loss of plant moisture in arid conditions. At the other end of the scale, as we have seen, many aquatic plants develop buoyant stems and leaves, and expose to the atmosphere organs, roots even, which allow air to pass freely through them.

Competition and Co-existence

The above are forms of adaptation to extreme conditions. But innumerable inherited features are to be seen in any large number of plants living together in any small fertile area, which enable each to survive the competition for space, light, and nutrients, and to flourish as a typical part of the local vegetation. Thus the plant population may include individuals which thrive in a light, but exposed, environment high above the ground, and others well adapted to a very shaded, but sheltered, location close to the soil. It is these communities existing together which we now examine as part of a particular type of natural vegetation.

Ecology is the study of the interrelationships between all the different members of the plant-animal community. So complex are the relationships, that any group making such a study can only begin to understand the balance of the whole, if it applies its investigations to tiny areas. We may, for convenience, distinguish between certain "types" of vegetation which occur over large areas of the earth's surface, but we need to understand the relationships of the plants one to another within our chosen units of vegetation,

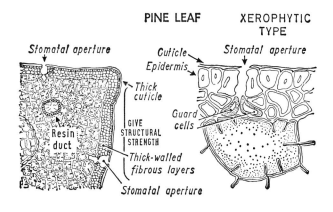

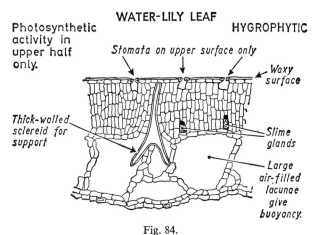

Fig. 84.

The leaf-structure of plants with very different habitats. The pine must conserve moisture for long periods. The leaf shows the thick cuticle and fibrous layer beneath; the guard cells below the level of the surface; and resin ducts within the chlorophyll-containing cells. The water-lily leaf floats, the plant rooted in its marshy environment. The stomata are exposed on the upper side of the waxy leaf surface; slime glands lie beneath; large inter-cellular air-spaces give buoyancy, and strong fibrous cells add rigidity.

and ecological studies may reveal whether or not a plant community is stable or undergoing modifications.

PLANT SUCCESSIONS

Plant populations vary in composition from one area to another; the key factors in their environment being climate, soils, the type of plant species present, plants available to invade an area, and competition among themselves. The nature of the competition depends on their habitat, and, in a sense, is itself an environmental factor; for one type of plant generally becomes dominant in the vegetation at any given time, and affects other plants in the vicinity, through, say, its shade, shelter, or effects on the humidity of the soil, and thus on their own, very local, atmosphere.

The Conception of "Climax Vegetation"

The composition of a local plant population is also apt to change with time. Communities generally become more complex, and lowly plants tend to give way to others of a higher form. Plants which are dominant at any given time may themselves be replaced during a process of continuous change, until eventually the plant community reaches a stable state known as the *climax*, when the composition of the vegetation remains more or less the same for a long period of time. But in the long run, even this may prove to be only a relative stability; for alteration in the climate, or soil make-up, may once more initiate a progressive or retrogressive change in the composition of the community.

Ecologists rightly regard the whole idea of a plant succession of this type reaching an ultimate climax as a convenience for the sake of study, rather than an inevitable natural process. But, even if it does not have absolute validity, the concept of a climax community is an extremely useful one in the study of vegetation.

From Initial Colonisation to Climax Vegetation

When plants colonise bare ground, through their usual processes of dispersion and plant migration, a number of families of a particular species, or colonies of two or more species, become established there at the outset. These compete for the available space, light, water, and plant nutrients. As they live and die within the area they help to change the existing habitat; affecting, for instance, the microclimate, the organic content of the soil and its humidity and texture. Thus, besides their struggle for existence, plants have indirect influence on each other. Other plants arrive from nearby areas to colonise the now altered habitat, and in turn affect the existing balance; new dominants take over, and again exert their own influence. Eventually a period of relative stability is achieved and a climax obtained, with dominants which have excluded rivals less suited to the prevailing conditions. The vegetation as a whole now maintains itself in balance with the climatic, physical, and biotic environment, though there are bound to be minor adjustments with time.

Occurrences of Broadly Similar Types of Climax Vegetation

Climate and soil both exert a strong control over the form of the dominant plants and those associated with them. Hence, in regions with roughly comparable climatic and edaphic (soil) conditions (the soils themselves being a reflection also of relief and drainage) there should be a noticeable correspondence between their types of climax vegetation, even if the regions are far distant from one another. The highest type of vegetation which can exist in a region under those climatic conditions is sometimes called the *regional climatic climax.*

Whether such a possible form of vegetation *will* establish itself there depends, of course, not only on climate, but on the other facts. Local soil conditions, the practice of burning vegetation, and the presence of grazing animals, are among the factors which often permit only dominants of lower life-forms to establish themselves. Where such lower forms of vegetation persist for long periods, however, the term *sub-climax vegetation* is sometimes used.

Any broad climatic region will contain innumerable variations in vegetation and in the plants associated with each type of vegetation. Nevertheless a study of world vegetation can be simplified by considering certain outstanding approximations to climax types which do tend to recur in comparable climate regions. Some ecologists would regard any attempt at preparing a simplified classification of vegetation on a regional, world-wide, basis as undesirable, or at least as highly dangerous. But provided we realise the limitations of any system of classification or regional division on such a broad basis (and of our own classification in particular), our studies of prevailing life-forms throughout the world must benefit initially from our appreciation of the distribution of types of vegetation.

Some Examples of Successions of Changes: The Sere

Before considering types of vegetation, let us examine a succession of changes which may follow the establishment of units of vegetation on a number of contrasting sites. The changes result in a successive series of communities—each known as a *sere*—leading to the climax.

Vegetation may have its origin in fresh water or salt water, on damp surfaces or dry surfaces. As higher life-forms develop, so there is a tendency for the habitat to be modified through soil-building, humus accumulation, and moisture changes. This often results in hygrophytic plants giving way to mesophytic; and in dry locations xerophytic plants may also be replaced by mesophytic ones.

A Hydrosere. In the case of the aquatic environment, this may be brought about by bottom-rooted and floating water plants gradually building up a bed of decaying plant matter and silt, until, in the shallowing water, swamp plants can enter the community and become dominant. Plant matter and debris continues to accumulate, until a soil surface with a humus content is sufficiently consolidated and aerated to support coarse grasses and, later, shrubs and trees.

A Xerosere. By contrast, a bare desert surface may first be colonised by simple life-forms which cling to, and help to corrode, rock surfaces. To the rock debris they add a small amount of organic matter, which supports incoming plants of a slightly higher life-form, capable of holding more water: lichens, for instance, may give way to small xerophytic herbs. Soil building and organic accumulation may continue, so that hardy herbaceous plants may be followed by larger, woody ones, and perhaps eventually a tree cover of sorts may be established.

These successions may be halted, of course, at any stage, by unfavourable conditions; but they illustrate the tendency of vegetation to establish higher life-forms and for less extreme water conditions to result.

CLASSIFICATION OF PLANTS

Though at the start of their studies geographers are usually more concerned with the classification and distribution of broad types of vegetation rather than with individual plants, at least in their local regional studies they must take regard of plant successions and realise that the vegetation present may be "sub-climax", or perhaps merely a stage in a succession. A knowledge of the order of classification of life-forms, and of the place of particular plants in that order, is thus a great asset to them. The highest groupings are the divisions which follow.

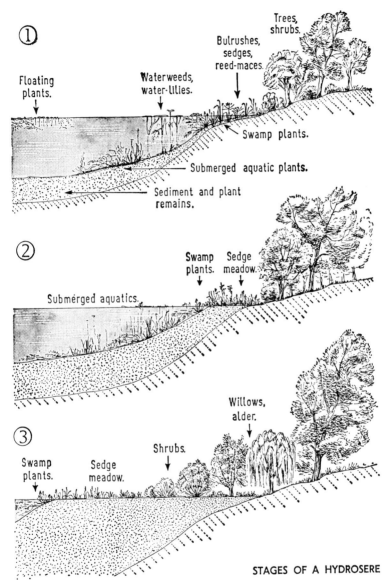

Fig. 85.

Water plants and marsh plants gradually build up a bed of decaying plant matter in silt: consolidation, and more aerated conditions, lead to the progressive establishment of marsh grasses, shrubs, and trees.

Divisions (or Phyla)

Schizophyta—minute organisms, like bacteria and simple algae.

Thallophyta—plants without properly differentiated roots, stems, or leaves; including large algae and seaweeds, fungi, moulds, and lichens.

Bryophyta—plants without true roots, but with the beginnings of stems and leaves.

None of these plant groups possesses the kind of structure, with cells forming tissue capable of distributing water, mineral salts, and nutrients via the roots, and through stems and leaf veins, that is found in the higher members of the following divisions. Mosses, for example, attached by rhizoids and without true roots, depend primarily on photo-synthesis for nutrition, and can take in dilute solutions through their leaves.

Pteridophyta—plants with roots, stems, leaves, and conducting tissues for the purposes described above; but reproducing through spores and not seeds. They include the horsetails and ferns.

Spermatophyta—seed plants. In this category are most of the plants which make up the vegetation formations of the present time.

Some recognise sub-divisions; but, generally, below the main phyla the grouping is into **Classes.** Thus the phylum spermatophyta consists of *Gymnosperms,* which are woody plants with ovules not enclosed in an ovary (conifers, for example), and *Angiosperms,* which are flowering plants with enclosed ovules: to some, therefore, these are sub-divisions, to others classes.

Each class is made up of various **Orders** (usually with name endings of—*ales*); and these, in turn, of **Families** of plants with certain characteristics in common (with name endings of—*aceae*). The families are grouped into **Genera,** and the members of each genus have many obvious points of resemblance, and consist of one or more **Species.** The plants in the same species are very similar to one another, and are usually able to interbreed. The species are usually known by Latin names, using words which indicate the genus to which they belong together with a descriptive epithet. There are usually recognisable *sub-species* and *varieties* of plants within the species.

Not all authorities use precisely the same method of breaking down the classification; but the main pattern is followed and is a useful one from the point of view of description. We may thus identify a tree on a hillside in northern Britain, obviously, as a spermatophyte; on closer inspection as a gymnosperm, and one of the most numerous orders of these—coniferales; next as a member of the genus "pinus"; and if we have sufficient knowledge we may then identify it as a *Pinus sylvestris*, or a Scots Pine.

The final identification of a plant in this way must call, of course, for considerable experience.

Raunkiaer's Classification

In order to describe the members of the vegetation in a certain location, or even in a broad climatic region, we can also adopt another type of classification, first made by the Danish professor C. Raunkiaer. This enables us to sum up the composition of the vegetation in terms of broad groups of life-forms. The plants' chief characteristics place them in one group or another, as follows:

(*a*) Perennial shrubs and trees with stems and renewal buds more than 250 mm above the soil and exposed to most climatic hazards (*Phanerophytes*);

(*b*) Perennial herbs and low shrubs with renewal buds between ground-level and 250 mm above: plants like thyme and the saxifrages (*Chamaephytes*);

(*c*) Herbs and grasses with resting buds at ground level or in the surface soil: plants like dandelion and nettles (*Hemicryptophytes*);

(*d*) Plants with underground bulbs, tubers, or rhizomes well buried in the soil: such as hyacinths and crocuses (*Geophytes*);

(*e*) Plants with a full life cycle under favourable conditions, but which survive later stringent conditions (as in an arid environment) in the form of resistant seeds or spores (*Therophytes*);

(*f*) Water plants and marsh plants (*Hydrophytes* and *Hygrophytes*);

This is a simple system which may be increased in complexity by adding further categories, and by the inclusion of certain special groups like the *Epiphytes*: these grow in debris on host-trees, using the latter as a means of elevation towards the light which they require for photosynthesis, and without harming their host.

Because this is a simple system, it can be used to present a broad "biological spectrum" of the percentage of the life-forms described to the total flora in any region, large or small. Fig. 86 shows a plot of the relative abundance of these forms in various places.

The Grouping of Plants on the Basis of Temperature Requirements

We have seen that one classification distinguishes between hygrophytes, mesophytes, and xerophytes in respect of the moisture

content of their environment; another classification may be made on
the basis of their temperature requirements. The following names

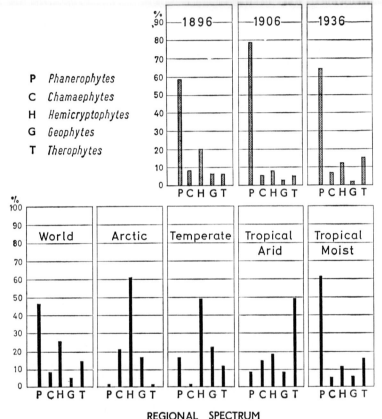

SPECTRUM SHOWING
RE-COLONISATION OF A VOLCANIC AREA

P *Phanerophytes*
C *Chamaephytes*
H *Hemicryptophytes*
G *Geophytes*
T *Therophytes*

REGIONAL SPECTRUM

Fig. 86.
    The composition of vegetation in various broad climatic regions as described
in Raunkaier's classification. Mean values for such broad regions provide
spectra, for principal vascular plants, from which highly generalised comparisons
of their distribution may be made.
    The spectra showing the colonisation of a relatively small area in which the
previous vegetation had been destroyed by volcanic activity, are more revealing.
Fluctuations in the proportion of life-forms suggest, among other things, the
effects of competition among themselves. (Plots are from figures by D. van
Leeuwen: *The Recolonisation of Krakatoa*.)

are used to describe plants which flourish in areas within the mean monthly temperature limits described:

Temperature Limits (Mean Monthly—°C)	*Name*
(*a*) All months above 18° C.	*Megatherms*
(*b*) Coldest months 6°-18° C.	*Mesotherms*
Warmest months above 22° C.	
(*c*) Coldest months above 6° C.	*Microtherms*
Warmest months 10°-22° C.	
(*d*) Warmest months below 10° C.	*Hekistotherms*

Such groups are, of course, extremely broad ones: and because plant environments vary enormously from one tiny locality to the next, they can be of only limited value in description.

Units of Vegetation Classified by Status

The following chapter considers the types of vegetation and their distribution over the earth's surface. But because (stressing this point once again) large units of vegetation include a variety of different plant communities, it is useful to refer to smaller plant groups within the larger unit. In terms of status these can be classified as follows:

Formations are the large distinctive units such as tundra, coniferous forest, heathlands.

Associations combine to make up these formations, being various climax units each with its characteristic dominant species. Thus a mixed deciduous forest formation may include an oak-beech association; or there may be a single dominant, as in a beech forest on chalk country.

Societies of other plants, often of lower life-forms, may occur within these major groupings. In these one or two species predominate; usually because some particular feature of the environment especially suits them—a certain type of soil perhaps. There may also be plants of several species, grouped together within a major vegetation unit, which have come in as a colony of invaders.

On a smaller scale there may be groups, or clans, of a single species which have local dominance in a certain part of the environment which suits them really well; or even a small group which has spread from a single invading plant.

CHAPTER XII

TYPES OF VEGETATION (I): TROPICAL

While the exact nature of the plant-life depends on numerous environmental factors, climate has a very great influence on the vegetation, both directly and indirectly (through soils, for instance). It is not surprising that there are areas remote from each other where like forms of vegetation flourish in broadly similar climatic conditions. These areas have sufficient features of their habitats in common for many characteristics of the plant communities to resemble one another. But though they may contain similar plant families, the individual plants may not be the same in each case. We can, for instance, distinguish broad vegetation types common to the near-equatorial lowlands of the Amazon Basin of South America and those of the Zaïre Basin in Africa; and also formations on pediplains of East Africa which have much in common with those on the tablelands of eastern Brazil; but we find that the actual plant species vary considerably from place to place. We will, in fact, be sure to find that any large "vegetation region" includes areas which bear a very different type of vegetation. We cannot, for instance, assume that the soils, which often exert a dominant effect on the form of vegetation, have been formed under present climatic conditions: often plants are growing in soils which have remained unchanged for enormously long periods (especially on tropical tablelands), so that quite a different kind of vegetation occurs where the soils are disturbed. Nevertheless, many formations are almost continuous over large areas, and their main features and variants are described below.

The Low Latitude Rainforest (Equatorial Forest)

Fig. 89 shows parts of the world where such forests of the low latitudes (sometimes called "Equatorial Forests") occupy almost all of the moist lowlands and slopes up to about 1 000 m; here high temperatures (mean monthly figures of the order of 25-6° C), and a small annual range, combine with high humidities and frequent rainfall to produce hot-house conditions.

The Composition of the Forests

These forests are sometimes called "evergreen", and may give that general impression; for, with the lack of seasonal variations, individual plants lose their leaves at intervals, and there is not the general leaf-fall among most species that there is in temperate deciduous forests; though the trees of some species all lose their leaves at roughly the same time. Among plants as a whole, however, leaf-growth, flowering, fruiting, and leaf-fall go on all the time, so that the overall impression is of a close green forest.

Seen from above, the crowns of the trees appear to form a continuous canopy, except over rivers, swamp areas, or clearings. The tree heights are irregular, however, and the very tallest, which may rise to some 30-40 metres, are often widely spaced; and, having

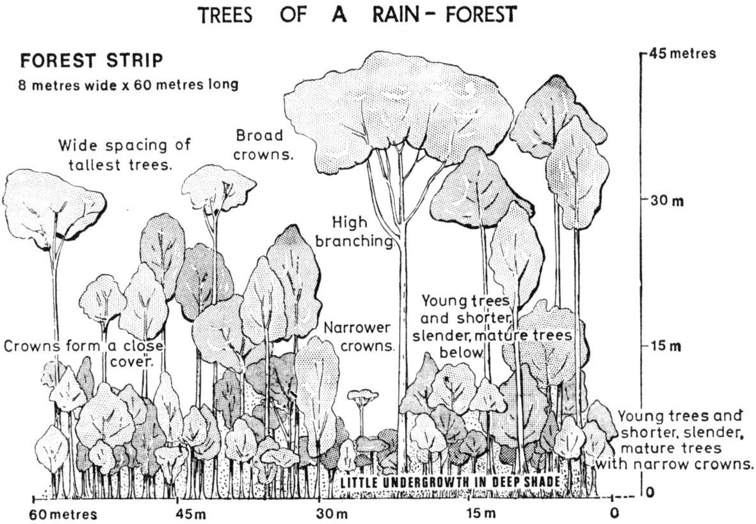

TREES OF A RAIN - FOREST

Fig. 87.
The composition of a strip of rainforest in southern Nigeria (after Richards).

sufficient space, these develop wide crowns. Beneath them, trees rising to a height of 20 m or so form a second "stratum", their crowns usually making a close cover. Beneath are shorter, more slender trees with narrower crowns; their heights vary from about 5-15 m. The lower trees include, of course, young forms which may grow to reach the highest level; but most species here are different from those above. The use of the terms "strata" or "layers", is in fact misleading. Such "layers" are usually revealed only by statistical investigation and plottings of height frequencies; a ground-level observer sees rather, a mass of branches and foliage belonging to lower trees and saplings, and amid them the soaring, creeper-festooned trunks of the taller species. The average height of the "layers" also varies from one rainforest area to another; so that the figures quoted serve only to give a general picture.

When the forest is fairly open at higher levels, palms, bamboos, tree-ferns, and well-developed shrubs may flourish; as they do in clearings which have been abandoned. Light plays a great part in aiding or retarding plant development at lower levels, where plant successions depend a great deal on the light intensity. At the edge of rivers, clearings, or on hillsides, where light penetrates more readily, there is often a dense lower growth, with ferns, shrubs, and grasses; on the other hand in the gloom near the ground, in a well-canopied forest, only flecks of light pass through the leaves above, and there is little undergrowth. Full grown trees stand at heights which largely depend on their tolerance to shading from above, and most have straight trunks with little branching below crown-level. Throughout the forest, and at all levels, there is the struggle for light, space, and nutrients from the soil, which helps to determine the make-up of plant communities.

These are indeed mixed forests, with literally thousands of species of trees, lianes, and epiphytes; though there is not the huge abundance of flowering species in the African formations as in those of the Americas and south-east Asia. Unlike most forest formations, there are few distinctive dominant trees in the rain-forests; the many different species exist side by side, though in a sense there are often a number of co-dominants. This is a forest mixed both horizontally and vertically.

Plant Forms

The great weight of the tall trees, with spreading crowns above their thick, branchless trunks is, in some species, partly supported on the moist ground by buttresses of woody material spreading from the lower part of the trunk and the upper sides of lateral roots. The trees, generally, are shallow-rooted. A number of the smaller trees have stilt-like projections from the lower parts of the trunk. Many have thin bark, and some, like the cacao, bear flowers and fruit on the trunk. The glossy, often leathery, leaves are usually of medium or large size, and adapted to shed water, so that photosynthesis may proceed; many of the lower trees have long, pointed, or channelled, tips ("drip-tips") from which the water is shed. Should transpira-tion be checked by surface water on the leaf, the process by which soil water is drawn up is also checked; so that, on this score also, the loss of water from the leaves is important. As there is usually very strong insolation in the middle part of the day, the dark green leaves are also protected from the excessive loss of moisture by their thick, "leathery", cuticles.

Green climbers and vines abound, twining about trees and inter-twining with the thick, woody, climbing lianes, in an upward

CHARACTERISTIC ELEMENTS OF LOW - LATITUDE FORESTS

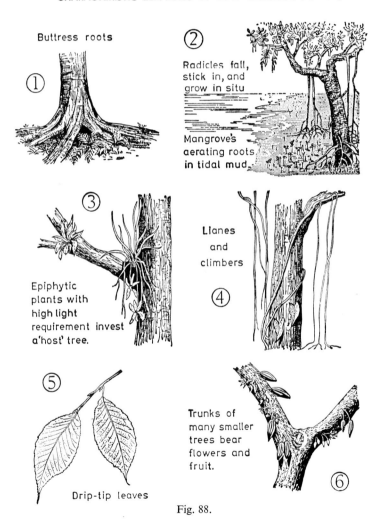

Buttress roots

② Radicles fall, stick in, and grow in situ

Mangrove's aerating roots in tidal mud

③ Epiphytic plants with high light requirement invest a'host' tree.

Llanes and climbers ④

⑤ Drip-tip leaves

Trunks of many smaller trees bear flowers and fruit. ⑥

Fig. 88.

competition for light. Lianes are often looped between trees, and, forming links from tree to tree, help to support them. There are also many families of climbers which enmesh trees and shrubs at their various levels.

These rainforests support a wide range of *epiphytes*—plants which thrive above ground level on various parts of trees and shrubs (without harm to their hosts, which help to support them in positions with the required intensity of light). Some are rooted in debris held in the fork of a branch; others thrive on decaying remains of other plants they have trapped; and some catch and hold water. Many of them are adapted to live with only a small intake of soluble minerals.

Besides these, there are *parasites,* taking their nutrients from the roots, trunks, or branches of a host plant. Many orchids grow attached to trees as epiphytes do; others live and thrive on dead organic matter on the forest floor, as *saprophytes.* There are also many "in-between" plants: some start as epiphytes, but later root themselves and become independent of their host, which may be strangled by them as they develop. Specialised means of survival are found at all levels in the forest.

Secondary Forest. Large areas of the present tropical lowland rainforests are really secondary growth, especially in Asia. After man has cleared and then moved on, the forest apparently takes control again very rapidly: but this is a different forest; and, although species of the primary forest gradually invade the area, the re-establishment of a climax vegetation is a slow process. The changes in environment, perhaps with depleted soils, favour shorter trees, shrubs, and climbing plants; these may produce a thick tangle of vegetation again, but one with a different proportion of species. Soil variation may cause differences within a broad region of low latitude rainforest: as there are areas of tropical podsols as well as the more usual ferralitic soils, these often support a distinct vegetation type, like the heath-forests in parts of south-east Asia, and on lowlands bordering the Guiana Highlands.

The Vegetation of Tropical Shores and Coastlands

In places where sediment accumulates near the shores, as deltaic deposits or mudflats, and where there is tidal salt water, or brackish water, mangrove swamps and forests often form a thick fringe of green or greyish vegetation. The mangrove is the main dominant of this halophytic evergreen vegetation: the trees, of low to moderate height, form an apparently tangled mass, whose stems and roots, often visible above the waters, bear reddish algae and

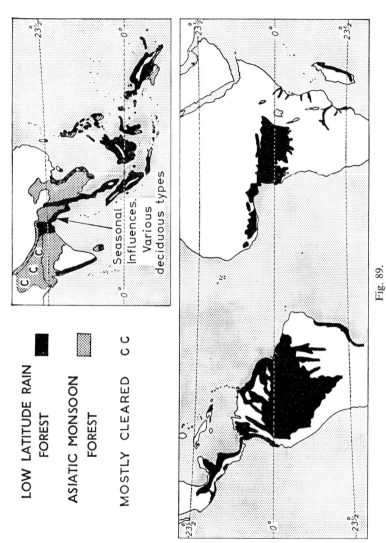

LOW LATITUDE RAIN
FOREST

ASIATIC MONSOON
FOREST

MOSTLY CLEARED C C

Seasonal
Influences.
Various
deciduous types

Fig. 89.

The tropical seasonal forests of southern Asia vary greatly in their composition, and have been much modified by long periods of continuous occupation by man. In the areas in northern India marked C, little remains of the former dry monsoon forests, except along the Himalayan foothills.

various lichens. There are few other vascular plants; but, like the mangroves, most have prop-roots, sharply arched, or growing erect from the mud, and capable of taking in air. The tangle of roots helps to retain silt, and this builds up a surface on which other, sometimes larger, forms of mangroves develop; later stages of a hydrosere, developing from hydrophytic to mesophytic forms, may then follow (p. 200). Again, the noon-day intensity of the insolation is usually great and, despite the aquatic surroundings, the thick, shiny, and often leathery, leaves of the vegetation are adaptations guarding against excessive transpiration.

In many mangrove species seeds germinate in the fruit while still on the plant, and as the seedling breaks through it extends downwards like a dagger, eventually falling and embedding the radicle in the mud, to form anchoring roots. Other seedlings may be carried away by water, perhaps to root elsewhere.

On salty marshes the roots of coarse grasses and other low plants help to bind sandy stretches; and the pandanus (screw-pine), with its clusters of strut-like prop-roots and tufts of thin, dry, leafy blades on a woody stem, is a typical tree-form adapted to salty conditions in the tropics. On firmer shores, low woody evergreens with dark green glossy leaves form a lower layer beneath the coconut palms. The fruit of the latter, with its thick fibrous layer and hard shell, can withstand a fall of well over 20 m, and, being buoyant, can be dispersed by water to develop on a distant beach, or beside some other creek or lagoon. The coconut palm is thus characteristic of tropical and near-tropical shores. The fruits and seeds, or seedlings, of most other swamp and shore dwellers are also dispersed by water.

Tropical Seasonal Forests

In humid tropical areas which, nevertheless, have a pronounced dry season, the forests have markedly different characteristics from the true rainforests. Such forests are found in the monsoon countries of southern Asia, on the central African plateaux, and in those parts of South America which lie poleward of the equatorial lowlands. The climates differ from those which support the low latitude rainforest in having dry periods lasting up to several months; there is often a smaller annual rainfall total, though in some monsoon locations the annual amounts are very large indeed. Almost always there are greater annual and diurnal temperature ranges, rather greater seasonal changes in the length of day and in intensity of light, and a tendency for stronger winds to set in at certain times of the year.

The vegetation varies from the rather luxuriant type of forest, in the better watered localities with a relatively short dry season, through drier deciduous seasonal forest, to the open woodland which is described below as "grassland-with-trees" rather than as forest.

The wetter type of forest is sometimes known as "semi-evergreen seasonal forest" and contains a fairly high proportion of evergreens, especially in the lower layer of the two main levels. Many trees are regularly deciduous, however, and shed their leaves in the dry season; some shed leaves regularly, but not always in direct response to drought conditions. Tall trees rise to about 25 m, some to over 30 m. In the drier forests with an annual rainfall between 1 000-2 000 mm, deciduous trees are the main species, usually with a lower discontinuous layer of evergreens. In northern Burma and eastern Assam, for instance, the wetter western parts have many evergreens, with the tall pyinkado as the chief deciduous tree; but in the drier parts of northern and central Burma teak takes over as the main dominant; and other deciduous trees, like sal and in, are prominent members of the higher "layer".

In many places where there is seasonal leaf-loss, or on hillsides, or where the leaf canopy is incomplete, light reaches the ground more readily, and the undergrowth may be very dense, with thick shrubs and bamboo clumps, so that the forests become difficult to penetrate on foot; and certainly in the dry season, as so many found in World War II, it is difficult to move with stealth between close, bare thickets over a carpet of dry, crackling leaves.

The trees themselves show seasonal growth-rings in their wood. Some have a dry, fissured bark. The trunks of the larger trees are still massive, but they do not have the buttressed base of many rainforest trees, and there is more branching and more trees with wide-spread crowns. The leaves are thin in many cases and vary in size between species; though many trees do have large leaves. On the whole there are fewer climbers, though the moist forests have many lianes; epiphytes are not nearly as numerous as in the low latitude rainforests. Flowering is most common during the dry season.

Tropical Grassland-with-Trees

Where the tropical forests give way to grass as the dominant vegetation form, there is, in a sense, a transition zone between close forest, with a complete tree cover, and true grassland: but the intermediate stages are "patchy" rather than regular; and in places tracts of forest lie within the extensive areas of grassland-with-trees. Large parts of the tropics are covered by "savannah woodland", "savannah parkland", or "scrub-savannah". Grasses clearly cover much of the countryside, but shrubs, trees, or tree clumps, occur, closely or sparsely, in various associations.

Climatic Influences—The Misconception of a "Savannah Climate". The idea of a "transition zone" suggests strong climatic influence; but the simple assumption that a progressive decrease in annual rainfall and increase in length of a drought period causes a gradual change from forest to grassland, with an in-between zone of dwindling tree cover, has too often been accepted as a complete explanation of the cause of variations in savannah vegetation. Obviously climatic influences are strong: and general vegetation maps of Africa show large areas of savannah lying between low latitude rainforest where the annual rainfall is high, and the thorn scrub and semi-desert lands of the sub-tropics, where little more than 250 mm of rain may fall in a year. But, in fact, in the savannah lands of Africa, Brazil, and Australia there are many anomalies: true forest often gives way to stretches of open grassland quite abruptly, and without any remarkable climatic changes; while elsewhere large areas of grassland-with-trees occur in the midst of widespread forests. Again, many tropical areas appear to receive rainfall sufficient to support forest, but yet carry only bush savannah: this applies to large parts of the tablelands of East Africa and Central and South America.

Undoubtedly, changes in soil conditions, and the progressive development of new landforms, are responsible for many of the variations in plant associations and vegetation types. Then, again, continuous grazing by wild animals (at first, perhaps, under drier climatic conditions), and subsequent interference by man, through his grazing animals and through burning, have long been important environmental influences: burning has affected, and still affects, enormous areas of the world's grasslands.

Though there is no such thing as a "savannah climate", the variation in plant composition of the "grassland-with-trees" has at least strong connections with the moisture content of the general environment and with present soils. This type of vegetation mostly appears where there is a fairly long, dry season; so, with a lower annual rainfall than in the regions of low latitude forest described above, there is a consequent seasonal deficiency in soil moisture. Where there is a high annual rainfall, mostly in the hot season, as in Mali in West Africa, savannah vegetation is often luxuriant, with close tree cover, and tussocky grasses more than 3 m tall. In other regions, with less moisture and poorer soils, the grasses tend to be less tall, shrubs and herbs cover a larger area, and the trees are fewer and show xerophilous characteristics. But there are many anomalies, which cannot be accounted for purely on a climatic basis.

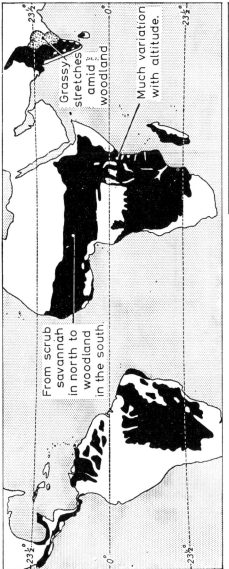

Fig. 90.

TROPICAL GRASSLAND

AND GRASSLAND WITH TREES

Woodland / Parkland   Savannah;

Grassland   and   Scrub   Savannah

A very general distribution map which includes the great diversity of vegetation forms described on pp. 213–221. Variations occur, often abruptly, within these broad regions, while elsewhere one vegetation "type", shades into another, especially at the outer limits defined here, so limiting the usefulness of any map of tropical grassland-with-trees. This is seen in Australia where no valid boundary may be drawn between "tropical" and "temperate" grasslands, and in northern India where the grassland-with-trees is seen encroaching on the monsoon forests shown Fig. 89.

The Variety of Deciduous and Evergreen Trees

The impression given by much of the "mid-savannahs" is of an open parkland of fairly tall tussock grasses with a number of moderately tall trees mingled with shorter ones. But many tree species have flattened crowns, and a number of them lose all, or most, of their leaves during the dry season. Others, especially in the South American savannah, are evergreen, and as adaptation to conditions of moisture deficiency and lack of certain salts, have hard, leathery leaves. Numerous bulbs and other geophytes live in the more open grasslands.

The trees may include various species of palm, especially in the Americas. In Australia there are many curious indigenous plants like the "blackboy" of the south-west, but most common are the eucalypts: there are hundreds of species, with adaptations ranging from a twisting leaf-stem, which turns the leaf edge-ways to intense sunlight and minimises loss by transpiration, to fire-resistant seed-cases: tall, high-branching eucalypts tend to be replaced by lower mallee forms on poorer soils in drier areas: the latter, each with many short stems rising from a single stock, also have various water-storing features. Among the dominant trees of the rather drier Australian grasslands, as in many similar parts of the tropics, are numerous species of acacia; in fact, plants of the pea family are common constituents of the drier grasslands. The flattened crowns of some of the acacias, and the flat, "layered", appearance of many savannah trees, may be a response to the persistent winds of the open grasslands, though this is debatable. The gnarled bark, seasonal loss of leaves, and well-protected buds guard against excessive loss of moisture; roots penetrate to reach deep ground-water. Most of the savannah trees are fire-resistant, which suggests that a former tree cover with less resistant species may have been removed by fire.

Where the rainy season is short, the more arid parts, and those with impoverished soils, may bear thorn woodland. Here the large, grotesquely shaped, deciduous baobab, with its unmistakable high branches, may stand out starkly; its water-storing trunk has a thick, corky bark, and its wood is spongy in texture. Many thorny plants occur in semi-arid regions (which are considered separately below), but in Africa, South America, and India low thorny trees are common in the drier grasslands.

Grasses—Their Competition with Trees and Shrubs

The grasses themselves, which are of course herbs, are mainly bunch or tussocky in form, distinct from neighbouring tussocks at their base; and though in the better watered tall-grass country the grass cover is fairly complete, in dry locations clumps are often separated by bare patches. These perennial grasses, whose stems and narrow blades spring from nodes near the ground, are very tolerant of seasonal drought and are resistant to wind. Their rapid growth in the wet season is not emulated by woody plants; and their seeds are widely distributed by the wind, or carried, like those of spear-grass, on the coats of animals. As a result, they are well fitted to develop at the expense of the seedlings of trees and shrubs—although once the latter have a hold they can shade large areas and kill out grasses.

Seasonal Changes

The whole appearance of the savannahs, especially those with lengthy droughts, changes with the season. The rains renew grass growth, shrubs and herbs blossom, and leaves appear on the deciduous trees. With the onset of the dry season many trees become bare, with a typically stark appearance; the grasses dry out from their tips downwards, and the grassland acquires a bleached look. Though many of the geophytes flower during the drought period, the overall impression of the dry savannahs is that of a parched landscape, saved from the desolate appearance of a desert by the amount of vegetation, the tree forms, and the movement of grasses in the wind.

The Influences of Soil Conditions

We have seen that soil conditions have a considerable influence on the vegetation, both by their nutrient content and through their texture. The changes in vegetation can be abrupt. The vegetation over various erosional levels in south-west Australia, for instance, changes suddenly from dominant eucalypts (jarrah) on lateric soils to heaths, with Banksia, on adjacent soils derived from sandstones. Elsewhere on river terraces coarse soils, which allow water to drain rapidly through them, may bear many succulents, while periodically flooded alluvial tracts with a high water-table, but not permanently marshy, may carry seasonal forests, or galleries of evergreen trees, and thick undergrowth.

Away from the main drainage flats and channels, the vegetation on plateaux surfaces is apt to vary markedly, and sometimes abruptly, with changes of slope and different soil characteristics. Plateau soils, remaining *in situ* on almost level surfaces for long periods under tropical wet and dry conditions often have little fertility; there is often a shortage of humus, and, sometimes, well-developed hard pans. A change of slope at a retreating plateau edge or a scarp face may break down the infertile layers, and, with soil movements on the slope, areas lower down may have mixed soils, and possibly receive water from a concentration of drainage. Hence poor grassland can give way to dry seasonal forest vegetation on slopes in the same climatic region. The occurrence of different types of parent rock may also cause variations in the

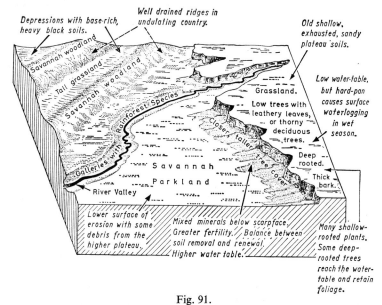

Fig. 91.

A diagrammatic representation of the variations in landforms, soils, height of water-table, and consequently, in forms of vegetation, which may occur in a broad area of upland with the same overall tropical, *Aw*, climatic conditions and a summer rainfall of some 700-1 400 mm.

composition of the grassland-with-trees vegetation: basaltic layers may break down to fertile intrazonal soils for instance. Variations in mineral content may also be reflected in the actual members present in a particular type of vegetation, and in the shape, size, or texture of the plant organs.

The Effects of Fires

The relative importance of climatic, edaphic, and human influences, including the effects of fire, on the nature of these tropical grasslands-with-trees is often very difficult to assess. Despite the obvious effects of climates, soils, relief, and drainage, described above, there is much evidence that fire and grazing have great significance on the composition of the vegetation, and the maintenance of grasslands, over large areas of savannah. In some parts of the African grasslands deliberate protection from fire and browsing animals has brought about a rapid increase in the proportion of woody plants. Where fires sweep over the savannahs fairly frequently—some are burnt annually to help the young grass and other herbs develop in the following season—it is not easy for bushes or trees to become established. Most of the savannah trees with thick bark are fire resistant once they are well established; it is possible that they and the herbaceous plants thrive here, rather than a more general forest vegetation, because of their ability to survive fire. Natural conditions so often seem to support tree cover where grass is now dominant, that it may be fire that has brought about the present balance in those regions.

Vegetation Classification and Ecological Studies

We have considered together, under the heading of "tropical grassland-with-trees", huge areas of vegetation in different parts of "savannah" grasslands and woodlands. This is a study of vegetation and not of plant geography; but, even so, some may query the desirability of making such a broad grouping of vegetation. Nevertheless, a student of geography in his preliminary studies must be able to ascertain whether a region is likely to bear mainly tundra or steppe, close rainforest, or types of xerophytic plants. At the same time it is essential for him to realise that most general regions include a variety of vegetation types and many different and *changing* plant associations; and that really satisfactory studies of the inter-dependence of climate, soils, and vegetation can only be carried out on the spot by trained ecologists. Even such a brief survey of the Tropical Savannahs cannot fail to emphasise these facts.

Tropical Thorn-bush and Semi-Arid Scrub

In tropical and near-tropical regions with prolonged droughts and low rainfall, and on coarse, readily permeable, soils, the clumps of grasses occur only sparsely, or may even be absent. Low thorn trees or thorn-bush with other xeromorphic shrubs and herbs may take over, and there are frequent bare earth patches between. In Africa, such country exists poleward of the grassy savannahs, though there tends to be a shading of one type into another. Elsewhere, with varying soil conditions, dry grasslands and semi-arid vegetation may intermingle. One of the major areas of thorn-bush and scrub country, known as "Caatinga", occurs on the dry north-eastern "shoulder" of Brazil.

ARID/SEMI ARID REGIONS: VARIATIONS IN VEGETATION.

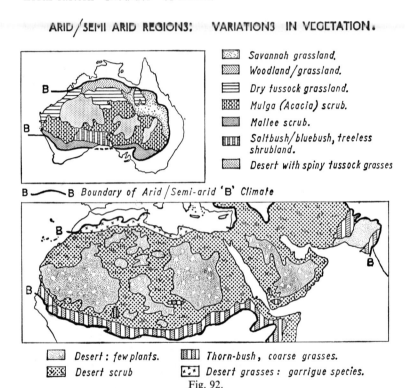

☒ *Savannah grassland.*

▨ *Woodland/grassland.*

☰ *Dry tussock grassland.*

▦ *Mulga (Acacia) scrub.*

■ *Mallee scrub.*

⊞ *Saltbush/bluebush, treeless shrubland.*

▦ *Desert with spiny tussock grasses*

B ——— B *Boundary of Arid/Semi-arid 'B' Climate*

▧ *Desert : few plants.*   ▦ *Thorn-bush, coarse grasses.*

▨ *Desert scrub*   ⊡ *Desert grasses : garrigue species.*

Fig. 92.

The distribution of vegetation within two of the *B* (arid and semi-arid) regions shown in Fig. 53, shows once again that many factors affect plant-life other than simple climatic controls. The merging of one form of vegetation with another can be seen in North Africa, where garrigue species occur, and to the south of the Sahara where thorn-bush and coarse grassland merge into the various savannahs. In Australia, thorn-bush, as such, is absent.

The dominant thorn vegetation is deciduous, losing its leaves as the drought sets in, and has many xerophilous features: deep, branched roots seek and compete for water, trunks and stems tend to be woody, and many stems are photosynthetic. Some evergreen species occur, and have the advantage that they need not wait for leaf-growth before photosynthesis can start in the short, wet season. Some trees, like the baobabs, or bottle trees, store water in swollen trunks, and other plants are capable of retaining water in their roots. There are usually succulents like the spurges and cacti, which are often very large; and beneath the soil geophytic herbs await the rainy season to develop, flower, and fruit.

Between the thicker thorn-bush cover and the true desert there is generally a transition through semi-desert with scrub, in which the plants are more widely spread, and where the proportion of succulents is higher. In some regions deep-rooted thorny acacias still occur, though of lower average height; they are particularly dominant on permeable soils where the infrequent rainfall soaks in deeply. The more shallow-rooted species compete most success-fully on less absorbent surfaces, where they can quickly use the water before it evaporates. Many, with organs swollen to store water, are curiously shaped, and without normal stem and leaf forms, though some, like the yuccas, have large leaves; in others the leaves are leathery.

Australia, without dominant thorny vegetation of this type, has many different species; in fact, the plant species in semi-arid scrub country vary from continent to continent; some are typical of both sub-tropical and temperate dry regions, like the creosote bush and bur-sages of North America.

Vegetation of the Hot Deserts

The quantity of dormant vegetation in hot deserts is often sur-prising. Showers of rain, infrequent though they are, may cause seeds, some of which may have lain dormant for years, to germin-ate and develop: the annuals rapidly bloom during their short life cycle, and hidden perennial geophytes may spring up and flower. These, however, are only one type of desert plant; they spend most of their life in the dormant state, as seeds protected by impervious coats, or bulbs protected by thick scale leaves. Other plants live where their deep roots may reach a relatively high water-table, and thus are found where water is held beneath the gravelly beds of wadis or depressions, or where ground-water seeps through.

The perennial rooted plants have small, thick, waxy leaves, or else thorns, and have a low, often bare and spiny appearance. But beneath the ground their roots penetrate perhaps to 10-15 m, and spread extensively to tap the water-table. Lines of low thorn bushes or deep-rooted tamarisks may indicate the general lie of underground water. In salty depressions, however, only tiny halophytic shrubs may be able to survive.

Other perennial plants depending largely on rainfall are the succulents, which in the short moist period store water in leaves and stems. Some of these spread a wide network of surface roots to absorb dew and occasional rain, and are otherwise adapted by fibrous tissues, thickened epidermis, waxy surfaces, and protected stomata to minimise the loss of water.

In some parts of an otherwise desert environment, surface and near-surface water may be plentiful: perhaps where artesian water emerges in springs or pools, or where a river from some distant source passes through the arid countryside. Here date palms may grow, and shrubs and coarse grasses provide grazing. But such well-watered regions are not likely to be left unoccupied, so that much of the vegetation in these favoured places has usually suffered modification, or else has been introduced by man.

Perennial irrigation transformed large areas of the Indus plains from desert to farmland. But even irrigated land can deteriorate. Excess water and percolation from canal "tails" can cause waterlogging (*above*) where the drainage is inadequate. High ground-water also allows salts to be concentrated by evaporation at the surface, making it salty and infertile (*below*). (*V. C. Robertson.*)

Grassland-with-trees: contrasts in plant forms, associations, and seasonal appearance
Above: The deciduous nature of the thickets, the low, dry grasses, and the gaunt baobab, emphasise the winter aspect of vegetation on infertile soils in the outer tropics of southern Africa. (*Paul Popper Ltd.*)

Below: Savannah grasses with flat-topped acacia in full leaf during a wet period in southern Kenya: maribou storks occupy the tree in the foreground. (*D. C. Money*)

CHAPTER XIII

TYPES OF VEGETATION (II): EXTRA-TROPICAL

Sclerophyllous Vegetation of the Warm Temperate Western Regions

The word "sclerophyll" is used to describe a plant which is able to survive dry conditions by means of the hard, leathery, thickened cuticles of its leaves. The leaves are usually small, and enable the plant to transpire and make carbohydrates in moist periods, but have various adaptations to allow them to survive long droughts: in particular the thick cuticle is a mechanical source of strength and prevents wilted cells from collapsing.

We have seen that one of the principal climatic characteristics of the so-called "Mediterranean Lands" is the alternation of a warm, moist winter season with a hot, dry summer. The air humidity varies greatly with the seasonal change, and the rate of evaporation is usually high in summer. As the precipitation is greatest during the cooler parts of the year, plants are able to make good use of the winter moisture, but need to resist long periods of drought; so that sclerophyllous formations occupy large areas around the Mediterranean Sea and in other warm temperate Western regions.

Woodland and the Effects of Clearance

In the vicinity of the Mediterranean itself man and his animals have been responsible for removing or disturbing much of the original vegetation. It is probable that a great deal of the land was once covered with mixed broad-leaved and coniferous forest; for, even with the lengthy period of annual drought, the present climate allows forest trees to re-establish themselves in specially protected areas amid an otherwise scrubby vegetation. Though to-day they are mainly scattered, forest trees are found to be widespread throughout the Mediterranean area. Where circumstances have protected stretches of land from common use, thick woodland still exists. In southern Italy there are still areas which have been maintained for centuries as hunting reserves. Here there are close woodlands with numerous evergreen oaks and well developed shrubs; though the dominant species of shrub seems to vary considerably with soils and location. Stands of pine and scattered pine trees are common: the maritime pines flourish below 450 m in the western parts of the basin, in southern France and Italy: the

Aleppo pines are common in the north-eastern parts of the Mediterranean; and umbrella pines occur up to some 900 m, among the hillside shrubs.   Like the evergreen oaks they have long, efficient rooting systems.

In those parts which have suffered clearance and then grazing by goats or sheep, but are not under present cultivation, former woodland has been replaced by a mixed deciduous and evergreen scrub, with shrubby herbs and a great many geophytes.   The scattered trees are mostly fairly short, sclerophyllous, and gnarled in

SCLEROPHYLLOUS VEGETATION OF THE 'MEDITERRANEAN' LANDS

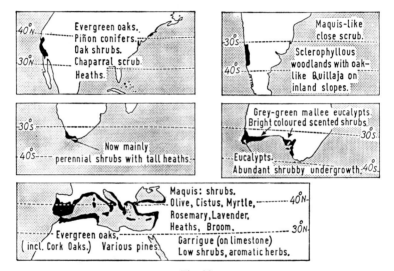

Fig. 93.

appearance: they include the thick-barked cork oaks and olives, trees whose real limits correspond closely to those of the Mediterranean climatic region.

Sclerophyllous Scrub Formations

Limestones occur widely in the lands about the Mediterranean and cause even greater surface aridity.   On much of the limestone a poor, low scrub known as *garrigue* occurs: in its most favourable state it includes a dense mass of shrubs such as lavender, thyme, myrtle, and rosemary, whose protective oils are sweet-scented; and many heaths are common.   Siliceous soils tend to bear the taller, denser *maquis* or *macchia*, containing most of the same evergreen, drought-resisting shrubs, with carobs and olives, cistus and heaths, gorse and broom.

In spring, when the ground is moist, the many flowers and fresh greenness of the vegetation give these lands a deceptively fertile and pleasant appearance: besides the shrubs and heaths, the numerous bulbs and tubers, cyclamen, tulips, and irises, are in flower. But, as the prolonged summer drought allows the water-table to fall, the greenness fades, and emphasises the bareness of many of the hillsides and the poverty of soils deficient in humus and prone to erosion. The very redness of the widespread terra rossa soils tells of a lack of humus. Deep-rooted vines thrive well in these lands of sunshine and periodic drought; the varieties producing currants have become especially important economically in the central Mediterranean. But a number of plants now regarded as "typically Mediterranean" have been introduced; the best known being the citrus trees.

Few succulents occur among the natural vegetation, except on the desert margins; though many have been introduced, and cactus hedges can be seen in many parts of the Mediterranean lands. In the natural vegetation grasses are also few, and tend to grow in wiry clumps; but again, sown grasses and cultivated grasses occupy surprisingly large areas.

Other "Mediterranean" Regions

Trees of different genera occur in those other parts of the world with a similar type of climate, though the actual form of vegetation tends to be similar: the Californian *chaparral*, for instance, resembles the thick shrubby Mediterranean maquis, but contains many species which are fire-resistant. In the moister parts of California grow the great coniferous red-woods, and there are evergreen oaks. These latter are restricted to the northern hemisphere, but Chile has a somewhat similar tree to the oak, although of a different genus—Quillaja—of common occurrence among its close-growing shrubs.

The Australian sclerophyllous scrub country has many species of eucalypts developed in mallee form. In parts these form a grey-green almost impenetrable scrub, difficult to clear. Here, too, are numerous aromatic shrubs found only in Australia. The sclero-phyllous vegetation of south-western Australia varies greatly between one part of the region and another. The better watered· country to the south-west has great forests of eucalypts, jarrah, and karri, though the light penetrates such close stands sufficiently for a rich undergrowth of hard-leafed shrubs. Further inland the jarrahs are smaller, but grow well amid an abundance of shrubs on the extensive level areas with old lateric horizons; and, as we have seen, on mixed soils beneath retreating scarps, or over adjoining sandstones, there may be an abrupt transition to heath-like formations or different sclerophyllous shrubs, with arboreal species of Banksia. It is worth noting the successful introduction of eucalypts to many other Mediterranean lands. In the south-west of South Africa yet another type of sclerophyllous scrub exists, with families and species peculiar to the region, but with few annual plants.

Warm Temperate Rainforests and their Great Variety

It is impossible to label as truly characteristic the types of vegetation which occur within the limits of what can be described as "warm temperate" or "sub-tropical" regions with a well-distributed, and often high annual rainfall (or even to define satisfactory limits to the regions). Broad-leaved evergreens occur, but so do broad-leaved deciduous trees, and in many places conifers are dominant, often for purely edaphic reasons or because of drainage conditions. The forests are often "mixed"; partly in the sense of a patchwork made up of broad-leaved associations and separate coniferous associations, and partly because stands of broad-leaved evergreens may alternate with broad-leaved deciduous trees. Again, as some of these forests verge on those of the tropical wet lands they have certain of the characteristics of the low latitude forests.

As already stated, there is value in building up a simplified picture of the general distribution pattern of vegetation on a world-wide basis provided that one appreciates the limitations of regional classifications. Here there is variety indeed, and generalisations must abound. With these reservations in mind, and remembering that in extra-tropical regions the pattern of vegetation has been affected by the great changes wrought by glaciations and recolonisations of glacially-affected soils, we will consider the various types of warm-temperate rainforests separately from the other temperate deciduous forests, and under a single heading.

These are regions of plentiful rainfall—receiving some 1 200–3 000 mm, distributed through the year (p. 125). Various characteristics of the different forms of vegetation point to their location between the tropical rainforests and the cool-temperate deciduous forests. Towards the tropics there tend to be numerous epiphytes and lianes, on and among the trees, and palms are fairly common:

the sub-tropical forests of eastern Brazil and parts of Florida merge into vegetation hardly distinguishable from that of low latitude rainforests. Poleward, however, the deciduous characteristics become more pronounced; yet, underlining the variety of associations found in this broad vegetation region, are the stands of

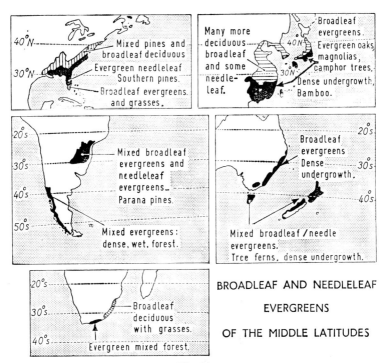

Fig. 94.
The range of latitude is great, and the variations in climate and soils are many; so that it is not surprising that there are many different plant associations, with dominant trees of different genera, as between eastern Australia and southern Japan. In the northern hemisphere, the forests of the poleward parts of these regions also contain many deciduous trees. The map includes the continuation of the evergreen forests into the cool-temperate lands of southern Chile.

coniferous pines, cedars, and cypresses which occur extensively in the south-eastern parts of the U.S.A., though usually on immature or sandy soils.

In general, the forests have many evergreen trees; though the presence of deciduous species give them a different summer and winter appearance. The broad-leaved woodlands do not have the overall luxuriance of tropical rainforests: their leaves tend to be smaller and thinner, and their canopy less complete; consequently, many smaller trees and shrubs occupy the lower levels. Climbers often festoon the trees and shrubs of the undergrowth, and beneath these are numerous herbs, ferns, and mosses.

Regional Variations

In the temperate rainforests of China, close stands of bamboos add to the density of the undergrowth, and there is the same wide variety of trees; conifers occur, even among the broad-leaved evergreens of central China. This is also true of Japan, where evergreen oaks, camphor trees, and magnolias stand among the close lower growth of smaller trees and shrubs, and are often draped about with woody climbers.

In south-eastern U.S.A., sweet chestnuts and evergreen oaks, magnolias, dense shrubby undergrowth, and numerous climbers are again characteristic, and the epiphytic "southern moss" festoons tree branches, giving the woods a remarkable appearance. On hillsides between 550-750 m, sweet chestnuts and beech occur together. The swamps of the near-coastal parts of the south and the south-east have their own dominants, which include the bald-cypress and pines; almost certainly part of the late stages of hydroseres. The high water-table prevents further invasion by the climatic climax dominants of the broad-leaved trees, so that this is really a sub-climax vegetation. Many other areas of pine forest exist in the south-east, with species like the loblolly, pitch, and slash pines peculiar to the region: both sandy areas and swamplands bear various species of conifer.

In south-eastern mainland Australia, huge tree-ferns grow among the dense lower layers of the warm temperate rainforest, whose dominants are tall eucalypts: in south-west Tasmania, the North Island of New Zealand, and the western coastlands of the South Island, they are even more plentiful, and the lower shrubs and climbers particularly dense. The New Zealand forests include the much exploited kauri, and more common native softwoods—the rimu, kahikatea, and totara.

The southern parts of the Brazilian Highlands have an evergreen mixed forest, though altitude modifies its form. Its main dominant is an araucaria pine, but many broad-leaved evergreen trees and shrubs are associated with it. The coastal forests and those of the lower, southern parts of the plateau are the most luxuriant. South of the "Mediterranean" parts of Middle Chile the evergreen forests are also dense and luxuriant, with araucaria pines, evergreen beech, larch, and Chilean cedar. In South Africa the occurrence of temperate rainforests is now restricted to a coastal area in the south-east, about a hundred kilometres long. These also contain both broad-leaved and coniferous evergreens, shrubs, ferns, climbers, and epiphytes.

Vegetation of the Middle Latitude Arid and Semi-Arid Lands

It is again difficult to make valid generalisations about the vegetation of these dry regions of the middle latitudes, or to define their limits accurately. Most of them lie far into the interior of the continents and at varying altitudes, like the plateaux of inner Asia and the intermontane plateaux and basins of western North America; though the semi-arid lands of Argentina, southern Australia, and South Africa, are rather differently situated. Equally, it is difficult to determine whether the present vegetation is a climatic climax type, or whether long periods of interference by man, as has undoubtedly occurred in central Asia and in dry lands adjacent to the Rockies, has been responsible for the present arid associations.

In North American semi-arid lands (Fig. 55) there is a characteristic vegetation of low, drab-coloured shrubs, of which the sagebrush is characteristic. In drier locations these give way to patches of wiry grass and creosote bush, woody stemmed, deep-rooted shrubs, and to others with widespreading root systems, narrow leathery leaves, and a bare, spiky appearance. There may be cacti, euphorbia, and other succulents; while in valleys the very deep-rooted acacias and mesquite bushes are able to make use of the relatively higher water-table.

The distribution of semi-arid associations in the U.S.A. varies not only with the rainfall and soils, but also with the degree of interference by man. Man's actions, for instance, seem to have allowed the degraded chaparral of the west, with bush oaks and scattered shrubs, or else sagebrush, to invade areas of overgrazed, dry prairie grassland.

In central Asia (Fig. 55) there are vast stretches of semi-arid deserts which bear a much greater covering of grasses than do lands with a similar degree of aridity in North America; most are tussock grasses, and in really dry regions they occur in widely spaced clumps. There are also shrubs resembling the sage-brush. But in slightly moister locations, poplars, willows, elms, and ash manage to survive the extremes of cold and heat; as in southern parts of central Asia, where, in the valleys of rivers fed by far distant snow-fields, such trees grow amid close grassy swards, forming green oases in an arid landscape. But some parts of central Asia have so little precipitation, and such extremes of cold and heat, that they are almost devoid of vegetation, and there remains a barren rock-strewn country with occasional sand-filled basins. Both in central Asia and North America salt flats occur in inland drainage areas, supporting occasional halophytic plants. Besides salt flats, there may also be areas with highly saline soils. Such soils, accumulating salt from oceanic sources, are widespread in southern Australia, for instance, where they support quite a close vegetation of salt-bush—a fact which has enabled sheep-rearing to extend into country with a remarkably low precipitation. Parts of central and western Australia are very arid, but support the sharp, tussocky species of Triodia grass, sometimes called "spinifex", xeromorphic shrubs, and occasional, low, deep-rooted acacias: there are thousands of square miles of what is sometimes referred to as "temperate desert" with acacia or mallee eucalypt scrub (though "temperate" is scarcely an appropriate description of the summer temperatures experienced in Australia's extra-tropical, arid and semi-arid lands).

Central and south-eastern Argentina has much semi-arid country, bearing a dry, tussock grassland and numerous thorny, or small-leaved, deciduous, shrubs. A semi-desert formation also borders the true desert of the Namib in south-west Africa; with xerophytic shrubs and many succulents. The Karroo plateau is also very dry and supports mainly shrubby plants.

Temperate Deciduous Forests

Before the period of man's intensive land-use, most, though not all, of the lowland parts of western Europe, north of the Mediterranean regions and south of the coniferous forests of Scandinavia and Russia, were covered with a natural vegetation in which broad-leaved deciduous trees were dominant. However, a belt of mixed coniferous-deciduous forest stretched across the North European Plain; and elsewhere the actual nature and distribution of the various types of woodland was complex. Minor climatic variations, differences of altitude and slope, parent rocks, drainage conditions, and soils would in any case have affected the character of vegetation locally; but an added variety has resulted from the series of climatic changes which caused ice-sheets to advance and retreat over the landscape. The nature of the deciduous forest associations varies with soils derived from different types of rocks, and also with their moisture content. Re-colonisation by stages resulted in many different woodland associations, and glacial soils added greatly to the variety of parent materials. In general, however, mature soils developed beneath such forests are podsolic, and rich with organic matter derived mainly from the annual leaf-fall. The sandy or immature soils which are more heavily leached tend to support conifers rather than deciduous hardwoods. Throughout western Europe, for one or more of these reasons, stretches of deciduous forest may lie adjacent to stands of conifers.

The Effects of Man's Interference

The spread of human settlement added immensely to the complexity of the vegetation pattern; and, as Europe became closely settled, the vegetation resulting from man's interference with the existing associations came to contain many introduced plants, and to include various stages of new successions. Little of the climax forest remains, and the use of pasture grasses and cereal grasses have so changed the landscapes as to give the impression that the climatic climax vegetation of many regions is grassland with wooded country, intermingled. The present grassland associations are mostly quite artificial, and when deprived of the grazing and treading of man's animals they usually revert to a scrubland of thorns, brambles, and briars, and eventually to secondary woodland. In one way or another, therefore, the climatic climax of deciduous vegetation (oaks, ash, birch, and elm in the northern lands, other forms of oaks, chestnut, sycamore, ash, elm, and beech in the southern) has been profoundly affected by man's activities.

Competition from Conifers

The dominants and associations vary with parent-material, altitude, soils, and drainage. The conifers are unable to compete with the broad-leaved trees on the majority of the lowlands, but tend to establish themselves on soils developed on sandy outcrops, or on areas of outwash sands and gravels. Coniferous competition is, of course, more successful at greater altitude and where the climate is more extreme. The mixed forests with intermittent areas of coniferous and broad-leaved deciduous trees are, therefore, particularly common in the northern and north-eastern parts of Europe and European Russia, where coniferous stretches occur within deciduous forest, and where deciduous communities are found within the boreal forests, whose main dominants are conifers (p. 241).

Regional Distribution

In North America, also, the deciduous forests have suffered from man's interference; though there are more extensive areas of relatively undisturbed woodland. Here, too, a zone of mixed forest lies between the summer deciduous forest formation and the more or less unbroken boreal forests. Oaks and hickory occur widely in the American deciduous woodlands: beech and maple are dominants of the north-east, and are joined by oaks, chestnut, the tulip tree, and hemlock further south; associated with them are a large number of smaller trees, shrubs, and herbs. Bordering the

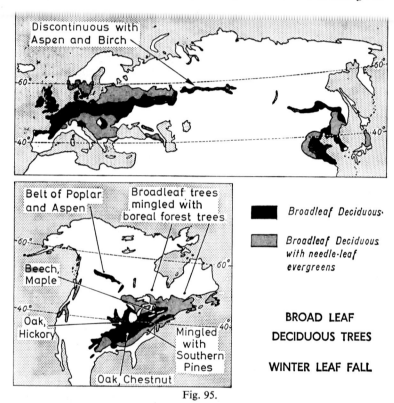

Fig. 95.

deep south, chestnut and oaks dominate; but inland, oaks and hickory are more suited to the drier conditions.

The deciduous forests of lowland Manchuria, north-eastern China, and western Korea also contain oaks, beech, ash, and birch. In Japan, and on parts of the mainland, they are co-dominant with conifers, and areas of coniferous forest mingle with them, or are separated by altitude zoning. In the southern hemisphere, the extensive forests of the south-western slopes and southern coastlands of New Zealand's South Island are of broad-leaved ever-greens—the southern beech (*Nothofagus* spp.). The denseness of these forests is increased by the presence of epiphytes and climbers. In southern Chile, there are again thick evergreen forests; there are also some continuous deciduous woodlands, though these are found only in sheltered valleys, and on the drier Patagonian slopes in the east.

Responses to Seasonal Variations

Before considering some of the chief associations, it is as well to examine the main characteristics of the plants in these deciduous forests, and the controlling factors. During the annual cold period, which may be up to six months in each year, the soil temperatures can fall low enough to hinder the absorption of water by the roots. When this happens, the broad leaves, through which free transpiration takes place, are shed; so avoiding the loss of water which cannot be replaced. Thus, forests with deciduous plants have quite a different appearance in summer and winter. In spring the leaves form quickly, so that growth may be renewed; the spring flowering enables fruit to develop gradually during the warm months.

Typical Associations

Various dominant deciduous trees form a main level, with young trees and tall shrubs at irregular heights beneath. The deciduous trees often grow close together; hence their many leaves may keep much light from the lower parts, thus reducing the numbers of woodland plants and affecting the composition of the undergrowth. Well spaced trees tend to promote a denser undergrowth; but many low perennial herbs and geophytes bloom early, fruit, and die down again before the leaf cover of the taller trees is fully developed. The degree of shade cast by various species is also important in determining which plants are associated with them. Some plants are much more shade-tolerant than others; for example, we find the tolerant yews regenerating themselves in the shade of beech, whereas the ash will not do so. On the other hand the ash can survive in competition with oaks which cast a dense shade, but not as dense as that of beeches. The early bud-ding of the beech also makes it difficult for a rich flora to develop beneath; whereas the oak, coming late into leaf, allows ground vegetation to become established, and bulbs to flower freely in spring; thus bluebells and wood anemones form a carpet of flowers in open oak woodland in early spring.

Open oakwoods are found scattered widely through western and central Europe: associated with them are ash, on drier soils, and birch and hazel on moister ones. Elms, cherries, alders, and poplars are others found in association, though their present occurrence in a particular location may well be due to man's conscious or unconscious interference in the past. Hazels, hawthorn, crab-apple, and holly are among the plants growing at lower levels, and the variety of shrubs and herbs is great; in open woodlands there may be plenty of coarse grasses. Climbers like honeysuckle and ivy are common, and parasitic plants like mistletoe fairly frequent. Beneath, may be various forms of fungi which do not need the light.

Beech forests tend to occur where the soil is rich in lime, where there is plenty of moisture in the growing season, and where temperatures are high enough to allow the fairly rapid decomposition of the thick carpet of fallen leaves. They flourish, for example, on the English chalk and soft oolitic scarplands; also in many parts of the Carpathians; but they do not tolerate wet soils. Yews may occur as a secondary layer, when the ground vegetation is very sparse indeed. Wood sorrel, dog's mercury, and wood barley-grass are among the species which occur in the thin lower level. But in the deep shade of the beech there may only be saprophytes, like the bird's nest orchid, and various fungi. The ash is the chief competitor, and probably gained a hold in many areas of northern Europe after the Ice Age, due to its ability to migrate more rapidly than the beech, which cannot disperse its seeds so efficiently. Oaks tend to disappear on calcareous soils, so that the ash, which is often co-dominant with oak on less limy soils, becomes the main dominant; ash forests were once widespread over areas which are now treeless limestone plateaux.

Forests of sweet chestnut are common in parts of southern and eastern Europe; they have been introduced into other parts of Europe, but mostly as single trees or in small woods.

Plants in the Open Downlands

We are concerned mainly with the forest associations, but the open chalk downlands, with their scattered trees and shrubs, and the almost treeless stretches of upland limestone form much of the countryside of northern Europe, and have their typical plant associations; though it is probable that they may have been more closely wooded in the past. Hawthorn, dogwood, and box are now common among the low trees and shrubs found on chalk, and roses—the dog rose and sweetbriar—abound on calcareous soils. Tiny yellow vetch, scabious, rock-rose, milkwort, and plantains are among the many plants which flourish amidst the short fine turf on open country with chalk-rich soils. But again, there are many variations in soil conditions within broad regions of calcareous rocks: in the wetter locations, leaching may be sufficient to lower the basic (alkaline) content of the upper soil; or clay-with-flints may provide a covering which supports plants less typical of the limestone countryside.

Sub-Climax Grasslands and Pasture Grasses

Finally, it bears repeating that, though to-day grasslands form a large part of the landscape within the broad areas of natural deciduous forest, especially in north-west Europe, they are usually maintained at a sub-climax stage by pasturing and mowing. Such cropping tends to form a compact turf; for the growth of the axillary buds and shoots, and of the fibrous roots, are thus encouraged. We have seen that the basic chalks and limestones often support grass, which is maintained against the vegetation of shrubs by being much grazed and manured by grazing animals. The dominant sheep's fescue is most common, and like other grasses on calcareous soils, is to some extent drought resistant.

The more nearly neutral soils carry much permanent pasture dominated by perennial rye grass, with wild white clover; cocksfoot, meadow foxtail, and rough stalked meadow grass are also common pasture grasses on such soils.

Acidic soils of a sandy nature may bear the fescues if well drained, and species of Agrostis where not. Where there is poor drainage and siliceous soils mat grass may be dominant, useful as hill pastures for rough grazing. On really wet uplands there may be only the purple moor grass with bog plants; but we will consider the vegetation of these damp uplands separately.

Heaths, Marsh, and Shore Vegetation of Cool Temperate Lands

Heaths and Upland Bog Formation

In north-western Europe, heaths and associated plants occur especially on acidic soils. Heaths occupy dry, loose soils over sands and gravels in lowland areas, where ling is particularly dominant. They also tend to form the vegetation on high moorlands where rocks, like granite, break down to a thin acidic soil, and where moist conditions produce damp peaty soils. There is usually a dense cover of ling, and heaths like "bell heather", with bilberries (wortle-berries) and cranberries, and thin cotton grass between, mingled on wet peaty moors with sphagnum moss (bog moss). Sometimes there are occasional taller shrubs, usually evergreens; junipers and gorse are typical. On drier areas, or slopes with better drainage, mat grass and purple moor grass may form a cover of close tussocks. The really wet undulating uplands above about 250 m tend to be covered with a "blanket bog" formation, with much bog moss and cotton grass and perhaps with rushes in water spill channels.

Many of Europe's heath-covered uplands were once forested; but the re-invasion by forest has been prevented by grazing and burning. In some neglected moors, where the soil has not deteriorated in the meantime, the heather and grass heath is soon rapidly overcome by bracken, and this first stage of a seral development is followed by shrub and forest colonisation. Heathlands associated with coniferous woodland in lower country may, on the other hand, be the result of more recent deforestation.

These types of vegetation exist under fairly extreme conditions. During dry spells in summer, heath soils may become very deficient in moisture, and species of plants flourish which are both tolerant of the deficiency in minerals and adapted, to some extent, to reduce transpiration and, structurally, to resist wilting. The leaves of the ling, crowberry, and bell heaths are rolled, with their lower surfaces reduced in area and with few, sunken, stomata; the cuticles are thick. These plants dominate areas where the upper parts of the soil are poor in nutrients: but the rapidity with which other plants take over is emphasised when fertilisers are added, or even where the droppings of sheep or rabbits are plentiful, and the heath cropped by sheep, or cut back. Grasses or grass-heath take over from the ling and bell heaths, and improved sown pastures can be established very quickly.

Lowland Bogs and Moors

The bog mosses, cushiony and absorptive, mentioned above as wet-moorland plants, may be found growing prolifically in other cool, badly drained areas with acidic peaty soils, and accompanied by cotton grass and various sedges. Many lowland moors are stages in a succession which has followed the drainage, or in-filling, of bog-land; heaths have taken over from the mosses, and may, perhaps, already be associated with scrubby bushes, silver birches, or conifers.

Other damp areas may not have notably acidic soils; for instance, where water comes from the drainage of limestone areas. Marshes with water-lilies, reeds, sedges, and various grasses may give way to scrub and damp elder woodland, along the lines of the hydrosere described on p. 200.

Shore Vegetation

Any detailed description of the vegetation of seas is beyond the scope of this book; but we may briefly notice that various forms of vegetation are to be found in zones roughly parallel with the shore, extending from the limits of photosynthesis beneath sea-level to the shingle or sandy shores, where colonisation by higher plants may occur and successions develop.

The great majority of marine plant life is made up of different types of algae, whose nutrients come from the sea-water, and which are attached to rocks and boulders beneath and just above water-level. The nature of the algae depends on such influences as light intensity, temperature, pressure, salinity, water movements (tides and currents) and, of course, competition. In temperate waters many species exhibit a noticeable change in form from summer to winter conditions.

It is possible to observe girdles of different green and red algae, and large kelps, extending from beneath tide-level to where they are exposed by particularly low tides. Above these are the more familiar types of brown algae, more common on the parts of the shore regularly covered and uncovered by the sea; and many of the forms, such as bladder wrack, are surprisingly large; here, too, eel-grasses may be found attached to the sides of rocks. Above this, again, where the shore receives only spray, or exceptionally high tides, the rocks may be covered with black lichens. Shingle banks bear plants with flat rosettes and swollen foliage, and with long, taproots.

Higher, dry, sandy areas, salty from spray or occasional sea-water, support halophytic plants like sea thrift. Coarse grasses, such as marram grass, inhabit dry dunes: these are often dune formers, holding sand and binding it. Marram grass, for instance, with long rhizomes and an abundant root system, reaches vertically and horizontally through the sands. If covered, fresh roots develop from higher levels of its stiff stems. The leaves are deeply corrugated, and open out fully only in moist atmospheric conditions. It is excellent for binding sands. Dunes held in this way by grassy vegetation may be fixed by other colonists, such as mosses or finer grasses: eventually shrubs and forest may be able to form part of a climax vegetation.

Temperate Grasslands

The clearance of forests in moist locations may lead to the temporary dominance of grasses, mostly in the form of close, broadleaved turf, though many other grasses may be present. As we have seen, meadows developed by clearance, mowing, pasturing, and, perhaps, improving, tend to revert to scrub and woodland when abandoned. There are, however, huge areas of natural grassland in the temperate zones, lying chiefly where the annual rainfall is some 250-750 mm, and situated mainly in the continental interiors. These include the North American prairies, the Russian steppes, and grasslands of somewhat different character in regions with less cold winters—the pampas of Argentina and Uruguay, the South African veld, and in southern Australia. Less extensive areas of the former type include the Hungarian and Manchurian plains. Tussock grassland in the eastern districts of the South Islands of New Zealand are in a milder climatic region, though their origin, as with some of the others, is certainly not entirely due to climatic influence. A great deal of the tussock grassland of the eastern hill country and plains in the South Island of New Zealand has taken over from woodland, which was disturbed, and probably fired, by early Moriori or Maori peoples; in other parts of the country much of the forest, cleared from hill country during the last hundred years, has degenerated to poor shrubland with coarse grasses.

Types of Grassland and Associated Plants

In all these regions grasses dominate; but many extend continuously through a wide range of latitude, and because of the differences in annual precipitation, winter temperatures, and soil structure, as well as interference by man, there are, understandably, a very wide range of genera, species, and associations within these grasslands. There are normally a number of perennial species with shallow roots which form a matted turf, except in really dry areas where bunch grass prevails. As the grass leaves die and dry out they remain attached to the stem, and with the root systems help to create a mat of fibres; this enables water to be held near the surface and also helps to prevent the germination of tree seeds. Their shallow root systems are able to maintain grasses where tree seedlings cannot survive. A great number of other plants, especially the numerous broad-leaved herbs, do thrive in the grasslands, however: daisies, poppies, mallow, and various crucifers, for example; with mosses in damp places, and small cacti in very dry ones. In

The effects of clearance and colonisation contrast with long-established climax vegetation of a major rainforest formation. *Above:* Fencing on a New Zealand hillside divides a sub-climax shrub vegetation from cleared, dangerously overgrazed land. The former has replaced mature forest cleared a century ago. (*D. C. Money*) *Below:* Tropical rainforest in Guyana which has been little disturbed. Tall trees stand above a crown cover so close that it masks the relief features - - - - - -, which includes a considerable scarp -x-x-, and a drainage pattern with falls at F. (*Huntings Surveys Ltd.*)

Above: Dense woodlands of evergreen beech, with lichen covered trunks, clothe valleys and hillsides of the mild, wet temperate south-west of New Zealand. (*D. C. Money*)

Below: A prospect mine near Leonora in the semi-arid interior of Western Australia, amid bluebush, mulga scrub and exposed red earth. (*D. C. Money*)

the heart of the northern grasslands, low trees and shrubs may occur along watercourses; but the warmer parts of the South African veld and the southern Australian grasslands include

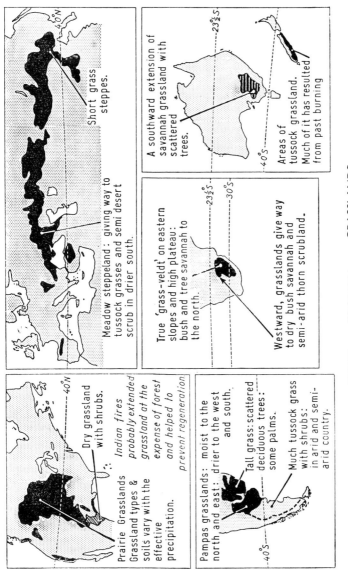

Short grass steppes.

Meadow steppeland: giving way to tussock grasses and semi desert scrub in drier south.

A southward extension of savannah grassland with scattered trees.

Areas of tussock grassland. Much of it has resulted from past burning.

True 'grass-veldt' on eastern slopes and high plateau: bush and tree savannah to the north.

Westward, grasslands give way to dry bush savannah and semi-arid thorn scrubland.

Dry grassland with shrubs.

Prairie Grasslands Grassland types & soils vary with the effective precipitation.

Indian fires probably extended grassland at the expense of forest and helped to prevent regeneration.

Pampas grasslands: moist to the north and east; drier to the west and south.

Tall grass: scattered deciduous trees: some palms.

Much tussock grass with shrubs: in arid and semi-arid country.

EXTRA — TROPICAL GRASSLANDS

Fig. 96.

scattered trees and patches of close shrubs; in this sense resembling the savannah grasslands.

Grassland/Forest Boundaries

Some boundaries between forest and steppe/prairie are quite clear-cut; but many of the grasslands intermingle with forest stretches in broad transition zones. Vegetation maps on a continental scale, such as Fig. 96, are necessary to show a general distribution, but are apt to be especially misleading in the border zones. The rolling countryside of mid-Uruguay has an extensive cover of rich grassland, but many of the moister valleys are well wooded: while there seems no reason, climatically, why the western parts of the Argentine pampas should not support close forest, and, indeed, trees of many species grow well when planted as wind-breaks or for decorative purposes on the tall grass pampas. We have already seen that much of New Zealand's tussock grassland may have taken over from forest. Caution is essential, therefore in treating the temperate grasslands as climatic climax vegetation; as it is when considering the causes of present tropical savannah distribution, which are not always what they seem.

Burning has long been a widespread practice by men wishing to ensure a plentiful regeneration of grass and other small herbs suitable for grazing. In marginal areas, with a rather delicate balance between grasses and shrub or forest forms, that balance may well have been tipped by mankind in favour of grassland associations, and maintained perhaps by grazing, or by the formation of a grass "mat", or the change in soil structure.

Rainfall, Soils, and Types of Prairie

The grasslands of the continental interiors receive rainfall during the summer months, and the northern ones have the advantage of snow melt-water, available after the resting period during the cold winters. The czernozem soils of North America and U.S.S.R., with their crumbly texture and richness of plant food, support a sward of tallish prairie grasses with many small herbs: trees near watercourses may include poplars. As rainfall amounts decrease further inland, shorter grasses are more common; eventually on the light brown soils with lime accumulations near the surface, xerophytic or halophytic plants appear among tussocks of drought-resisting species. In such regions of fairly slight and irregular rainfall grasses may remain dormant during drought periods, even though temperatures are high enough for growth.

Northern Coniferous Forests (Boreal Forests)

These forests, known also as "taiga", extend across huge areas of Eurasia, with northern limits about 50° N. in the east and 60° N. in the west, and across the Northern American continent, as far south as 45° N. in the east. Near their northern limits the trees are stunted and dispersed, so that forest gradually fades into, or is intermingled with, the tundra (p. 244). The climatic conditions are hard: winters are very cold, with little or no sunlight, and mean temperatures are usually below 6° C for six to nine months of the year. In the short summer, monthly averages are above 10° C, and the hours of daylight long. The precipitation varies with location, but is usually between 250-1 000 mm a year, though most of the boreal forest receives from 400-650 mm; mid-winter precipitation is mainly in the form of snow, of course.

Dominant Species and their Associations

In these conditions conifers are the main dominants; though at their southern limits they tend to grade into forests of broad-leaved deciduous trees, and in places with extremes of cold only small deciduous birch, larch, and aspen may be able to survive. The conifers are able to maintain themselves under the normal hard climatic conditions by virtue of their narrow, needle-like or scale-like, leaves, whose thick cuticles give strength in times of water deficiency; characteristics which enable them greatly to reduce transpiration and to retain their leaves during the winter, even when soil water is unavailable. The individual leaves usually last for a number of years, although the larches shed theirs in autumn. For this reason larches can exist with deciduous birch and aspen in colder locations than the evergreens. Generally, however, the boreal forest is an evergreen one, with the advantage that photosynthesis can take place whenever conditions allow. The trees are slow-growing, absorb few bases, and can thrive on soils which would not suit most broad-leafed trees: the latter are usually able to compete successfully only where soils are relatively rich in minerals, warm, and moist.

The conifers tend to be shallow rooting, and can flourish where the sub-soil remains frozen for long periods. They are softwooded, with thick, resinous bark and shortish springy branches, which help to shed snow; their overall, compact, conical shape also tends to prevent snow accumulation. They stand well against the wind, although, being shallow rooted, exceptionally strong winds are apt to uproot them. In the cones themselves the ovules are on the cone scales, and protected by the closing together of these scales, which, in favourable conditions, open out to free the seeds.

The forests usually have continuous softwood stands; although poor drainage may lead to stretches covered mainly with bog plants. The spruces, firs, and pines often have birch associated with them, though the composition varies from one region to another. The undergrowth in such forest is usually sparse, with relatively few plant species; for the evergreen canopy shades the ground through out the year, and beneath the trees a thick, slowly decaying carpet of resinous leaves makes it difficult for other seedlings to establish themselves. The trees have absorbed little mineral material, so that few bases are returned by the falling leaves, whose decay produces an acid "mor" or "raw humus", and favours podsol formation. The climate, of course, is a direct bar to the development of most other plants, and the frozen sub-soil is against the deeper rooted ones. Sometimes, however, small shrubs and berried herbs, or dwarf birch, form an undergrowth; and mosses and lichens are usually numerous. In the poorer coniferous forests, towards the limits of tree-growth, the mosses and lichens may form thick carpets amid the dominant trees, which are low, gnarled, and scattered; though even here drained soils may support clumps of stronger growth.

Felling for commercial purposes takes a great toll of these forests; although forest conservation, planning, and re-afforestation measures now help to treat the northern softwoods as a "crop". Where clearings are left, it is usually the birch and aspen, with wind-borne seeds, which first re-colonise the area. But, later, as the conifers, planted or invading, grow to mature trees, they tower above the deciduous invaders, shading them, and gradually ousting them from a dominant role in the community.

Regional Distribution

In north-western Europe the Scots pine and spruce are common forest trees, often the only dominants. Further east, passing into Asia, other species occur more frequently. In the very cold parts of central and eastern Siberia shallow rooted larches predominate, with pines only in dwarf form. On the eastern side of North America, between the boreal forests and the deciduous ones to the south, are various transitional types; in parts of these, the dominant pines, spruce, and hemlocks are associated with broad-leaved trees, with a mixed, though still fairly sparse, undergrowth. Throughout the North American boreal forests there are more species than are commonly found in such forests in Europe, though

the dominants vary: mainly spruce and firs on the southern
Laurentian shield, for example, but lodgepole pines and Alpine
firs in central Alaska. In the milder, humid climates of the north-
western Pacific coasts of America the dense coniferous forests
include huge trees like the Douglas fir and Redwoods, and the
undergrowth is often shrubby, with ferns growing plentifully. Their
presence, incidentally, shows how misleading, oversimplified, and
inaptly named, climatic and vegetation regions can be: many maps

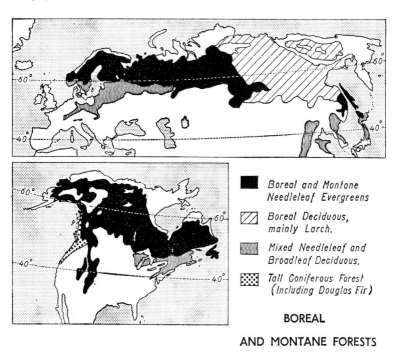

Boreal and Montane
Needleleaf Evergreens

Boreal Deciduous,
mainly Larch.

Mixed Needleleaf and
Broadleaf Deciduous.

Tall Coniferous Forest
(Including Douglas Fir)

BOREAL

AND MONTANE FORESTS

Fig. 97.

and classifications of climate and vegetation equate this part of North
America both with north-west Europe, and with western parts of
New Zealand's South Island. The differences are not so much of
climate as of availability of species for colonisation and competition.
In north-western U.S.A. the great conifers survived the Ice Age
where most deciduous species could not. Since then, the barriers of
mountains and the aridity to the east have restricted competition
from eastern deciduous trees.

Tundra

The literal meaning of tundra is a "treeless plain". The boreal forests do not abruptly, nor uniformly, give way to treeless tundra; but nevertheless the location of the isotherm of 10° C. for the warmest month has long been taken as a dividing line between the two types of vegetation, regardless of interpenetration of forest and tundra on either side of that limit. Like so many statements in connection with vegetation, this is only a generalisation, of course; other factors such as topography, soils, and microclimates are involved in determining the "tree-limit". While it does give us some idea of the climatic borderline of the treeless tundra, we should recognise that there is, rather, a forest/tundra zone, where boundaries between the two advance or retreat with changing circumstances. The northern forest trees are handicapped partly by the low density of their seed, away from areas of close tree cover; and more particularly by the fact that the capacity for germination is much reduced in these habitats.

In these regions the winters are dark and very cold, and winds are frequently strong. The summers are short, but with almost continuous insolation; so that, with some 50-60 days without severe frost, considerable plant growth occurs and much low vegetation is formed. The lower sub-soil remains permanently frozen, so that the spring melt produces swamp conditions in hollows. Most soils are peaty with gley characteristics (p. 168), and remain moist during the summer. Local environments have a marked effect on vegetation, and different "microhabitats" may support quite different associations of small plants.

Overall, the vegetation forms a close, almost continuous, sward, with hardy grasses and sedges, and many tiny hygrophilous herbs; small berry-bearing plants like the crowberry and bilberry form a carpet in places, with occasional under-shrubs and dwarf willows, or dwarf birches: the numerous mosses and lichens are usually well developed. Long hours of daylight allow almost continuous growth, and plants complete their life cycle during the brief summer period. The early summer is colourful, when the bright green vegetation bears many vivid flowers, as plants like saxifrage, Iceland poppies, anemones, and gentiàns come into bloom. For much of the time, however, the summer tundra has a rather drab appearance, partly because many plants bear the remains of the former year's growth. In the southern parts of the tundra the vegetation cover is almost continuous, and grasses and sedges, or mosses and lichens, are dominant over large areas. Poleward, the plant cover is less, and the perma-frost may be only just beneath the surface; finally, only the scattered plants may be found.

Much of the tundra landscape is hummocky in appearance and the surface is generally stony; sometimes it is patterned with polygons made up of fairly large stones. Alternate periods of freeze and thaw occur, entailing an expansion and frost-heaving of the ground in autumn, followed by shrinkage during the spring when the thaw occurs. Stones left behind during shrinkage, and others which, perhaps, were thrust out during the freezing and expansion, are distributed by gravity away from the centres of hummocky ground, and so may form the pattern of adjacent polygons.

Responses to Local Environments

Irregularities, large and small, cause variations in the make-up of the plant communities. The higher, drained parts, even only slightly above their surroundings, may bear heathy plants and lichens, above patches of lower ground covered with sedges: grassy hummocks may stand out about water-filled hollows. South-facing aspects favour plant development, and there are often notable differences in plants on opposite sides of tiny depressions or of rocks. In the more southerly parts of the northern tundra, damp depressions and favourable slopes may enable willow or birch scrub to grow to about a metre high—taller nearer the southern margins; while drier, better drained, localities often bear heathland. Snow gives good protection during the winter months, but in the mid-tundra, where snow remains for long periods, the late melting on northern slopes may reduce the growing period, and so restrict the number of plants which can become dominant: Arctic bell-heather is a plant often found in such places.

Consequently, there are numerous variations in plant types and associations in the tundra formations, partly due to their extent, from the taiga borderlands to the ice-caps, and partly due to different microhabitats within the main tundra areas. Even the nesting grounds of wildfowl may develop relatively luxuriant vegetation forms, with dominants differing from those of surrounding tundra, as birds manure the soil and introduce seeds.

These tundra lands belong mainly to the Arctic regions. The Antarctic Continent is mostly covered by ice-sheets, though a few parts bear a vegetation of lichens, mosses, and algae; and in southern South America, and on ice-free islands in the extreme south, are heaths and grasses of a tundra nature.

MOUNTAIN VEGETATION

Earlier chapters have described various effects of altitude, aspect, and forms of relief on climatic features, and, directly and indirectly, upon soils (p. 186). These will obviously cause differences in the nature of the vegetation in mountainous country, and broad vegetation zones can be identified between various altitudes on mountain slopes.

There is, however, a tendency to assume that the changes in the form of vegetation with altitude closely resemble the changes encountered on a poleward journey through successive tropical, temperate, and polar regions. There is a germ of truth in this; but the type of vegetation and plant species occurring at a given altitude depend on factors other than temperature. Mountainous regions in themselves often act as barriers to migrating species, and so may restrict the number of competitors. Not the least of the factors is the climatic regime of the whole area, with its seasonal variations, or lack of seasonal change, affecting both plant organs and competition between plants. At 2 000 m in a near-equatorial location the temperatures throughout the year may resemble those of northern Britain in summer; but the climatic regimes, the light intensity, and the hours of daylight are quite different in each case, and so there are considerable differences in their respective flora.

Mountain Vegetation in the Low Latitudes

On Lower Slopes under Humid Conditions

The vegetation of the lower parts of a mountainous area will broadly resemble that of the surrounding lowland, though there are likely to be local differences. A tendency for precipitation to increase on mountain slopes may well cause the proportion of water-tolerant species to be greater there, even allowing for rapid drainage. Often the sunlight penetrates more easily on the lower slopes and so gives rise to a denser undergrowth than on the flatter lowlands. Where the mountains rise above tropical rainforests, there is a tendency for the three-tiered tree system to give rise to a poorer forest, in which an upper layer of trees, less tall than those of the lowlands, rises above a single lower layer of vegetation; and at the greater altitude there may be tree species related to those more usually found in temperate regions.

At Higher Altitudes Under Humid Conditions

A number of factors combine to give the higher montane forests a distinct character. Hillsides high above the true rainforest are

usually in a zone of high humidity, much cloudiness, and precipitation. On the other hand, with little seasonal variation, growth is
continuous. Branching and leafiness is favoured, and the trees,
some identical with those of lowland rainforests, many related to
sub-tropical species, are a mass of foliage, and often covered with
mosses and lichens. The abundance of ferns, climbers, and epiphytic mosses is particularly characteristic, and their blanketing
so effective, that these are often called "moss-forests". The trees
are not usually more than 12 m high. Many of the plants have an
unusual form or structure, and the trunks and boughs are often
contorted. On some of the higher slopes of the mountains of the
western parts of the East African plateau, Ruwenzori for example,
fleshy groundsel, lobelia, and heaths grow to giant size; the whole
landscape of the leafy trees, rotting vegetation, abundant mosses,
and the curious shrublands and heathy vegetation nearer the snow-
line, has an unreal appearance. Between the tree limit and the
snow-line there are often grassy tracts, as well as shrubs and heathy
vegetation.

Rain-shadow Effects

Such are the modifications which may occur with increasing
altitude in humid regions in the low latitudes; but *within* mountain
areas the barrier effect of huge ranges can be marked, and give rise
locally to unusually dry climates. In the central and western Andes,
very dry conditions occur at high altitudes; and in these highlands in
low latitudes at about 3 000-4 500 m are the *paramos*, or extensive areas of dry grassland with many xeromorphic plants. Soil
conditions also affect the vegetation, of course; in Ecuador, for
example, volcanic deposits in the high basins are porous and
extremely dry, so that grass forms are tussocky and wiry, and other
xeromorphic plants are common. The eastern slopes of these
mountain systems carry montane forest, yet deep river canyons
between the eastern mountain ranges are so sheltered that their
valleys bear arid scrub. In a sense the great mountain masses make
their own climates; and as these are numerous, so, of course, are
the types of vegetation found there.

On High Plateaux—A Wide Variety of Influences

We have already seen the variety of savannah vegetation which
occurs on tropical plateaux (p. 218). Here we consider plateaux
which may extend also through equatorial regions. One set of
influences are, therefore, those of latitude—the temperature and
rainfall regimes, duration of daylight, intensity of insolation, and

so on. Others are those of altitude, and exposure, involving the factors described in the previous paragraphs; for broad plateaux often include outstanding ranges, or high erosion levels. Then, of course, on tropical plateaux there are the different types of vegetation associated with older surfaces and relic soils, and with areas of intrusive rock, as well as the catenas associated with retreating scarps. Besides these, there are the factors of human interference, of clearing, grazing, and burning, which can affect plateau surfaces so drastically.

Fig. 98 shows the vegetation of parts of Kenya, Uganda, and Tanzania; and, even this, of course, is a much simplified map. Nevertheless, it shows a pattern which climate alone cannot account for. Areas of outstanding relief in the Kenya Highlands, and about Mt Kilimanjaro, are shown bearing high altitude forest (although there are vegetation zones between the snows of Kilimanjaro and the open savannah around, which cannot be shown on a map of this kind; and there is considerable variety in the Kenya Highlands).

Along one latitude, we can see the light woodlands of western Tanzania, the dry bushlands of the broad, flat interfluves near Tabora, the variations of savannah associations with the different slopes and soils of the eastern rift-valley system, and the bushland and dry thickets of the eastern lateritic plains.

And, in other parts of the world as well, we find variety in the vegetation of low latitude high plains—in the surprisingly open grasslands of the Rupununi savannahs of the Guiana Highlands and the grassy basins of the central highlands of New Guinea.

Mountain Vegetation in the Middle Latitudes

Away from the low latitudes, mountain vegetation shows characteristics which are partly due to seasonal variations; and many latitudinal influences, such as the intensity and duration of light, are important. Taking examples from the Andes once more, the type of vegetation, and the height and extent of vegetation zones, and of the snow-line, are seen to vary with latitude and altitude, and also with aspect and relative humidity. Near the equator in the eastern Andes the snow-line averages a little over 4 500 m; yet in the dry zone of the central Andes, near latitude 20° S., it stands at some 6 400 m, with arid scrub beneath; while in the moist lands of the extreme south of Chile permanent snow lies at less than 1 000 m; beneath it there is close temperate evergreen forest in the west, but temperate grassland with only a little mountain forest in the drier east.

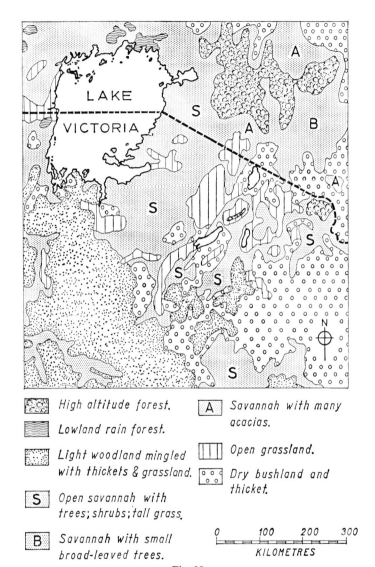

| | High altitude forest. | A | Savannah with many acacias. |

High altitude forest.

Lowland rain forest.

Light woodland mingled with thickets & grassland.

S Open savannah with trees; shrubs; tall grass.

B Savannah with small broad-leaved trees.

A Savannah with many acacias.

Open grassland.

Dry bushland and thicket.

0   100   200   300
KILOMETRES

Fig. 98.

Even on this scale, the variety of vegetation in Kenya and Tanzania is obvious, In fact, of course, there is a complicated mosaic of vegetation which is in perpetual change, varying with the changing landforms, with erosion and deposition and their consequent effects on drainage and soils.

The actual plants found in altitude zones depend on the location of the mountain region. Even in an east-west mountain system like the Himalayas, there are many differences in the species living at comparable heights in the drier eastern and wetter western parts of the ranges. As an example of zoning in a mid-latitude location, we will briefly look at the eastern parts of the Himalayas (Fig. 99). Here, at lat. 27° N., the low level vegetation is a mixture of tropical evergreens and mixed deciduous forest with sal, bamboo, and tall grasses, and shows pronounced seasonal changes. Above about 1 500 m, the deciduous forest contains many trees found in the cool temperate latitudes: oaks, magnolias, alder, and birch give way to evergreen conifers and rhododendrons, some of which flourish as high as 3 000 m. Above these are often quite luxuriant grassy swards, with many small herbs, and tiny, brightly-coloured tundra plants and lichens: alpine plants flower at nearly 6 000 m in these mountains. But, again, the type of vegetation often varies from one high valley to another; whereas a cool, damp slope may bear coniferous forest, drier slopes, nearby, may well support mainly grass and scattered bushes; so that, of course, the vertical vegetation zones tend to merge with one another. The actual vegetation depends again on the slopes and their soil cover. There are frequently differences in vegetation on old and new screes, according to their origin, porosity, and age *in situ*.

Another example of altitude zoning, involving different temperature and humidity conditions, and different plant species, is shown in Fig. 99. In those parts of western U.S.A., where high sierras stand above the low scrub of the arid foothills and intermontane plateaux, the lower slopes with rainfall between 250-500 mm a year bear scattered groves of dwarf piñon, juniper, and cedar. These give way to closer stands of ponderosa pines where the precipitation exceeds 500 m, though these pines occupy fairly dry soils; the Douglas fir occurs on the moister slopes, extending upwards in places to nearly 3 000 m; above this is a sub-alpine forest with white fir, Englemann spruce, and lodgepole pine. With increasing altitude, the trees now tend to become stunted and gnarled. Above this again is alpine tundra, and rock, bare except for lichens; and finally the zone of permanent snow.

In other extra-tropical mountain regions, the lower forests may be deciduous, and the middle belts mixed forest, giving way to coniferous trees above: at higher levels, depending on the latitude, there may be upland heaths or Arctic alpine grassland, as a transition to the tundra zone.

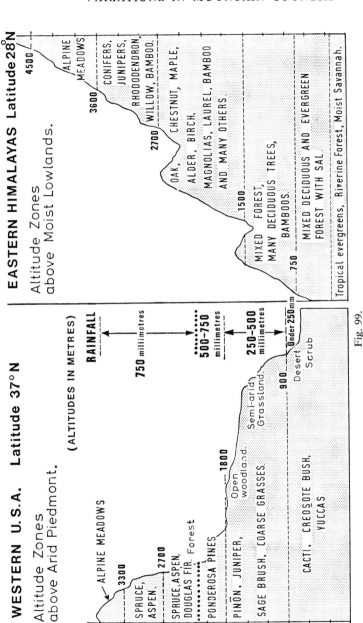

Fig. 99.

The rainfall figures are not given for the Eastern Himalayas, for they vary a great deal with position and aspect. Parts of the lowlands of the north-east may receive well over 2 500 mm a year, others as little as 1 000 mm. Rainfall is heavy in the summer months, and in the north-east the winters are not as dry as they are over most of the sub-continent (Table 3). There is, generally, no lack of moisture for plant growth, although certain slopes or valleys may be much drier than others.

The effect of different aspects is very apparent on many of the prominences on the high plateaux of central Asia, where the air is very dry and extremes of temperature are experienced. Outstanding landforms sometimes have sparse, dry, tussocky grasses on their southern slopes, where insolation is stronger and evaporation greater, but support close Alpine grassland at the same altitude on the northern slopes. In other mountains of the middle and higher middle latitudes, there are contrasts between the vegetation and the height of the tree-line on slopes exposed to, or, shaded from, the sun; especially in east-west valleys like the Swiss Lötschental, where, after mid-day, the northern "adret" slopes receive much more light and warmth than the southern slopes. But many individual local habitats exist, influenced perhaps by exposure to prevailing or local winds, by the movements of soil on slopes, or by the accumulation of rock debris in fans or talus.

In contrast to Arctic conditions, the light in Alpine locations is often intense, but intermittent. The rarefied air causes increased transpiration; and the fact that the light is richer in blue and violet rays than that which reaches the lowlands may cause differences in plant form and colour. Plants tend to be dwarfed, with narrow leaves arranged in rosettes. Plants also tend to be protected against loss of radiant heat: many have thick leaves; some, like the Edelweiss, are hairy.

CHAPTER XIV

STUDIES OF SMALL AREAS

So far we have considered the distribution of climatic regions and vegetation formations in a highly generalised way, which is unavoidable in any treatment on a world scale. It has been apparent, however, that local climates may be very different from those of the broad surrounding region; and that climatic, relief, and edaphic variations can produce a patchwork of different types of vegetation within a given formation. Man can also play havoc with the natural vegetation over large areas in a very short time. We now know something of the general environment in various parts of the world, and can appreciate why such and such a type of climate, or vegetation formation, is found in a particular area. This gives us an overall framework into which much greater detail can be fitted by sample studies or local surveys.

Though the types of climates, soils, and vegetation have been considered in separate chapters, there have been numerous illustrations of their interdependence. When we examine smaller areas this interdependence becomes even more apparent: we see that small plants may help to create a "climate" of their own very close to the ground (often a matter of millimetres rather than metres), and that this "climate" will influence the humidity of the soil, the development of seedlings, and so on. But before we consider such microhabitats, let us first reduce the scale of study gradually, from a major region to a much smaller area, and then examine on a very local basis two typical, but contrasting, hill-slope-valley profiles.

Changing relationships within the dry intermontane country of north-western U.S.A.

Like so much of the intermontane plateau of western U.S.A., the north-west has extensive areas of semi-arid country. But these northern dissected tablelands, with various ranges, like the Blue Mountains, rising above the general level, are affected by cyclonic systems moving in from the Pacific, especially during winter; even though they are sheltered to a great extent by the Cascade Range to the west. Parent materials for the soils vary: they include the great basalt sheets, which cover so much of the north-west, loess deposits, alluvium in the valleys, and colluvial materials beneath the slopes. The soils themselves tend to be arranged in belts, and individually display some of the characteristics of the profiles described in Chapter X.

Fig. 100 shows a diagrammatic profile of the country stretching north-westward from the Blue Mountains of Oregon towards the Columbia river. The foothills and slopes of the Blue Mountains receive an annual precipitation of over 700 mm: but as the country drops away westwards towards the Cascades, which act as a partial barrier to Pacific influences, the annual rainfall decreases until it is less than 200 mm in the western districts. There are also some well-marked temperature differences: and although, as a whole, the westerly influences help to preserve moderate temperatures during winter, the frost-free period tends to contract towards the interior.

Streams rising on the mountains of the interior unite to form larger tributaries to the Columbia river; so that a pattern of dendritic drainage has developed, which dissects the main upland surfaces and produces deep valleys in the otherwise smooth, or rolling, tablelands. These differences in the relief, precipitation, and soils lead to considerable variety in the vegetation and land-use of even relatively small areas.

Variations in Vegetation and Soils

The diagram shows the general fall westward for some 50 km, across undulating country of the basalt-capped plateau to the terraces bordering the Columbia river, about 75 m above sea-level. As the rainfall decreases westward, the vegetation can be seen to change from the pine-clad slopes and the rather close and luxuriant bunch grass of the foothills to the poor grass cover and sage-brush country in the west. The soils which are described on pp. 170 to 178, as responses to differences in climate and vegetation across half a continent (Fig. 74), are seen to occur in the same kind of sequence across this relatively small area (Fig. 100). Those in the western and central parts are lime-accumulating, and vary from sierozems, of the lands with low rainfall and sparse vegetation, to the much richer czernozems, beneath the grasslands near the eastern foothills. Prairie soils of the type described on pp. 173–5 tend to occur on the better watered lands. Within this general sequence there are variations again; immature scree soils on the foothills and alluvium along the wider valleys, have, respectively, been ignored and exploited agriculturally.

Variations in Land-Use

During the last hundred years, at first by trial and error, and later more scientifically, men have established forms of land-use

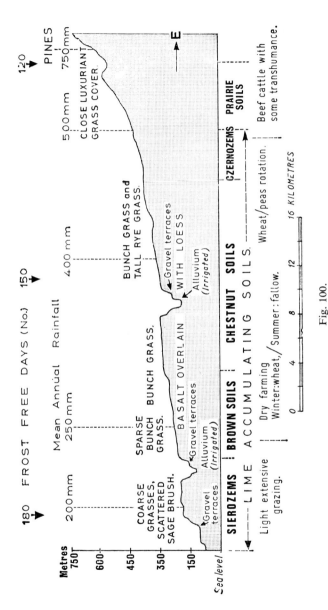

Fig. 100.

Profile of intermontane country in north-western U.S.A.: from the Blue Mountains in the east towards the Columbia river, near the borders of Washington and Oregon.

which still reflect the natural conditions. The western zone can stand only light grazing, and is now uncultivated, except where tributary valleys are successfully irrigated for fruit growing. The central areas have long been wheat farming lands; though their drier western parts, with brown soils and a low organic content, grow winter wheat in alternate years, with the help of summer fallow and a heavy application of fertilisers; the moister lands towards the interior, with chestnut brown soils and a belt of czernozem, yield an annual wheat crop, but with leguminous crops—usually green peas—in rotation; even here, fertilisers are used to-day. Much of the hill country forms pasture for beef-cattle, and some transhumance occurs beween plateau farms and hillside grazing lands.

Here, then, we see the influences of relief, climate, soils, and vegetation on a fairly local, regional, basis: but even within the land-use belts described, there are local peculiarities—coarse gravelly terraces, and skeletal soils on steep valley slopes, occur within the belt of fertile chestnut-brown soils: scrub vegetation grows amid the well-grassed lower slopes of the Blue Mountains. In this region man's actions in the past must also be taken into account. If we could look more closely at the drier western countryside, we would find areas of serious soil erosion: while earlier accounts tell us that the grassland was once much richer, and, even in these districts of low rainfall, supported large herds. Man's overgrazing and poor attempts at cultivation have led to the present regenerated cover of coarse grasses and sage-brush.

Now let us turn from profiles extending over many kilometres to study those measured rather in hundreds of metres.

Moorland and Valley in Western Britain

The area in north-western U.S.A. described above is sufficiently large to allow considerable differences in rainfall, temperatures, and length of growing season; and we have seen striking variations produced by their combined effects on soils, vegetation, and land-use. But even a small area can show remarkable contrasts in these respects; and to illustrate this Fig. 101 gives an idealised picture of climatic, soil, and vegetation conditions on a typical sequence of upland slopes and adjacent lowland in western Britain.

Drainage and Soils

The diagram shows high moorland, with soils formed on parent material derived from the resistant rocks of the upland itself. Here are wet conditions: cloud and rain for much of the year give an excess of precipitation over evaporation. Here, too, the growing period is a shortish one. As wet moorland plants rot down, and acidic organic matter accumulates, hill peat is formed, and beneath it is a greyish-green gley horizon, saturated with water held above an iron pan developed in the top of the B layer.

The rest of the countryside is taken as having a typical covering of drift as parent material; this is thin on the upper slopes, thicker

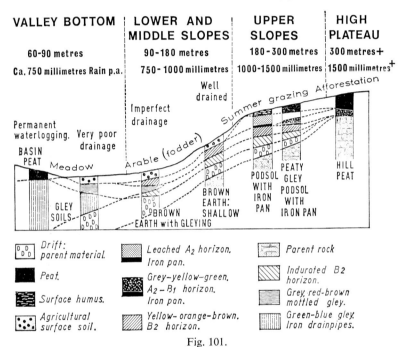

Fig. 101.

Idealised section showing soil profiles, under moist conditions in western Britain, from a high moorland to an adjacent valley bottom.

After James A. Taylor, "Methods of Soil Study", *Geography*, 45, p. 55.

on the lowland. As the slope increases and drainage improves, the peat gives way to peaty gley podsols, and then to the more strongly leached podsols, with perhaps traces of peaty matter and iron pan development in their profile. The lower and middle slopes receive somewhat less rainfall, and have the advantages of adequate drainage, better aerated soils, and a rather longer growing season. Shallow brown earths on the slope give way to deeper brown earths lower down, on the more gentle, but less well drained, inclines.

In particularly wet locations, the flat, or concave, relief of the adjacent lowlands may again lead to waterlogging. In these conditions, soils are wet and heavy, and the growing season is apt to be reduced by valley frosts. Where the drainage is very poor, gley horizons are again developed; and in valley bottoms which are fully waterlogged, basin peat is sometimes formed above thick, gleyed layers.

Land-use

The high plateau country may be useful only for afforestation purposes, or for maintaining reservoirs; while the upper slopes are likely to be used for summer grazing. In a land like Britain, with a long history of rural settlement, men will probably have used the lower slopes and the upper parts of the valley for arable farming for generations, producing a top soil with characteristics depending on their methods of cultivation (in Fig. 101 this is simply shown as an "agricultural horizon"); the crops grown are likely to be used for fodder purposes. In the valley itself there will probably be meadowland, and perhaps some of the very poorly drained parts will be useless for agriculture.

This type of sequence shows that, as we break down the scale of our investigations, the inter relationships of climate, soils, and vegetation are complex; and it is not until we consider microhabitats that we can really appreciate just how finely balanced are the factors which allow a given plant association to exist virtually unchanged, or a particular crop to yield to its full capacity.

Chalk Downlands and Valleys in Southern England

Chalk, with its shallow soils, lies at the surface over much of southern England, and we may take examples from its downlands and valleys to illustrate how vegetation may be affected by differences in the character of its soils. For instance, on its downlands and summits above steep slopes leaching is at its most intense. As calcium is thus removed from the surface layers the measured pH value drops (p. 160); and as a result alkalinity becomes greater with depth. This "layering" takes place even in the few inches of its shallow soils. Many species of plants have a narrow range of tolerance of acidity/alkalinity; so that one of the consequences of such leaching is that very shallow-rooted acid-tolerant species, such as members of a heath community, like ling, are found growing side by side with deeper-rooted plants which thrive on basic calcareous soils (calcicoles). Beech trees tend to check developing acidity, by returning much calcium in their leaf litter; but where high chalk country has been cleared and leaching has been intense, heath moorland and not beech woodland may take over any land which has been abandoned. Oakwood and bracken are often the dominants in the vegetation under these conditions.

Fig. 102 shows, diagrammatically, a typical downland/valley profile. The oak and bracken vegetation is established at the summit where pH values are low. On the drop of the downland, near the shoulder, chalky debris tends to accumulate, permitting a restricted area of beech woods on the upper slopes, with trees rooted in the chalk. The eroded sides of the valley are not leached in the same

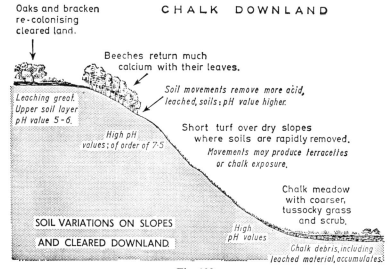

Fig. 102.

way, and provide dry, chalky pasturelands of short turf; except perhaps where the slope is too great for soil formation. At the foot of the downs the leached material and chalk, which have been washed down, accumulate, and here chalk meadow with coarser tussocky grass and scrub is likely to be found.

The actual vegetation will depend also, of course, on the degree of land-use. Since the early clearing of higher plant forms, grazing has tended to prevent the regeneration of small trees and shrubs on many slopes and downs. Nevertheless, much chalk country bears characteristic shrubs; dogwood, hawthorn, and roses, with the climbing Traveller's Joy, may be scattered over the less closely grazed hillsides. There may also be other plant associations suited to superficial deposits such as clay-with-flints (itself the result of protracted processes of leaching). However, the simple profile will suffice to illustrate that present soil characteristics may be due either to their development *in situ*, or to mechanical processes, and that in quite a small area with one type of parent rock there can be significant soil differences, which are reflected by the various forms of vegetation.

Microhabitats

In even more restricted areas than those considered above, quite small variations of climatic and edaphic factors can be of very great importance to plant life, and so influence crop growth and agricultural practices. Near ground level, a small ridge, or an isolated boulder, may have one side well lit and directly heated by the sun, the other shaded and cooler, and perhaps moister: one side may be more sheltered from the wind; and there may also be a difference of humidity on, and immediately above, the surface on either side. In high latitudes, the north and south sides of tussocks can differ in temperature in summer by as much as 20 C°.

Surface Colouration and Texture

At the lowest levels the surface albedo is important, and hence the colour and texture of soil affects its temperatures. In Bedfordshire, in early summer, thermometers buried to 100 mm under loam, loam and soot, and loam and lime, showed in mid-afternoon the following readings: beneath the normal loam surface 18° C; beneath the black surface 22° C; beneath the whiter surface 15·5° C. Also, whether the surface is smooth or broken can affect both the temperature and humidity of the air in immediate contact with it: a rough surface may cause turbulence in these very low "levels" of the atmosphere. Air conditions may be quite different at a few millimetres, and several metres above the surface. This is obvious when we consider that surface temperatures in the tropics can reach over 80° C, whereas only exceptionally would a thermometer in a Stevenson screen record 50° C. Even in England surfaces may reach 60° C in summer when air temperatures of 20°–30° C are usual a metre or so above the ground. Vegetation cover will itself influence surface temperatures: typical figures recorded in summer in southern England for adjacent surfaces of open sand and of lawn were 55° C and 44° C, respectively: at Poona, freshly turned "black cotton soil" was found to absorb 86 per cent. of radiation received, compared with 60 per cent. by an adjacent grass surface.

The Local Environment of Individual Plants

The terms micrometeorology and microclimatology are often used to refer to conditions of the lower air, a hundred metres or so from the surface; and many micrometeorological observations are now made in order to give a clear picture of the environment of the vegetation as a whole (including tall trees). But it is the climate of the really low levels of the atmosphere, in which plants germinate and develop their youthful forms, which is so important to their well-being, and to the composition of vegetation as a whole. Thermometers placed near the ground and about a metre above it can show temperatures affecting the aerial parts of the young plants, and also indicate air turbulence, by recording the lapse rate in the first metre or so of the atmosphere. In clear, warm weather the lapse rate over vegetation cover may be many hundreds of times the adiabatic value. O. G. Sutton has pointed out that in the first 25 mm a value of nearly 2 000 times the adiabatic rate has been recorded. During daylight hours, there is thus a continuous exchange of the lower air with that above it. The resulting turbulence, and the effect on the evaporation rate is therefore of great importance to plants, even when there is little horizontal air movement. Conversely, on those nights when the ground loses heat rapidly by radiation, the air in contact is chilled; it becomes denser than the air above, and thus stable; as it contains moisture from the plants, it may soon become saturated.

Sensitive anemometers and hygrometers have been developed to record wind speed and humidity at low levels on days when there is horizontal movement; and formulae have been devised to express the rates of evaporation in terms of such readings. Local figures may thus be available, for agriculturalists or conservancy experts, which are more reliable than calculations based on broad climatological data.

Evapo-transpiration and its Measurement

There are also more direct means of estimating the evapo-transpiration—the loss of water from soil and plants. The actual loss can only be estimated of course; but instrument readings enable the potential loss from the surface of a short, green, growing crop of uniform height to be measured. This is done by sinking a gauge in a reasonably level, open, grassed plot, in such a way that it becomes a typical part of the surface.

The *evapo-transpirometer*, as the gauge is known, is a simple arrangement of two watertight tanks, filled with soil above a layer of gravel, and sunk into the ground: their surfaces are sown with a grass cover resembling their surroundings. The base of each of these tanks is connected to collecting cans housed in a third water-tight tank. Water can only enter the soil tanks from the atmosphere, and can leave only by the outlets at the bottom. The tanks receive, daily, a known amount of water from precipitation—measured by a rain gauge—and from sprinkling (which is used initially to saturate the soil in the tanks and then to maintain sufficient soil moisture to satisfy plant needs). The amount of percolate in the collecting cans is measured, and can be converted into depth in mm. for each soil tank. The difference between the amount entering and the amount leaving the tanks represents that lost by evapo-transpiration. Details of the apparatus, its installation and maintenance are described by Dr R. C. Ward in *Geography,* 48, pp. 49-55.

Variations within a Growing Crop

Other work has been done by meteorologists to enable them to estimate the energy absorbed and radiated by particular surfaces, and to find how the ground conducts energy. Formulae have been derived to estimate temperatures at a given depth : but there are so many variable factors in nature—the water content of the soils, for example—that fresh constants need to be determined for each locality before the average environmental conditions affecting the crops can be appreciated. Even in a single crop on uniform soil with a level surface, the facts of temperature, humidity, and air movement near ground level will be different in the middle of the field from that at the sides. Besides these horizontal variations, there will be vertical ones; which means that stem, leaves, and various parts of the root system, each live in a different environment. Readings taken in eastern Java show a mean annual temperature of 26·1° C at 1 200 mm above the surface, and 29·2° C and 29·5° C at 30 mm and 900 mm beneath the surface, respectively. Absolute maximum and minimum figures show 18·3/35·8° C in the atmosphere; 23·4/31·5° C at 30 mm depth; and 26·9/30·1° C at 900 mm depth. Tall plants, therefore, live under different temperature conditions at different stages of their growth.

Different Parts of a Plant Respond in Different Ways

One further illustration of the difficulties of estimating the effects of environmental conditions is the fact that not all parts of the plant are affected in the same way by changes of, say, light intensity or humidity; nor do seeds, seedlings, and mature plants react similarly to environmental changes. There are also minimum optimum, and maximum conditions for plant functioning and sur- vival. Man sets about measuring light by its duration and intensity, by means of sensitised papers and photo-electric cells, but still has no valid estimate of its effectiveness for the growth of particular plants; for it is known that certain wavelengths of light are more effective for some functions of plant development than for others.

Mineral Contents of Soils

We must not lose sight of the importance of local edaphic variations. A narrow rock outcrop may provide minerals to which some plants are tolerant, but which do not suit the development of other plants: as a result a type of plant community may occur only along the outcrop concerned, and be surrounded by plant associa- tions of a different nature. This has proved most useful in the field in identifying rocks bearing certain minerals.

It should now be obvious that for a satisfactory study of even a tiny area there must be careful preparation, followed by numerous observations in the field. Specialists, like the geologist, soil scientist, botanist, zoologist, and meteorologist, are all required to contribute to the presentation of a true ecological picture.

Man-Made Climates and Soils

There are so many ways in which man exercises control over the rural scene, that here we can only point to a few examples of his deliberate interference, from the climatic and edaphic points of view. In glasshouses he provides the required conditions of temperature, humidity, and light: more than this, direct soil-heat- ing by electrical methods is now used indoors and out; overhead sprays provide moisture and nutrients necessary for his crops, which are preserved from undesirable competition by weeding, and given chemical protection against insects and fungi. Selection and artificial pollination improve the stock. The various methods of large-scale irrigation, and the prevention of soil erosion need no more than a mention here; and the necessity for drainage, as well as irrigation, according to local circumstances, has been empha- sised in the discussion of soil types. Men learn from experience and protect what reserves of soil nutrients and moisture they have by conservation methods, by chemical skins on reservoirs, and in a host of other ways.

But some of the large-scale modifications are not conscious ones. The evils of soil erosion due to deforestation or overgrazing are known to "scientific" man: and yet the very schemes he insti- gates to guard against them, and the scientific methods he uses to reclaim arid areas for cultivation, may themselves produce undesirable conditions elsewhere. The irrigation of hot, arid country can lead to an increase in soil salinity at or near the surface; and as streams return some of the irrigation water to the main river system the salinity may increase further downstream. Such has been the case in the south-western interior of the U.S.A.; and has already caused disputes between Mexico, whose irrigation water from the Colorado has become undesirably saline, and the U.S.A., whose own irrigation schemes are held responsible.

Climatic changes caused in and near large urban areas are also significant; these are mostly involuntary as far as the inhabitants are concerned. The extent and nature of the changes depend, of course, on the climatic region in which the large built-up area lies. The following considerations are based on observations in temperate zones, and special reference is made to London.

"Urban Climates"

A really large city can so modify the climatic elements that it may be said to have its own urban climate. The following climatic elements are all modified to some extent by an urban environment.

The Atmospheric Contents

Atmospheric pollution from chimneys and exhausts provide a vast quantity of gaseous and solid impurities. It was estimated that London was coated annually with upwards of a hundred thousand tons of soot and dust before smokeless zones were established. Such pollution varies seasonally according to the number of household fires, though many large cities in the temperate regions now have smokeless zones. Meteorological conditions affect the nature and concentration of the impurities; which may be quite different under conditions of strong winds, turbulence, or still, stable air. There are also likely to be variations between different industrial and residential areas, and with differences of relief.

The incidence and density of fog is also, of course, greatly affected by pollution on this scale. There is evidence from Britain that skies over large built-up areas tend to be cloudier than those of surrounding rural areas, due to the special effects of turbulence and to additional condensation caused by pollution nuclei.

Sunshine Received

This, too, will depend partly on the factors affecting pollution, and the frequency and density of fogs. Tall buildings, of course, cast their shade over considerable areas, although modern town-planning aims to prevent the canyon-like streets and the gloom so often found in city centres. When open spaces, other than parks, receive direct insolation, they may well become considerably hotter than a similar area of rural countryside, being unshaded by trees and unprotected by a vegetation cover.

Air Movements

The jumble of buildings and open spaces also have the general effect of reducing wind-speed over large areas; though they may also funnel air into gusty passages and cause eddies in the channels of streets. The uneven surface as a whole makes for turbulence, and an extra warmth within the city may well cause thermal winds.

Urban Temperatures—"Heat Islands"

These generally tend to be above those of the surrounding rural areas, creating what has been termed "a heat island". The following mean figures were obtained for London and its immediate surroundings over the period 1921-50.

	Max. (°C)	Min. (°C)	Mean (°C)
Central London	14·6	7·3	10·9
The Suburbs	14·3	6·2	10·2
Surrounding Country	14·0	5·5	9·7

There are also, of course, variations within the city, depending on the housing density, size of parks, sites near the river, and so on.

It is thought that at dawn London's temperatures are frequently greater than those of the surroundings; but that the latter warm more quickly in the early part of the day, when buildings shade the ground in the city and turbulence has not yet dispersed the haze. At night there again seem to be differences: the shade effect does not apply, but buildings and roads release heat to the air about them: the air of the city therefore tends to cool more slowly. These facts are, of course, more likely to be true under fairly calm conditions; their magnitude must depend on the time of the year; for the length of daylight, and the intensity of insolation have direct bearing on them.

Humidity

Cities, on the whole, tend to have both lower relative and absolute humidities than their rural environment; due mainly to their higher temperatures and lack of vegetation. However, many large cities are ports, and many have sizeable rivers in their midst, which affect atmospheric humidity; and some, like San Francisco, are in locations peculiarly liable to fogs. Nevertheless, it seems probable that these facts are true for large urban areas in the cool temperate zone, and certainly apply to suburban London away from the river and estuary.

MINIMUM TEMPERATURES (°C) LONDON

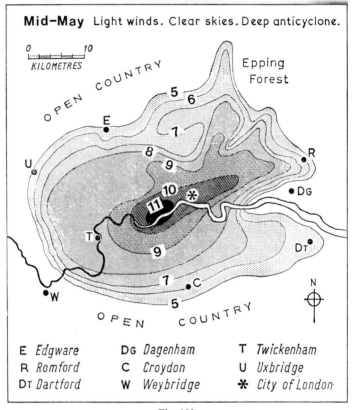

Fig. 103.
Minimum temperatures (° C) for a day in mid-May, indicating, under anti-cyclonic conditions, an urban "heat island". (After Chandler.)

Precipitation

It is difficult to generalise about this, for so much depends on the amount and normal causes of precipitation in the region as a whole, and on the relief of the city and variations within it. For instance, in London there seems a tendency for summer thunder-storms to develop and intensify to an unusual extent in the northern parts of the city; however, this part of London includes ridges of higher ground, whose edges would probably favour the creation of thermals even if they were set in rural surroundings.

The nature of the precipitation is undoubtedly affected by urban conditions, and even in the excessive snowfall of 1962-3 there was a noticeable tendency for sleet rather than snow to fall in central London; and when snow did fall it cleared more quickly from open undisturbed areas in the city than from open land in the surrounding countryside.

Studies of Natural Conditions on a World-Wide Basis: "Case Studies" Seen in Perspective

The number of "case studies" of local, rural, and urban environments may be multiplied indefinitely. Even studies of primary interrelationships of climates, soils, and vegetation show the complexity of any existing natural order. But when we observe the interactions of the fauna, and above all of man himself, with the natural elements of the environment, and then consider the additional impacts of some of the end-products of man's actions—his agriculture, housing, industries, forms of transportation, and communication, for instance—we realise that the ecology of any territory, and the interactions there between man and his environment, are unlikely to be repeated exactly in any other area.

Generalisations concerning the ways in which climates, soils, and vegetation affect one another are bound to be wide of the mark when applied to certain precise areas. This leads to a fear of over-simplification; and there are those who condemn the rigid classification and mapping of types of climate, soil, or vegetation. But just because they *are* so intricately inter-dependent, we can, to begin with, gain a great deal by viewing their relationships in a fairly simple way; even if we have to consider broad "natural regions" which we know have no precise boundaries in reality. But then, having obtained a general knowledge of the climates, soils, and vegetation of the world in this way, it is extremely important to realise the limitations of our methods of classification; to break down our studies by examining smaller regions in more detail, and making use of case studies, or an accurate ecological survey of small areas within a chosen region. In fact, it is often the *exception* within a climatic or vegetation region which excites interest; and this may, as in the case of unusual plant species revealing mineral deposits, be of practical as well as academic value.

FURTHER READING

CHAPTERS I-IV

1. "Meteorology and Climatology in Schools." R. H. C. CARR-GREGG, *Geography*, **46**, p. 301.
2. "Teaching Climate." M. DOVER, *Geography*, **47**, p. 285.
3. "Some Developments in Climatology during the Last Decade." G. B. TUCKER, *Geography*, **46**, p. 198.
4. "The General Circulation of the Atmosphere." P. A. SHEPPARD, *Weather*, **13**, p. 377.
5. "Solar Radiation and Temperature." W. H. RANSOM, *Weather*, **18**, p. 18.
6. "Frost and the Fruit Grower." R. BUSH, *Geography*, **30**, p. 80.
7. "An Example of the Coriolis Effect." J. R. D. FRANCIS, *Weather*, **15**, p. 339.
8. "The Structure of Rain Clouds." F. H. LUDLAM, *Weather*, **11**, p. 187.
9. "Atmospheric Convection." M. SIMONS, *Geography*, **55**, p. 196.
10. "Aspect of Geographical Hydrology." R. C. WARD, *Geography*, **55**, p. 390.
11. "Changing Weather to meet the needs of Man." W. R. D. SEWELL, *Geogr. Mag.*, **43**, p. 91.
12. "Coastal Fogs and Clouds." D. H. MILLER, *Geogr. Review*, **47**, p. 591.
13. "Cloud Cover of the U.S.S.R." M. SCHLOSS, *Geogr. Review*, **52**, p. 389.
14. "The Chinook Arch in Western Alberta and North-West Montana." T. M. THOMAS, *Weather*, **18**, p. 166.
15. "Warm Blast Across the Snow-covered Prairie" (Chinook). I. ASHWELL, *Geogr. Mag.*, **43**, p. 858.
16. "The Occurrence of Föhn Winds in the British Isles." J. GLOCKWOOD, *Met. Mag.*, **91**, p. 57.
17. "The Khamsin in Northern Egypt." A. BIRTWISTLE, *Geography*, **31**, p. 59.
18. "The Hailstorm." F. H. LUDLAM, *Weather*, **16**, p. 152.
19. "Hurricanes." D. L. NIDDRIE, *Geogr. Mag.*, **37**, p. 228.

20. "An Aerial Observation of a Tornado and Its Parent Cloud." F. C. BATES, *Weather,* **18,** p. 12.
21. "Windiness and the Weather." DR A. G. FORSDYKE, *Geogr. Mag.,* **35,** p. 611.
22. "Energy Changes and General Circulation." F. K. HARE, *Geography,* **50,** p. 229.
23. "Atmospheric Circulation, Climate, and Climatic Variations." H. H. LAMB, *Geography,* **46,** p. 208.
24. "The Atmosphere in Perpetual Motion." T. J. CHANDLER and L. F. MUSK, *Geogr. Mag.,* **49,** p. 93.
25. "High and Low Elevations as Thermal Source Regions." P. B. MACREADY, *Weather,* **10,** p. 35.
26. "Structure of the Upper Westerlies." *Q. J. Royal Met. Soc.,* **78,** p. 198.
27. "The Westerlies." F. K. HARE, *Geogr. Review,* **50,** p. 345.
28. "The Polar Night Westerlies." F. K. HARE, *Weather,* **17,** p. 256.
29. "Jet Streams in relation to Fronts and Flows at Low Levels." C. J. BOYDEN, *Met. Mag.,* **92,** p. 319.
30. "The Structure of the Arctic Winter Stratosphere." C. V. WILSON and W. L. GODSON, *Q. J. Royal Met. Soc.,* **89,** p. 205.
31. "Jet Stream Features of the Earth's Atmosphere." J. S. SAWYER, *Weather,* **12,** p. 333.
32. "The Jet Stream." D. H. JOHNSON, *Weather,* **8,** p. 270 and p. 325.
33. "The Tracks of Depressions over the Eastern Half of the North Atlantic." T. M. THOMAS, *Weather,* **15,** p. 325.
34. "Variations in Energy Exchange between Sea and Air in the Trades." H. RIEHL, *Weather,* **9,** p. 335.
35. "Satellite Meteorology and the Geographer." E. C. BARRETT, *Geography,* **49,** p. 377.
36. "Climatology in Arid Zone Research." J. L. MONTIETH, *Weather,* **12,** p. 203.
37. "Climate and the Geomorphic Cycle." A. A. MILLER, *Geography,* **46,** p. 185.
38. "Maps and the Meteorologist." J. B. RIGG, *Weather,* **12,** p. 154.
39. "Global Atmospheric Research." P. A. SHEPPARD, *Weather,* **23,** p. 262.

CHAPTERS V-VIII

1. "A Human Classification of Climate." W. J. MAUNDER, *Weather,* **17**, p. 3.
2. "The Use of Monthly Mean Climate Charts for the Study of Large-Scale Weather Patterns and Their Seasonal Development." H. H. LAMB and A. I. JOHNSON, *Weather,* **15**, p. 83.
3. "Three New Climatic Maps." A. A. MILLER, *I.B.G. Publication,* **17**, p. 15.
4. "Köppen Definitions of Climatic Types and Their Mapped Representations—Some Remarks." H. P. BAILEY, *Geogr. Review,* **52**, p. 444 and p. 447.
5. "Measuring Potential Evapo-Transpiration." R. C. WARD, *Geography,* **48**, p. 49.
6. "The Evaporation—Precipitation Fallacy." J. E. McDONALD, *Weather,* **17**, p. 168.
7. "Delimitation of the Humid Tropics." F. R. FOSBERG, B. J. GARNIER, A. W. KÜCHLER, *Geogr. Review,* **51**, p. 331.
8. "Some Problems of Agricultural Climatology in Tropical Africa." A. H. BUNTING, *Geography,* **46**, p. 283.
9. "Wind and Weather in the Equatorial Zone." *I.B.G. Publication,* **17**, p. 23.
10. "On the role of the tropics in the general circulation of the atmosphere." H. RIEHL, *Weather,* **24**, p. 288.
11. "Tropical Weather Disturbances." J. S. MALKUS, *Weather,* **13**, p. 75.
12. "Pattern of East African Rain." G. SUMNER and A. Q. ORCHARD, *Geogr. Mag.,* **43**, p. 129.
13. "The Climate of Nigeria." (I.T.C. Movements.) R. MILLER, *Geography,* **37**, p. 198.
14. "Variations in Energy Exchange Between Sea and Air in the Trades." H. RIEHL, *Weather,* **9**, p. 335.
15. "Rainfall, Rice Yields, and Irrigation Needs in Western Bengal." (Use of Climographs.) P. N. HORE, *Geography,* **49**, p. 114.
16. "The Monsoon of South Asia." J. M. WALKER, *Weather,* **27**, p. 178
17. "The Indian Monsoon." J. G. LOCKWOOD, *Weather,* **20**, p 2.
18. "Solar Influences on Monsoon Storms in the Bay of Bengal." K. RAGHAVAN, *Weather,* **16**, p. 59.
19. "Shadow on the Indus Plain." (Irrigation and Salinity.) V. C. ROBERTSON, *Geogr. Mag.,* **37**, p. 98.

20. "Irrigation Systems of Sind." L. H. GULICK, *Geogr. Review*, **53**, p. 79.
21. "Air Mass Maps of China Proper and Manchuria." J. H. CHANG, *Geography*, **42**, p. 142.
22. "Climatology in Arid Zone Research." J. L. MONTIETH, *Weather*, **12**, p. 203.
23. "Some Aspects of Desert Geomorphology." R. F. PEEL, *Geography*, **45**, p. 241.
24. "Reducing Water Loss in South Australia." G. R. COCHRANE, *Geography*, **45**, p. 297.
25. "Between the Tasman Sea and the Blue Mountains." S. R. EYRE, *Geography*, **35**, p. 155.
26. "Problems of Florida's Water Resources." R. B. MARCUS and D. MOOKHERJEE, *Geography*, **47**, p. 368.
27. "Winter Temperatures of a Mid-Latitude Desert Mountain Range." R. F. LOGAN, *Geogr. Review*, **51**, p. 236.
28. "Precipitation Within the British Isles in Relation to Depression Tracks." T. M. THOMAS, *Weather*, **15**, p. 361.
29. "Climate in Britain over 10 000 years." G. MANLEY. *Geogr. Mag.*, 43, p. 100.
30. "The Treelessness of the Tundra." D. L. LINTON, *Geography*, **48**, p. 80.
31. "Distribution of the Albedo over Arctic Surfaces." P. LARSSON, *Geogr. Review*, **53**, p. 573.
32. "Antarctic Prospect." L. M. GOULD, *Geogr. Review*, **47**, p. 1.
33. "The General Circulation over the Far South." G. P. BRITTON and H. H. LAMB, *Weather*, **11**, p. 281 and p. 337.
34. "The Structure of the Arctic Winter Stratosphere." C. V. WILSON and W. L. GODSON, *Q. J. Royal Met. Soc.*, **89**, p. 205.
35. "Differences in the Meteorology of the North and South Polar Regions." H. H. LAMB, *Met. Mag.*, **87**, p. 364.

CHAPTERS IX-XIII

1. "Methods of Soil Study." J. A. TAYLOR, *Geography*, **45**, p. 52.
2. "Soil Fertility and Biotic Geography." W. A. ALBRECHT, *Geogr. Review*, **47**, p. 86.
3. "The Humid Soil: Process and Time." G. F. CARTER and R.

L. Pendleton, *Geogr. Review*, **46**, p. 488.

4. "Soil Warmth in Sunny and Shaded Situations." G. M. Howe, *Weather*, **10**, p. 49.

5. "The Loess in European Life." H. J. Fleure, *Geography*, **45**, p. 200.

6. "A Soil Map of Great Britain." E. M. Bridges, *Geography*, **49**, p. 105.

7. "The Importance of Biogeography." K. C. Edwards, *Geography*, **49**, p. 85.

8. "Vegetation and the Teaching of Geography in the Field." C. A. Sinker, *Geography*, **59**, p. 105.

9. "Production Ecology and the International Biological Programme." P. J. Newbould, *Geography*, **49**, p. 98.

10. "Determinism and the Ecological Approach to Geography." S. R. Eyre, *Geography*, **49**, p. 369.

11. "Delimitation of the Humid Tropics." F. R. Fosberg, B. J. Garnier, A. W. Kuchler. *Geogr. Review*, **51**, p. 331.

12. "Some Problems of Agricultural Climatology in Tropical Africa." A. H. Bunting, *Geography*, **46**, p. 283.

13. "Physiognomy of Tropical Vegetation." C. D. Harris, *Geogr. Review*, **50**, p. 284.

14. "Recent Hydrological Changes in the Rema Basin, Northern Nigeria." (Relations between Climate, Soils, and Vegetation.) D. C. Ledger, *Geogr. Journal*, **127**, p. 477.

15. "Mangrove Succession in South-West Malaya." *I.B.G. Publication*, **26**, p. 79.

16. "Bamboo as an Economic Resource in Southern Asia." J. Oliver, *Geography*, **41**, p. 49.

17. "Grass Roots of a Continent's Prosperity" (Africa). R. A. Pullan, *Geogr. Mag.*, **43**, p. 197.

18. "Man's Impact on Savannah Vegetation." B. J. Maclean, *Geogr. Mag.*, **43**, p. 243

19. "Cerrado, Caatinga, Pantanal: Distribution and Origin of the Savanna Vegetation of Brazil." M. M. Cole, *Geogr. Journal*, **126**, p. 168.

20. "Vegetation and Geomorphology in Northern Rhodesia: An Aspect of the Distribution of the Savanna of Central Africa." M. M. Cole, *Geogr. Journal*, **129**, p. 290.

21. "Vegetation Studies in South Africa." M. M. Cole, *Geography*, **41**, p. 114.

22. "Natural and Artificial Zonation in Vegetation Cover—Chiapas, Mexico." P. L. WAGNER, *Geogr. Review*, **52**, p. 253.

23. "A History of Land-Use in Arid Regions." Arid Zone Research, UNESCO Publication XVIII, Ed L. D. STAMP.

24. "Some Aspects of Desert Geomorphology." R. F. PEEL, *Geography*, **45**, p. 241.

25. "Oak Woodlands of South-West Spain,—Acorn, Hog Economy." J. T. PARSON, *Geogr. Review*, **52**, p. 211.

26. "New Zealand's Tussock Grasslands." L. W. MCCASKILL, *Geography*, **49**, p. 422.

27 "Some Effects of Rainfall on Tree Growth and Forest Fires." G. D. ROUSE, *Weather*, **16**, p. 304.

28. "The Climatic Resources of Intensive Grassland Farming (New Zealand)." L. CURRY, *Geogr. Review*, **52**, p. 174.

29. "Grass of the Great Plains." J. E. WEAVER and F. W. ALBERTSON, *Geogr. Review*, **47**, p. 120.

30. "Grazing as a Natural Ecological Factor." W. C. ROBINSON, *Geogr. Review*, **51**, p. 308.

31. "The Vegetation of Blackdown, Sussex." E. M. YATES, *Geography*, **40**, p. 84.

32. "Vegetation in Shore Stabilisation." C. KIDSON, *Geography*, **45**, p. 241.

33. "The Southern Cold Temperate Zone, Plant and Animal Geography." H. J. FLEURE, *Geography*, **47**, p. 179.

34. "Man and Environment in the South Chilean Islands." M. W. HOLDGATE, *Geogr. Journal*, **127**, p. 401.

35. "The Influence of Open Pine Forest on Daytime Temperatures in the Sierra Nevada." D. H. MILLER, *Geogr. Review*, **46**, p. 209.

36. "Burning in the Boreal Forest of North America." E. ROSTLUND, *Geogr. Review*, **51**, p. 127.

37. "The Treelessness of the Tundra." D. L. LINTON, *Geography*, **48**, p. 80.

CHAPTER XIV

1. "Microclimatology and Town Planning." E. N. LAWRENCE, *Weather*, **9**, p. 227.

2. "Microclimatology and Hydroponics." E. N. LAWRENCE, *Weather*, **9**, p. 147.

3. "Soil Warmth in Sunny and Shaded Situations." G. M. HOWE, *Weather*, **10**, p. 49.

4. "Horticultural Climatology at the Natural Vegetation Research Station." E. T. WINTER and G. STANHILL, *Weather*, **12**, p. 218.

5. "Frost and the Fruit Grower." R. BUSH, *Geography*, **30**, p. 80.

6. "Microclimates of Cultivated Crops." J. R. MATHER, *Geogr. Review*, **53**, p. 315.

7. "Natural and Artificial Modifications of Microclimate." L. A. RAMDAS, *Weather*, **12**, p. 237.

8. "Measuring Potential Evapo-Transpiration." R. C. WARD, *Geography*, **48**, p. 49.

9 "A Note on the Physics of Soil Temperatures." N. E. RIDER, *Weather*, **12**, p. 241.

10. "Variations in Visibility over Urban and Rural Areas." G. REYNOLDS, *Weather*, **12**, p. 314.

11. "Temperature Variations in a Welsh Valley." D. J. GEORGE, *Weather*, **13**, p. 325.

12. "London's Urban Climate." T. J. CHANDLER, *Geogr. Journal*, **128**, p. 279.

13. "Diurnal, Seasonal, and Annual Change, in the Intensity of London's Heat Island." T. J. CHANDLER, *Met. Mag.*, **91**, p. 146.

14. "Temperature and Humidity Traverse Across London." T. J. CHANDLER, *Weather*, **17**, p. 235.

15. "The Changing Form of London's Heat Island." T. J. CHANDLER, *Geography*, **46**, p. 295.

16. "Wind as a Factor of Urban Temperature—A Survey in North-East London." T. J. CHANDLER, *Weather*, **15**, p. 204.

17. "Man's Impact on the Atmosphere." T. J. CHANDLER, *Geogr. Mag.*, **43**, p. 83.

18. "Sheffield Emerges from Smoke and Grime." A. GARNETT, *Geogr. Mag.*, **43**, p. 123.

GENERAL READING

The Challenge of the Atmosphere. O. G. SUTTON. (Hutchinson.)

Understanding Weather. O. G. SUTTON. (Pelican Books.)

Atmosphere, Weather and Climate. R. G. BARRY and R. J. CHORLEY. (Methuen.)

Introduction to Climate. G. T. TREWARTHA. (McGraw-Hill.)
Modern Meteorology and Climatology. T. S. CHANDLER. (Nelson.)
Climatology. W. G. KENDREW. (O.U.P.)
World Climatology. J. G. LOCKWOOD. (Arnold.)
Concept in Climatology. P. R. CROWE. (Longman.)
The Climates of the Continents. W. G. KENDREW. (O.U.P.)
Global Climate. K. BOUCHER. (E.U.P.)
The Earth's Problem Climates. G. T. TREWARTHA. (Methuen.)
Everyday Meteorology. A. A. MILLER and M. PARRY. (Hutchinson.)
Weather Elements. T. A. BLAIR. (McGraw-Hill.)
The Restless Atmosphere. F. K. HARE. (Hutchinson.)
General Climatology. H. J. CRITCHFIELD. (Prentice-Hall.)
Clouds, Rain, and Rainmaking. B. J. MASON. (C.U.P.)
Cloud Types for Observers. (H.M.S.O.: Meteorological Office.)
Cloud Study. F. H. LUDLAM and R. S. SCORER. (John Murray.)
Viewing Weather from Space. E. C. BARRETT. (Longman.)
Climatology of the Mediterranean Area. E. R. BIEL. (Chicago.)
The Monsoon. P. PÉDELABORDE. (Methuen.)
Monsoon Asia. E. H. G. DOBBY. (University of London Press.)
The World of Soil. SIR E. JOHN RUSSELL. (Fontana Library.)
World Soils. E. M. BRIDGES. (C. U. P.)
The Geography of Soil. D. STEILA. (Prentice-Hall.)
Soils. D. BRIGGS. (Butterworth.)
Soils in the British Isles. L. F. CURTIS, F. M. COURTNEY and S. TRUDGILL. (Longman.)
Soil Geography. J. G. CRUICKSHANK. (David & Charles.)
The Geography of Soil. B. T. BUNTING. (Hutchinson.)
Soil Conditions and Plant Growth. SIR E. JOHN RUSSELL. (Longmans.)
Introduction to Plant Geography. N. POLUNIN. (Longman.)
Vegetation and Soils. S. R. EYRE. (Arnold.)
Plant Ecology. J. E. WEAVER and F. E. CLEMENTS. (McGraw-Hill.)
The Geography of Flowering Plants. R. GOOD. (Longman.)
The Life Form of Plants. C. RAUNKIAER. (Clarendon Press.)
Plant and Animal Geography. M. I. NEWBIGIN. (Methuen.)
World Vegetation. D. RILEY and A. YOUNG. (C.U.P.)
Elements of Ecology. G. L. CLARKE. (Wiley.)
Outline of Plant Geography. (Macmillan.)

Plant Ecology. W. B. McDougall. (Kimpton.)

Plant Ecology. W. Leach. (Methuen.)

Ecology and Resource Management. K. E. F. Watt. (McGraw-Hill.)

Environmental Conservation. R. F. Dasmann. (Wiley.)

The History of British Flora. H. D. Godwin. (C.U.P.)

The Tropical Rainforest: An Ecological Study. P. W. Richards. (C.U.P.)

The Tropical World. P. Gourou. (Longman.)

Plant Life in Malaya. R. E. Holttum. (Longman.)

The Australian Environment. C.S.I.R.O. (Melbourne.)

Salt Marshes and Salt Deserts of the World. V. J. Chapman. (Leonard Hill.)

APPENDIX
EQUIVALENTS

° C.	° F.	° C.	° F.	° C.	° F.	° C.	° F.	° C.	° F.	° C.	° F.
−70	−94	+1	+34	11	52	21	70	31	88	41	106
−60	−76	2	36	12	54	22	72	32	90	42	108
−50	−58	3	37	13	55	23	73	33	91	43	109
−40	−40	4	39	14	57	24	75	34	93	44	111
−30	−22	5	41	15	59	25	77	35	95	45	113
−20	−4	6	43	16	61	26	79	36	97	46	115
−15	+5	7	45	17	63	27	81	37	99	47	117
−10	+14	8	46	18	64	28	82	38	100	48	118
−5	+23	9	48	19	66	29	84	39	102	49	120
0	+32	10	50	20	68	30	86	40	104	50	122

(Fahrenheit Equivalents are shown to the nearest whole number.)

km	ft	knots	m p h	ins	mb
1	3 300	10	11·5	28·0	948
2	6 600	50	58	28·5	965
3	9 800	60	69	29·0	982
4	13 100	70	81	29·5	999
5	16 400	80	92	30·0	1 016
6	19 700	90	104	30·5	1 034
7	23 000	100	115	(1 000 mb = 29·53 ins)	
8	26 200	110	127		
9	29 500	120	138		
10	32 800	130	149		
15	49 200	140	161		
20	65 600	150	173		
25	82 000	200	230		
(1 metre = 3·281 ft)		250	288		

GENERAL INDEX

INDEX TO PLACE NAMES